COLLEGE ACCOUNTING
NINTH EDITION

WORKING PAPERS WITH STUDY GUIDE

Chapters 1–13

Douglas J. McQuaig
Wenatchee Valley College, Emeritus

Patricia A. Bille
Highline Community College

SOUTH-WESTERN
CENGAGE Learning

Australia • Brazil • Japan • Korea • Mexico • Singapore • Spain • United Kingdom • United States

SOUTH-WESTERN
CENGAGE Learning™

College Accounting: Working Papers with Study Guide Chapters 1–13, Ninth Edition
Douglas J. McQuaig, Patricia A. Bille

Executive Publisher: George Hoffman

Senior Sponsoring Editor: Ann West

Senior Marketing Manager: Mike Schenk

Senior Development Editor: Chere Bemelmans

Project Editor: Paula Kmetz

New Title Project Manager: Susan Brooks-Peltier

Editorial Assistant: Diane Akerman

Marketing Coordinator: Erin Lane

For product information and technology assistance, contact us at
Cengage Learning Customer & Sales Support, 1-800-354-9706

For permission to use material from this text or product, submit all requests online at **www.cengage.com/permissions**
Further permissions questions can be emailed to
permissionrequest@cengage.com

ISBN-13: 978-0-618-82419-9

ISBN-10: 0-618-82419-7

South-Western
5191 Natorp Boulevard
Mason, OH 45040
USA

Cengage Learning is a leading provider of customized learning solutions with office locations around the globe, including Singapore, the United Kingdom, Australia, Mexico, Brazil, and Japan. Locate your local office at **international.cengage.com/region**

Cengage Learning products are represented in Canada by Nelson Education, Ltd.

To learn more about South-Western, visit **www.cengage.com/southwestern**

Purchase any of our products at your local college store or at our preferred online store **www.ichapters.com**

Printed in the United States of America
3 4 5 6 7 11 10 09

Contents

To the Student

As you study *College Accounting,* Ninth Edition, you will find these Working Papers helpful in many ways. The first part of the book contains the following selections to assist you in your study of accounting.

- Review of T Account Placement and Representative Transactions
- How to Study Accounting
- How to Solve Accounting Problems
- Ten-Key Skills Review
- Introduction to Spreadsheets
- Review of Business Mathematics
- How to Work a Practice Set
- Suggested Abbreviations for Account Titles

Then for each chapter in the textbook, the Working Papers with Study Guide provide the following:

- **Performance Objectives and Key Terms** The Performance Objectives duplicate your textbook. When you begin your study session, read the objectives and try to recall the text explanations. If you do not feel you can fulfill a performance objective, look for the performance objective in the margin of your textbook and review the corresponding material before trying to complete your homework assignments. Use the list of key terms to test your recall of vocabulary in the end-of-chapter glossaries. Look in the glossary at the end of the chapter in your textbook to find the definition of any term you do not know. If you still don't understand the term, note the page number in the glossary and look for the term itself in the body of the chapter. Each key term is printed in red type when it is first used and defined. Make sure you understand all the key terms before going on to the next chapter.

- **Study Guide Questions** After you read each chapter in the textbook, try answering these short questions. They will show how well you have learned the material in the text. Answers are provided at the back of the Working Papers with Study Guide, so you can find out right away whether you are correct. If you missed a few questions, go back to the text and review those areas where your understanding is incomplete. If you have mastered the material, you are ready to move ahead.

- **Demonstration Problem and Solution** Important concepts are illustrated by a self-study program and its solution. Test yourself by working this sample problem. Next, verify your answer with the solution presented. Also, as you work your homework assignments, you may want to refer to the Demonstration Problem as well as to the text.

- **Accounting Forms** Blank forms are provided for every exercise and problem in the textbook. Sometimes information is provided to help you get started. The pages are perforated so that you can tear them out if the instructor asks for them.

In addition, all the information you need to complete the Accounting Cycle Review Problems (following Chapter 5), the Comprehensive Review Problem (following Chapter 13), and the Before a Test Checks is provided in the Working Papers with Study Guide, including the required blank accounting forms. A selection of blank forms is also provided for you to use to solve supplement problems. If you photocopy these forms as you need them, you shouldn't ever run out of forms.

We hope that the Working Papers will make it easier for you to learn the fundamentals of accounting. Please write to us in care of Cengage Learning if you have suggestions about the text or other learning materials in your course.

Good luck in your college accounting class!

Douglas J. McQuaig
Patricia A. Bille

Review of T Account Placement and Representative Transactions

PART I
CHAPTERS 2 THROUGH 5

Review of T Account Placement

The following display sums up the placement of T accounts covered in Part I, Chapters 2–5, in relation to the fundamental accounting equation. Italicized accounts are contra accounts.

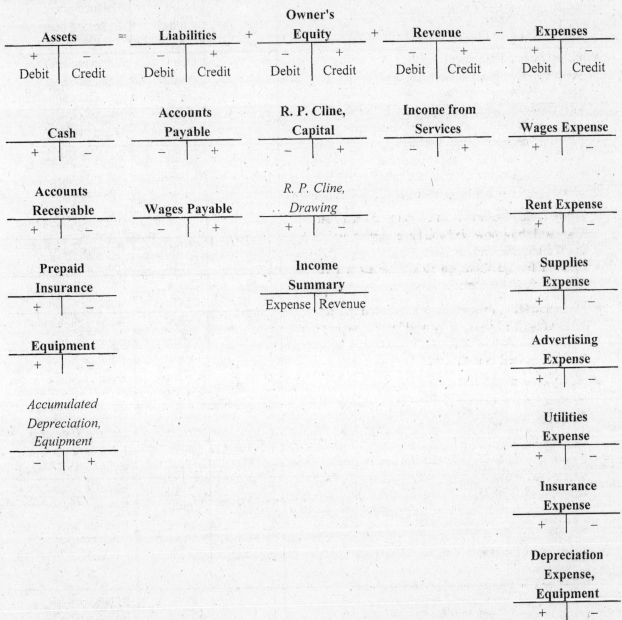

Review of Representative Transactions

The following table summarizes the recording of the various transactions described in Part I, Chapters 2–5, and the classification of the accounts involved.

Transaction	Accounts Involved	Class.	Increase or Decrease	Therefore Debit or Credit	Financial Statement
Owner invested cash in business	Cash R. P. Cline, Capital	A OE	I I	Debit Credit	Balance Sheet and Statement of Owner's Equity
Bought equipment for cash	Equipment Cash	A A	I D	Debit Credit	Balance Sheet Balance Sheet
Bought equipment on account	Equipment Accounts Payable	A L	I I	Debit Credit	Balance Sheet Balance Sheet
Paid creditor on account	Accounts Payable Cash	L A	D D	Debit Credit	Balance Sheet Balance Sheet
Owner invested equipment in business	Equipment R. P. Cline, Capital	A OE	I I	Debit Credit	Balance Sheet and Statement of Owner's Equity
Sold services for cash	Cash Income from Services	A R	I I	Debit Credit	Balance Sheet Income Statement
Paid rent for month	Rent Expense Cash	E A	I D	Debit Credit	Income Statement Balance Sheet
Bought supplies on account	Supplies Expense Accounts Payable	E L	I I	Debit Credit	Income Statement Balance Sheet
Paid premium for insurance policy	Prepaid Insurance Cash	A A	I D	Debit Credit	Balance Sheet Balance Sheet
Sold services on account	Accounts Receivable Income from Services	A R	I I	Debit Credit	Balance Sheet Income Statement
Paid wages to employees	Wages Expense Cash	E A	I D	Debit Credit	Income Statement Balance Sheet
Bought equipment, paying a down payment with the remainder on account	Equipment Cash Accounts Payable	A A L	I D I	Debit Credit Credit	Balance Sheet Balance Sheet Balance Sheet
Received cash from charge customer to apply on account	Cash Accounts Receivable	A A	I D	Debit Credit	Balance Sheet Balance Sheet

Review of Representative Transactions

(Part I, Chapters 2–5, concluded)

Transaction	Accounts Involved	Class.	Increase or Decrease	Therefore Debit or Credit	Financial Statement
Owner withdrew cash for personal use	R. P. Cline, Drawing	OE	I	Debit	Statement of Owner's Equity
	Cash	A	D	Credit	Balance Sheet
Adjusting entry for insurance expired	Insurance Expense	E	I	Debit	Income Statement
	Prepaid Insurance	A	D	Credit	Balance Sheet
Adjusting entry for depreciation of assets	Depreciation Expense	E	I	Debit	Income Statement
	Accumulated Depreciation	A	I	Credit	Balance Sheet
Adjusting entry for accrued wages	Wages Expense	E	I	Debit	Income Statement
	Wages Payable	L	I	Credit	Balance Sheet
Closing entry for revenue accounts	Revenue accounts	R	D	Debit	Income Statement
	Income Summary	OE	—	Credit	—
Closing entry for expense accounts	Income Summary	OE	—	Debit	—
	Expense accounts	E	D	Credit	Income Statement
Closing entry for Income Summary account (Net Income)	Income Summary	OE	—	Debit	—
	R. P. Cline, Capital	OE	I	Credit	Balance Sheet and Statement of Owner's Equity
Closing entry for Drawing account	R. P. Cline, Capital	OE	D	Debit	Balance Sheet and Statement of Owner's Equity
	R. P. Cline, Drawing	OE	D	Credit	

Review of T Account Placement

The following display sums up the placement of T accounts covered in Part II, Chapters 7–9, in relation to the fundamental accounting equation.

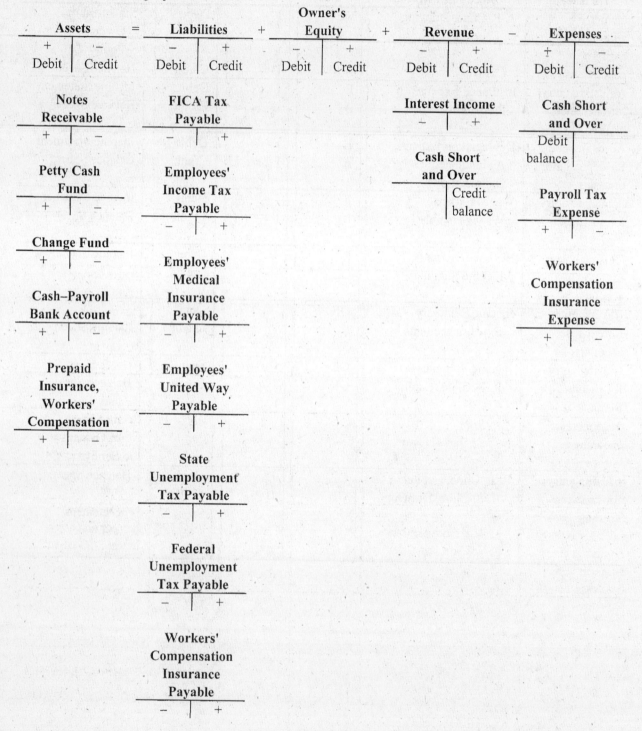

Review of Representative Transactions

The following table summarizes the recording of transactions covered in Part II, Chapters 7–9, along with a classification of the accounts involved.

Transaction	Accounts Involved	Class.	Increase or Decrease	Therefore Debit or Credit	Financial Statement
Recorded non-interest-bearing note receivable collected by our bank	Cash Notes Receivable	A A	I D	Debit Credit	Balance Sheet Balance Sheet
Recorded service charge on bank account	Miscellaneous Expense Cash	E A	I D	Debit Credit	Income Statement Balance Sheet
Recorded interest-bearing note receivable collected by our bank	Cash Notes Receivable Interest Income	A A R	I D I	Debit Credit Credit	Balance Sheet Balance Sheet Income Statement
Recorded NSF check received from customer	Accounts Receivable Cash	A A	I D	Debit Credit	Balance Sheet Balance Sheet
Established a Petty Cash Fund	Petty Cash Fund Cash	A A	I D	Debit Credit	Balance Sheet Balance Sheet
Reimbursed Petty Cash Fund	Expenses or Assets or Drawing Cash	E A OE A	I D	Debit Debit Debit Credit	Income Statement Balance Sheet Statement of O. E. Balance Sheet
Established a Change Fund	Change Fund Cash	A A	I D	Debit Credit	Balance Sheet Balance Sheet
Recorded cash sales (amount on cash register tape was greater than cash count)	Cash Cash Short and Over Income from Services	A E R	I — I	Debit Debit Credit	Balance Sheet Income Statement Income Statement
Recorded cash sales (amount on cash register tape was less than cash count)	Cash Income from Services Cash Short and Over	A R R	I I —	Debit Credit Credit	Balance Sheet Income Statement Income Statement

ix

eview of T Account Placement and Representative Transactions

Review of Representative Transactions

(Part II, Chapters 7–9, concluded)

Transaction	Accounts Involved	Class.	Increase or Decrease	Therefore Debit or Credit	Financial Statement
Recorded the payroll entry from the payroll register	Sales Wages Expense	E	I	Debit	Income Statement
	Office Wages Expense	E	I	Debit	Income Statement
	FICA Tax Payable	L	I	Credit	Balance Sheet
	Employees' Income Tax Payable	L	I	Credit	Balance Sheet
	Employees' Medical Insurance Payable	L	I	Credit	Balance Sheet
	Employees' United Way Payable	L	I	Credit	Balance Sheet
	Wages Payable	L	I	Credit	Balance Sheet
Issued check payable to Cash to pay payroll	Wages Payable	L	D	Debit	Balance Sheet
	Cash	A	D	Credit	Balance Sheet
Issued check to transfer cash to the payroll bank account	Cash-Payroll Bank Account	A	I	Debit	Balance Sheet
	Cash	A	D	Credit	Balance Sheet
Recorded employer's payroll taxes	Payroll Tax Expense	E	I	Debit	Income Statement
	FICA Tax Payable	L	I	Credit	Balance Sheet
	State Unemployment Tax Payable	L	I	Credit	Balance Sheet
	Federal Unemployment Tax Payable	L	I	Credit	Balance Sheet
Recorded deposit of FICA taxes and employees' income tax withheld	Employee's Income Tax Payable	L	D	Debit	Balance Sheet
	FICA Tax Payable	L	D	Debit	Balance Sheet
	Cash	A	D	Credit	Balance Sheet
Paid state unemployment tax	State Unemployment Tax Payable	L	D	Debit	Balance Sheet
	Cash	A	D	Credit	Balance Sheet
Recorded deposit of federal unemployment tax	Federal Unemployment Tax Payable	L	D	Debit	Balance Sheet
	Cash	A	D	Credit	Balance Sheet
Paid for workers' compensation insurance in advance	Prepaid Insurance, Workers' Compensation	A	I	Debit	Balance Sheet
	Cash	A	D	Credit	Balance Sheet
Adjusting entry for workers' compensation insurance, assuming an additional amount is owed	Workers' Compensation Insurance Expense	E	I	Debit	Income Statement
	Prepaid Insurance, Workers' Compensation	A	D	Credit	Balance Sheet
	Workers' Compensation Insurance Payable	L	I	Credit	Balance Sheet

x

opyright © South-Western, Cengage Learning. All rights reserved.

PART III
CHAPTERS 10 THROUGH 13

Review of T Account Placement

The following sums up the placement of T accounts covered in Part III, Chapters 10–13, in relation to the fundamental accounting equation. Italics indicates those accounts that are treated as deductions from the related accounts above them.

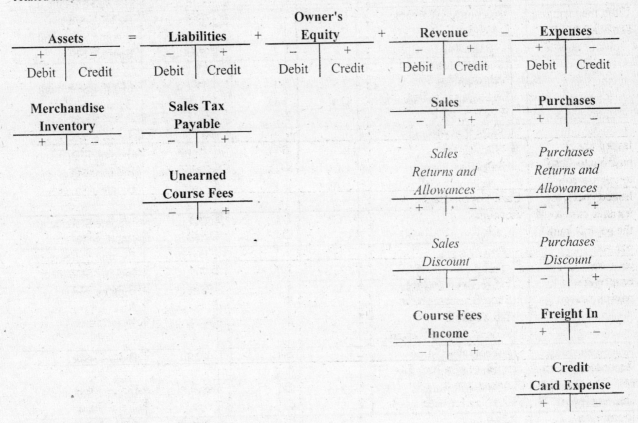

Review of Representative Transactions

The following table summarizes the recording of transactions covered in Part III, Chapters 10–13, along with a classification of the accounts involved.

Classifications

	Balance Sheet		Income Statement
CA	Current Assets	S	Revenue from Sales
P & E	Property and Equipment	CGS	Cost of Goods Sold
CL	Current Liabilities	SE	Selling Expense
LTL	Long-Term Liabilities	GE	General Expenses
		OI	Other Income
		OE	Other Expenses

Review of Representative Transactions

(Part III, Chapters 10–13, continued)

Transaction	Accounts Involved	Class.	Increase or Decrease	Therefore Debit or Credit	Financial Statement
Sold merchandise on account	Accounts Receivable	CA	I	Debit	Balance Sheet
	Sales	S	I	Credit	Income Statement
Sold merchandise on account involving sales tax	Accounts Receivable	CA	I	Debit	Balance Sheet
	Sales	S	I	Credit	Income Statement
	Sales Tax Payable	CL	I	Credit	Balance Sheet
Issued credit memo to customer for merchandise returned	Sales Returns and Allowances	S	I	Debit	Income Statement
	Accounts Receivable	CA	D	Credit	Balance Sheet
Issued credit memo to customer for merchandise returned with sales tax	Sales Returns and Allowances	S	I	Debit	Income Statement
	Sales Tax Payable	CL	D	Debit	Balance Sheet
	Accounts Receivable	CA	D	Credit	Balance Sheet
Bought merchandise on account	Purchases	CGS	I	Debit	Income Statement
	Accounts Payable	CL	I	Credit	Balance Sheet
Bought merchandise on account with freight prepaid as a convenience to the buyer	Purchases	CGS	I	Debit	Income Statement
	Freight In	CGS	I	Debit	Income Statement
	Accounts Payable	CL	I	Credit	Balance Sheet
Received credit memo from supplier for merchandise returned	Accounts Payable	CL	D	Debit	Balance Sheet
	Purchases Returns and Allowances	CGS	I	Credit	Income Statement
Paid for transportation charges on incoming merchandise	Freight In	CGS	I	Debit	Income Statement
	Cash	CA	D	Credit	Balance Sheet
Sold merchandise, involving sales tax, for cash	Cash	CA	I	Debit	Balance Sheet
	Sales	S	I	Credit	Income Statement
	Sales Tax Payable	CL	I	Credit	Balance Sheet
Sold merchandise involving sales tax and the customer used a bank charge card	Cash	CA	I	Debit	Balance Sheet
	Credit Card Expense	SE	I	Debit	Income Statement
	Sales	S	I	Credit	Income Statement
	Sales Tax Payable	CL	I	Credit	Balance Sheet
Charge customer paid bill within the discount period	Cash	CA	I	Debit	Balance Sheet
	Sales Discounts	S	I	Debit	Income Statement
	Accounts Receivable	CA	D	Credit	Balance Sheet

Review of Representative Transactions

(Part III, Chapters 10–13, concluded)

Transaction	Accounts Involved	Class.	Increase or Decrease	Therefore Debit or Credit	Financial Statement
Paid invoice for the purchase of merchandise within the discount period	Accounts Payable Cash Purchases Discounts	CL CA CGS	D D I	Debit Credit Credit	Balance Sheet Balance Sheet Income Statement
First adjusting entry for merchandise inventory—periodic	Income Summary Merchandise Inventory	— CA & CGS	— D	Debit Credit	— Balance Sheet and Income Statement
Second adjusting entry for merchandise inventory—periodic	Merchandise Inventory Income Summary	CA & CGS —	I —	Debit Credit	Balance Sheet and Income Statement —
Adjusting entry for course fees earned (Course Fees Income)	Unearned Course Fees Course Fees Income	CL OI	D I	Debit Credit	Balance Sheet Income Statement
Adjusting entry for merchandise inventory—perpetual, if physical count is less than ledger balance of merchandise inventory	Costs of Goods Sold Merchandise Inventory	CGS CA	I D	Debit Credit	Income Statement Balance Sheet
Adjusting entry for merchandise inventory—perpetual, if physical count is greater than ledger balance of merchandise inventory	Merchandise Inventory Cost of Goods Sold	CA CGS	I D	Debit Credit	Balance Sheet Income Statement
Reversing entry for adjustment for accrued wages	Wages Payable Wages Expense	CL SE or GE	D D	Debit Credit	Balance Sheet Income Statement

How to Study Accounting

Studying is defined as applying oneself to learning.

The purpose of studying accounting is to obtain the textbook and technical knowledge of accounting plus the experience necessary to succeed in the accounting profession.

Research has shown that the greater your involvement in studying, the more you retain. Retention means how long you are able to remember the concepts and practices. The four groups of study activities are shown from the lowest percentage of retention (about 10%) to the highest level of retention (about 98%):

- Hearing
- Seeing
- Saying
- Doing

Let's also look at why you are studying manual accounting when you hear so much about the use of the computer to complete accounting tasks in business. It is true that computers have become an integral part of accounting. However, you must first know the basics of accounting, the language of the profession, and the flow of the accounting cycle before you can effectively enlist the aid of a computer. A computer is only a tool to perform routine accounting tasks and print the results more quickly and attractively.

Now, let's begin our journey learning manual accounting. To do so, we shall work our way through the hierarchy of retention.

Hearing alone will only take you to the lowest level of retention. This means that if the only activity you enlist in your learning process is listening, you will retain very little. However, this does not mean that listening is not important as a learning tool. There are several things you can do in the area of listening.

Attend class equipped with paper and pencil to **take notes**. Use a tape recorder or digital recorder if this fits your needs and the instructor agrees. Also, take your textbook to class to refer to as the presentation progresses.

Be prepared to listen to questions asked and answers given, as well as classroom discussion.

The second level of retention adds **seeing** to hearing to increase the amount you remember. Two resources are critical to this level: your instructor and your textbook.

First, **observe your instructor** carefully. Take note when he or she makes references to textbook examples, shows illustrations on handouts, distributes material on transparencies or overhead projections, or shows examples drawn in chalkboard presentations.

Second, **know your textbook** and what it contains, how it is structured, and where you can find various tools.

So far, we have looked at only half of the retention hierarchy. Hearing allows you to retain the least. Hearing and seeing together increase your chances for retention. However, if you add saying or **verbal participation** at the third level, you will significantly increase what you remember. There are several ways in which you can strengthen your learning by hearing the sound of your own voice speaking about the subject.

Ask questions. Sometimes you may feel confused and feel unable to formulate a question. Don't let that stop you. Try to avoid the sweeping negative statement, "I just don't get this." Narrow your question to the place your understanding went off the track.

Volunteer answers. Be an active and enthusiastic learner!

Participate in classroom discussions. You may be surprised how your own life experiences have prepared you for this course in accounting. You have owned things, owed money, bought items, sold things, incurred expenses, and earned an income. You may have filled out a W-4 form when you went to work for an employer, and received a W-2 form from the employer at the end of a calendar year. You may have had a checking account. Each of the activities mentioned are ones that you will experience in accounting. Your experience is valuable—share it in class. Use your personal experiences to visualize accounting tasks. See how each task fits into the accounting cycle. The **discussion questions** at the end of each chapter provide material to spark conversations and support discussions.

Study with a partner or group. It will serve not only as a way to get acquainted, but it will also provide you with support. The give-and-take of studying as a team will help both of you learn. You both win because your voice is a powerful tool for teaching others as well as strengthening your own learning.

Finally, outside of class, **talk to yourself.** Yes, talk to yourself! For example, study glossary terms aloud, reread your notes aloud, talk your way through an accounting transaction. Let your brain hear you. You will decrease your journalizing and posting errors considerably with this technique. Don't be bashful. It will be much easier for you to speak up in class as the terminology becomes more familiar.

Let's add the last retention builder to the hierarchy—**doing.** So far, we have investigated

- hearing only
- hearing plus seeing
- hearing plus seeing plus saying

and now,

- hearing plus seeing plus saying plus **doing.**

You may have heard it said that accounting is best learned through the end of a pencil. In other words, you can read and listen all you wish, but until you actually do it, it does not become yours. An analogy might be one of studying to become a surgeon or an auto mechanic by only reading and hearing about your profession—until you try it, you do not have a working knowledge of the subject. Therefore, let us suggest that you thoughtfully and conscientiously complete all assignments your instructor makes whether they are questions, exercises, or problems.

Accounting is like a pyramid. What you learn in each new chapter builds on knowledge from previous chapters. If the base of the pyramid is not firmly in place, your accounting skills will be weak.

To summarize, in looking at "How to Study Accounting," you have seen that you need to put into force all levels of action to give yourself the highest level of retention—hearing plus seeing plus saying plus doing. You have also seen how important it is that you know your textbook—how it is structured and where to find the things you need.

How to Solve Accounting Problems

Solving means finding or providing a satisfactory answer or explanation for a problem. A solution to a problem, whether in accounting or in any other discipline, involves more than just "getting the answer." This is what most of us search for, but other preliminary steps lead to the final solution.

Before you can solve any problem, you need to understand accounting fundamentals and strategies for solving problems. First, we will look at these fundamentals, then we will review problem-solving strategies.

The **fundamental accounting equation** (Assets = Liabilities + Owner's Equity) is the basis for **double-entry accounting. Assets** are things owned. **Liabilities** are amounts owed to creditors. **Owner's equity** is the financial interest of the owner in the company.

We can think of owner's equity as an umbrella that covers the **Capital account**. The Capital account increases with investments and revenues, and decreases with withdrawals by the owner and expenses incurred.

Revenues, expenses, and the **Drawing account** are considered temporary owner's equity accounts, or nominal accounts. They are open for the accounting period to keep track of changes to owner's equity due to revenue earned and expenses incurred. At the end of the accounting period, they are closed out and the difference between the revenue and expenses is transferred to the Capital account. A net profit increases Capital, and a net loss decreases it.

Our expanded fundamental accounting equation now reads:

$$\text{Assets} = \text{Liabilities} + \text{Owner's Equity} + \text{Revenue} - \text{Expenses}$$

Both sides of any equation must balance.

The equation elements or classifications are broken down into subdivisions called **accounts**. Each account can be represented by a **T account**—a visualization of the information presented in a formal ledger account. The T account provides a structure to demonstrate the rules of **debit** and **credit.** It has two sides, a left side called the debit side and a right side called the credit side. You must clear your mind of your emotional attachment to the term credit. A credit is neither good nor bad, plus nor minus. Increases can be shown by debits or credits, depending on which account is involved.

The first accounting rule is that **debits must equal credits** in any entry.

Another rule is that the **normal balance** of an account is the plus side, which can be either the debit or credit side.

The problems at the end of the chapter provide the opportunity to apply the fundamentals that you have learned. Now let's look at some basic problem-solving techniques.

Scan the entire problem to get an overview of what is involved and what is expected. Most of the problem sets in your textbook have three sections that you must read carefully.

The first section includes a list of learning objectives, a problem number, and information about the problem and the business.

There is a list of transactions or other information providing the basis for solving the problem.

There are step-by-step instructions to guide you through the problem.

Read and follow each instruction carefully. Do them in order and do not skip any. Write down any questions you have and remember to ask your instructor to clarify them.

Most of the problems in your book include **narrative transactions**—sentences describing the transaction. The secret for solving this kind of problem is finding and understanding **key words**. Here are some translations of some of the more common words you will encounter in the problems:

Paid means cash going out, cash decreased.

Invested may mean cash was invested by the owner, but an investment can also mean another asset besides cash, such as personal equipment, one's law library, or other assets which are then given a fair market value.

Received cash means cash coming in, cash increased.

Bought means purchased something with cash or maybe on account or with a promissory note. In either of the latter two cases, a promise has been made to pay cash at a later date agreed upon by both parties.

Received and paid a bill is the same as paid. Cash went out, cash decreased.

Received a bill, without any reference to paying, means cash is not paid out at this time. The bill has been put away for payment at a later date.

Billed customers for services means no cash was received, but customers have promised to pay after they receive the bill. (The **accrual basis** of accounting allows us to book revenue when earned and expenses when incurred, the opposite of the cash basis most people use for their personal accounting.)

Another way of looking at key words in transactions is to group phrases which you can expect to see together in certain types of transactions. Here are some words and phrases that you might encounter in a problem involving a customer:

Issued a credit memo	*Sales Returns and Allowances*
Sales	*Accounts Receivable*
Sold	*Accounts Receivable Ledger*
Sales Discount	

You will not see these customer-related key phrases mixed with phrases involving vendors and suppliers.

Here are some words and phrases associated with vendors and suppliers:

Received a credit memo	*Purchases Returns and Allowances*
Purchases	*Accounts Payable*
Purchases Discount	*Accounts Payable Ledger*

We have just looked at key words in transactions described in sentences, but in real-world situations, transactions are primarily generated by **source documents.** A source document is a piece of paper that evidenses a transaction—some change in the financial condition of the business—for example, an invoice or a check. However, most of the problems in your book are based on sentences describing transactions. Whether the transaction is generated by a sentence or a document, analyze the transaction to decide what accounts are debited and credited. The steps taken to analyze a transaction are:

1. Which accounts are involved?
2. Where do the accounts fall in the fundamental accounting equation: Assets, Liabilities, Owner's Equity, Revenues, or Expenses?
3. Are the accounts increased or decreased?
4. Which accounts are debited, and which accounts are credited?
5. Do total debits equal total credits?

These steps work for every transaction, no matter how complex. Analyzing each transaction using these steps is critical to your success in accounting.

In summary, you need a firm base in accounting fundamentals before you begin to journalize transactions. You need to understand the fundamental accounting equation, the rules of debiting and crediting, and how to analyze each transaction based on these rules. Next you must understand the problem posed. Scan the problem, and then read it carefully. Follow, in order, the specific instructions listed at the end of each problem.

If you follow these rules and steps, your accounting experience will be more successful and satisfying. Try them—they work.

Ten-Key Skills Review

Keyboard arrangement:

Finger/thumb locations

Index	Middle	Ring
7	8	9
4	5	6
1	2	3
0	00	decimal
Thumb	Thumb	Thumb

Home Row ⟶

5 may be more deeply recessed
   than other keys or be
   marked by a bump

Finger used	Number keys
Index	7 4 1
Middle	8 5 2
Ring	9 6 3
Thumb	0's decimal

Steps to complete each addition problem:
a. Clear the machine by pressing the total bar.
b. Use the correct fingers to enter each digit, keep your eyes on the copy, and move steadily.
c. Tap the plus (+) key after each entry.
d. When all entries are made, tap the total bar and check your answer.

Ten-Key Skill Review Problems

Practice 1, 2, and 3

1.	2.	3.
31	21	32
22	32	13
12	11	11
13	23	22
32	31	21
110	118	99

Practice 4, 5, and 6

4.	5.	6.
44	55	66
45	56	65
64	65	46
66	44	45
55	54	44
274	274	266

Practice 7, 8, and 9

7.	8.	9.
78	89	77
88	87	89
79	79	78
89	78	87
98	99	98
432	432	429

Practice Index Finger

10.	11.	12.
11	47	44
44	74	71
77	17	17
71	14	11
41	77	14
244	229	157

Practice Middle Finger

13.	14.	15.
22	58	82
55	85	58
88	52	25
28	25	85
25	28	22
218	248	272

Practice Ring Finger

16.	17.	18.
33	36	39
66	39	36
99	93	93
96	69	63
63	63	93
357	300	324

Introduction to Spreadsheets

Definition: A type of computer application software made up of rows and columns that lets users perform calculations electronically rather than writing on a paper spreadsheet.

Purpose: A spreadsheet is an essential business tool because users can quickly recalculate computations after a change in a value. This feature enables users to engage in "what if" sessions, that is, to try out different numbers, let the spreadsheet recalculate; and then consider the new results.

Example: Think of a spreadsheet as columnar working paper with rows displayed on a screen.

Appearance: In addition to the powerful capability of spreadsheets to calculate and recalculate instantly, the appearance of the spreadsheet information can be enhanced with borders, shading, different sizes and shapes of print, as well as charts and graphs to illustrate the data.

Illustration: This generic spreadsheet includes the major areas of most spreadsheets.

File name

Column headings

Row headings

A cell is the intersection of a row and a column; B3, C4, and D5 are the addresses of the cells shown.

Examples of text entries vs. numeric or symbolic or formula entries

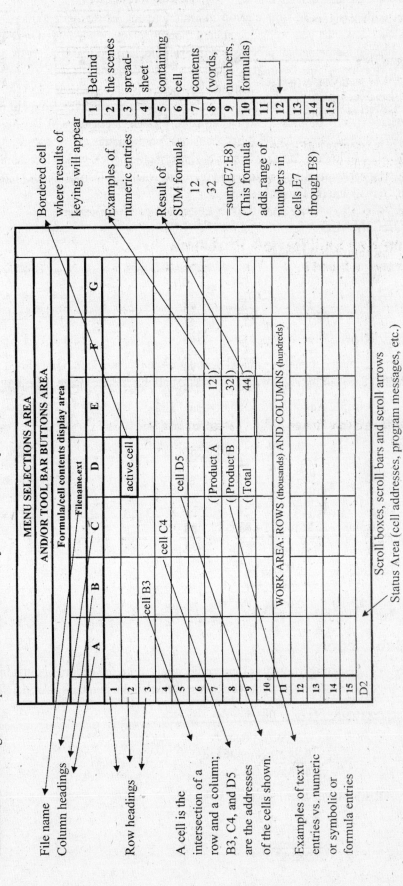

MENU SELECTIONS AREA

AND/OR TOOL BAR BUTTONS AREA

Formula/cell contents display area

Filename.ext

	A	B	C	D	E	F	G
1							
2							
3		cell B3					
4			cell C4				
5				cell D5			
6				active cell			
7				(Product A	12)		
8				(Product B	32)		
9				(Total	44)		
10							
11	WORK AREA: ROWS (thousands) AND COLUMNS (hundreds)						
12							
13							
14							
15							
D2							

Scroll boxes, scroll bars and scroll arrows

Status Area (cell addresses, program messages, etc.)

1	Behind
2	the scenes
3	spread-sheet
4	
5	containing
6	cell
7	contents
8	(words,
9	numbers,
10	formulas)
11	
12	
13	
14	
15	

Bordered cell where results of keying will appear

Examples of numeric entries

Result of SUM formula
12
32
=sum(E7:E8)
(This formula adds range of numbers in cells E7 through E8)

Review of Business Mathematics

People assume that anyone who is an accountant is good at mathematics. But accountants are like anyone else; they can make simple errors in arithmetic that cause them hours of searching later on. The thing that slows down the beginning accountant more than any other single factor is not being really sure about certain common mathematical processes. For example, how do you convert from fractions to percentages? What do you do with the decimal point when you are dividing?

Of course, we all agree that an electronic calculator capable of performing the arithmetic functions is an invaluable aid in accounting. However, even with a calculator, you still need to know what to divide by what, what to multiply by what, and so forth. The calculator will do only what you tell it to do, so you will always need a knowledge of basic business mathematics.

The following short review of business mathematics, which has items labeled so that you can better identify them, is designed to help you recall what you learned about mathematics long ago. In other words, it's a mathematical booster shot.

DECIMALS

Examples of terms:

Whole number	12
Decimal	0.62
Mixed decimal	4.15

Addition

When adding decimals or mixed decimals, keep the decimal points lined up, one under the other. Fill in any blank places to the right with zeros so that all the addends have the same number of decimal places.

Example Add 4.2, 16.53, 0.004, and 322.

$$
\begin{array}{r}
4.200 \\
16.530 \\
0.004 \\
+\ 322.000 \\
\hline
342.734
\end{array}
\ \Big\}\ \text{Addends}
$$

Example Add 16.02, 4.035, 40, and 0.06.

$$
\begin{array}{r}
16.020 \\
4.035 \\
40.000 \\
+\ 0.060 \\
\hline
60.115
\end{array}
$$

Subtraction

When subtracting decimals or mixed decimals, keep the decimal points lined up, one under the other. Fill in any blank places to the right with zeros so that all the numbers have the same number of decimal places.

Example 5.378 minus 0.8421.

$$
\begin{array}{r}
5.3780 \quad \text{Minuend} \\
-\ 0.8421 \quad \text{Subtrahend} \\
\hline
4.5359
\end{array}
$$

Example 624.1 minus 16.003.

$$
\begin{array}{r}
624.100 \\
-\ 16.003 \\
\hline
608.097
\end{array}
$$

Multiplication

When multiplying decimals or mixed decimals, find the position of the decimal point in the product (answer) by adding the number of decimal places in the multiplicand (number to be multiplied) and in the multiplier (number of times to multiply), and count off the same number of places from right to left in the product.

Example Multiply 0.62 by 0.4.

```
      0.62   Multiplicand
x      0.4   Multiplier
      0.248  Product
```

Example Multiply 626.231 by 2.87.

```
      626.231
x        2.87
      43 83617
     500 9848
    1252 462
    1,797.28297
```

When the number of decimal places required is greater than the number of places in the product, add as many zeros to the left of the product as necessary.

Example Multiply 0.049 by 0.02.

```
      0.049
x      0.02
      0.00098
```

Example Multiply 0.26 by 0.0091.

```
       0.26
x     0.0091
         26
        234
      0.002366
```

Division

When the divisor (dividing number) is a whole number and the dividend (number to be divided) is a mixed decimal, place the decimal point in the quotient (answer) directly above the decimal point in the dividend.

Example Divide 172.64 by 4.

```
                    43.16   Quotient
Divisor     4 ) 172.64   Dividend
                16
                12
                12
                 6
                 4
                24
                24
```

Example Divide 6.39 by 15.

```
                   0.426
           15 ) 6.390
                6 0
                 39
                 30
                 90
                 90
```

When the divisor is a decimal, move the decimal point in the divisor as many places to the right as necessary to make the divisor a whole number, and move the decimal point in the dividend to the right also, the same number of places.

Example Divide 14.406 by 0.007.

```
                   2,058
       0.007 ) 14.406
               14
               40
               35
               56
               56
```

Example Divide 8.3927 by .943.

```
                  8.9
       0.943 ) 8.3927
               7 544
               8487
               8487
```

FRACTIONS

Examples of terms:

$$\frac{\text{Numerator} \longrightarrow 6}{\text{Denominator} \longrightarrow 39}$$

Proper fraction: 8/9

Improper fraction: 13/6

Mixed number: 2 3/8

Like fractions: 2/5, 3/5, 4/5

Unlike fractions: 1/2, 1/4, 5/6

Addition of Fractions

To add like fractions, add their numerators.

Example Add 1/5 and 3/5.

$$+ \frac{\begin{array}{r} 1/5 \\ 3/5 \end{array}}{4/5}$$

To add unlike fractions, you must convert them to like fractions. First, find the least common denominator (the smallest number that is exactly divisible by each denominator),

Next, divide the least common denominator by the denominator of each original fraction. Then multiply both the numerator and the denominator of each original fraction by this number. Add the numerators of the like fractions and, if necessary, reduce the sum to lowest terms.

Example Add 3/4 and 2/3. The least common denominator is 12.

$$4 \,\overline{)\,12} \quad \frac{3}{4} = \frac{3 \times 3}{4 \times 3} = \frac{9}{12}$$

$$3 \,\overline{)\,12} \quad \frac{2}{3} = \frac{2 \times 4}{3 \times 4} = +\frac{8}{12}$$

$$\frac{17}{12} = 1\frac{5}{12}$$

Example Add 1/3, 1/6, and 3/8. The least common denominator is 24.

$$3 \,\overline{)\,24} \quad \frac{1}{3} = \frac{1 \times 8}{3 \times 8} = \frac{8}{24}$$

$$6 \,\overline{)\,24} \quad \frac{1}{6} = \frac{1 \times 4}{6 \times 4} = \frac{4}{24}$$

$$8 \,\overline{)\,24} \quad \frac{3}{8} = \frac{3 \times 3}{8 \times 3} = +\frac{9}{24}$$

$$\frac{21}{24} = \frac{7}{8}$$

Subtraction of Fractions

To subtract like fractions, subtract their numerators.

Example 7/8 minus 3/8.

$$
\begin{array}{r}
7/8 \\
- \quad 3/8 \\
\hline
4/8 = 1/2
\end{array}
$$

To subtract unlike fractions, you must convert them to like fractions. First, find the least common denominator and divide it by the denominator of each original fraction. Then multiply both the numerator and the denominator of each original fraction by this number and subtract. When subtracting mixed numbers, change each mixed number to an improper like fraction.

Example 8/9 minus 5/12. The common denominator is 36.

$$
\begin{array}{l}
9\,\overline{)\,36} \quad \dfrac{4}{} \qquad \dfrac{8}{9} = \dfrac{8 \times 4}{9 \times 4} = \dfrac{32}{36} \\[2em]
12\,\overline{)\,36} \quad \dfrac{3}{} \qquad \dfrac{5}{12} = \dfrac{5 \times 3}{12 \times 3} = -\dfrac{15}{36} \\[1em]
\hline
\qquad\qquad\qquad\qquad\qquad\qquad\qquad \dfrac{17}{36}
\end{array}
$$

Example 4 1/6 minus 2 3/8. The common denominator is 24.

$$
\begin{array}{l}
6\,\overline{)\,24} \quad \dfrac{4}{} \qquad 4\dfrac{1}{6} = \dfrac{25 \times 4}{6 \times 4} = \dfrac{100}{24} \\[2em]
8\,\overline{)\,24} \quad \dfrac{3}{} \qquad 2\dfrac{3}{8} = \dfrac{19 \times 3}{8 \times 3} = -\dfrac{57}{24} \\[1em]
\hline
\qquad\qquad\qquad\qquad\qquad\qquad\qquad \dfrac{43}{24} = 1\dfrac{19}{24}
\end{array}
$$

Multiplication of Fractions

When multiplying fractions, first simplify by canceling (dividing one numerator and one denominator, regardless of their positions, by the same number). Next multiply the numerators, multiply the denominators, and reduce the results to the lowest terms.

Example 5/16 x 1/5 x 9/8.

$$
\dfrac{\cancel{5}^{\,1}}{16} \times \dfrac{1}{\cancel{5}_{\,1}} \times \dfrac{9}{8} = \dfrac{1 \times 1 \times 9}{16 \times 1 \times 8} = \dfrac{9}{128}
$$

Example 140 x 4/25 x 5/18.

$$
\dfrac{\cancel{\cancel{\cancel{140}}}^{\,14}}{1} \times \dfrac{4}{\cancel{25}_{\,5}} \times \dfrac{\cancel{5}^{\,1}}{\cancel{18}_{\,9}} = \dfrac{14 \times 4 \times 1}{1 \times 1 \times 9} = \dfrac{56}{9} = 6\dfrac{2}{9}
$$

Division of Fractions

When dividing fractions, invert the divisor (turn the fraction upside down) and multiply.

Example Divide 7/16 by 3/4.

$$\frac{7}{16} \div \frac{3}{4} = \frac{7}{\underset{4}{\cancel{16}}} = \frac{\cancel{4}}{3} = \frac{7}{4} \times \frac{1}{3} = \frac{7}{12}$$

Example Divide 36 by 2/3.

$$36 \div \frac{2}{3} = \frac{\overset{18}{\cancel{36}}}{1} \times \frac{3}{\underset{1}{\cancel{2}}} = 54$$

Changing a Fraction to a Decimal

Divide the numerator by the denominator.

Example Change 7/8 to a decimal.

```
       0.875
  8 ) 7.000
       6 4
        60
        56
        40
        40
```

Example Change 146/42 to a decimal.

$$\frac{146}{42} = \frac{146 \div 2}{42 \div 2} = \frac{73}{21}$$

```
          3.476 +
  21 ) 73.000
        63
        10 0
         8 4
         1 60
         1 47
           130
           126
             4
```

Changing a Decimal to a Fraction

Draw a line under the decimal. Write a 1 immediately below the decimal point and a 0 below each number in the decimal. Then drop the decimal point. Reduce to lowest terms.

Example Change 0.72 to a fraction.

$$0.72 = \frac{72}{100} = \frac{72 \div 4}{100 \div 4} = \frac{18}{25}$$

Example Change 0.8125 to a fraction.

$$0.8125 = \frac{8,125}{10,000} = \frac{8,125 \div 625}{10,000 \div 625} = \frac{13}{16}$$

Common Decimal Equivalents

The following equivalents are rounded off at the fourth decimal place.

1/2 = 0.5	1/6 = 0.1667	1/10 = 0.1
1/3 = 0.3333	1/7 = 0.1429	1/11 = 0.0909
2/3 = 0.6667	1/8 = 0.125	1/12 = 0.0833
1/4 = 0.25	3/8 = 0.375	1/15 = 0.0667
3/4 = 0.75	5/8 = 0.625	1/16 = 0.0625
1/5 = 0.2	7/8 = 0.875	1/20 = 0.05
3/5 = 0.6	1/9 = 0.1111	1/25 = 0.04

PERCENTAGES

Percentages are fractions that have 100 for their denominators.

Changing a Percentage to a Decimal

Drop the percent sign and move the decimal point two places to the left. If the percentage consists of only one digit, add a 0 to the left of the digit.

Example Change 36 percent to a decimal.

$$36\% = 36. = 0.36$$

Example Change 5.85 percent to a decimal.

$$5.85\% = 05.85 = 0.0585$$

Changing a Decimal to a Percentage

Move the decimal point two places to the right and add the percent sign.

Example Change 0.48 to a percentage.

$$0.48 = 0.48 = 48\%$$

Example Change 1.495 to a percentage.

$$1.495 = 1.495 = 149.5\%$$

Changing a Percentage to a Fraction

Drop the percent sign, make a fraction with the percentage as numerator and 100 as denominator, and reduce to lowest terms.

Example Change 25 percent to a fraction.

$$25\% = \frac{25}{100} = \frac{25 \div 25}{100 \div 25} = \frac{1}{4}$$

Example Change 31.5% to a fraction.

$$31.5\% = \frac{31.5}{100} = \frac{315}{1,000} = \frac{315 \div 5}{1,000 \div 5} = \frac{63}{200}$$

Changing a Fraction to a Percentage

Reduce to lowest terms. Divide the numerator by the denominator, move the decimal point two places to the right, and add the percent sign.

Example Change 5/8 to a percentage.

$$
\begin{array}{r}
0.625 \\
8 \overline{)\ 5.000} \\
\underline{4\,8} \\
20 \\
\underline{16} \\
40 \\
\underline{40}
\end{array}
\qquad = \ 0.625 \ = \ 62.5\%
$$

Example Change 46/8 to a percentage.

$$
\frac{46}{8} = \frac{46 \div 2}{8 \div 2} = \frac{23}{4}
$$

$$
\begin{array}{r}
5.75 \\
4 \overline{)\ 23.00} \\
\underline{20} \\
3\,0 \\
\underline{2\,8} \\
20 \\
\underline{20}
\end{array}
\qquad = \ 0.575 \ = \ 575\%
$$

Finding the Ratio of ... to ...

This is the same thing as finding the percentage that one thing is of another. Write the "of ..." amount in the numerator and the "to ..." amount in the denominator. Reduce to lowest terms and divide the numerator by the denominator.

Example Find the ratio of current assets ($69,000) to current liabilities ($27,000).

$$
\frac{69,000}{27,000} = \frac{69,000 \div 3,000}{27,000 \div 3,000} = \frac{23}{9}
$$

$$
\begin{array}{r}
2.555 \\
9 \overline{)\ 23.000} \\
\underline{18} \\
5\,0 \\
\underline{4\,5} \\
50 \\
\underline{45} \\
50 \\
\underline{45} \\
5
\end{array}
\qquad = \ 2.555 \ \ \text{or} \ \ 2.56
$$

Review of Business Mathematics

Example Find the ratio of salesroom floor space (6,000 square feet) to office floor space (900 square feet).

$$\frac{6,000}{900} = \frac{6,000 \div 300}{900 \div 300} = \frac{20}{3}$$

$$3,000 \overline{)\,20.000} = 6.666 \quad = \quad 6.666 \quad \text{or} \quad 6.67$$

```
      6.666
3,000 ) 20.000
        18
         2 0
         1 8
           20
           18
           20
           18
            2
```

Finding the Percentage of Increase or Decrease

Divide the amount of the change by the base (starting figure). Change the decimal to a percentage.

Example Moore's income increased from $12,000 to $15,000. Find the percentage of increase.

Amount of change = 15,000 − 12,000 = 3,000

```
          0.25
12,000 ) 3,000.00     = 0.25 = 25%
         2 400 0
           600 00
           600 00
```

Example Arnold's grade-point average decreased from 3.6 to 3.1. Find the percentage of decrease.

Amount of change = 3.6 − 3.1 = 0.5

```
         0.1388          = 0.1388 = 0.139 = 13.9%
3.6 ) 0.50000
        36
        140
        108
        320
        288
        320
        288
         32
```

ROUNDING OFF

If the last number in a decimal is 5 or greater, drop it and add one to the next number on the left. If the last number in a decimal is less than 5, drop it and let the other number stay the same.

Example Round off to two decimal places.

1.825 = 1.83

Example Round off to three decimal places.

0.6923 = 0.692

xxviii

How to Work a Practice Set

A practice set is a packet of accounting materials involving one business. Its purpose is to give you the opportunity to practice on a hypothetical company's accounting records, using what you have learned from the text and presentations by your instructor.

The advantages of completing a practice set during your accounting education are:

1. You are working for the same company.
2. You are able to maintain the continuity of the accounting cycle.
3. The materials are designed to simulate the records you will see on an accounting job.
4. The practice set may provide source documents to generate transactions to bridge the gap between textbook materials and real-world experiences.
5. It is rewarding to see your studying of text topics come together in a complete picture.
6. Completing the practice set is an excellent review of accounting.

Whatever practice set or sets your instructor chooses for you, here are some tips for working a practice set.

You will be most confident and successful if you first open the practice set, find the introduction, and answer the following questions:

- Where is the business located?
- What is the owner's name?
- Is it a sole proprietorship, a partnership, or a corporation?
- Does the company sell services, products, or both?
- What is your job title?
- What are your duties?
- Where do your duties fall in the accounting cycle, or will you be involved in the entire cycle?
- What is the length of the fiscal period?
- Are the books on the accrual basis?
- What date are you beginning work?
- In what format are the directions? In narrative form or in memos written to you?
- Are the transactions in narrative form, or will source documents generate the transactions?
- Are there check figures?
- What is required by the practice set? That is, what is the story behind the set—recording, finding errors, organizing? What is it trying to emphasize?
- What subjects does it cover?
- Is it manual or computerized?
- How long is it expected to take?
- Are you expected to file paperwork? Are there checkpoints where you must submit work?

Now it is time to begin the practice set. Follow these steps throughout the practice set to help ensure a more pleasant and rewarding experience:

- Read the instructions carefully, sometimes more than once. As you read, circle or highlight important words or phrases. Use this same technique when reading documents as you analyze the transaction generated by the document.
- Check off each instruction as you complete it. In the case of documents, initial each document as it is journalized.
- List questions that occur to you, and take them to class to get answers.

- Write words and numbers clearly; this will avoid some errors. Remember, this is an opportunity to show your best work.
- Follow the rules of accounting precisely—the step-by-step procedures you learned during the prior weeks in class will save you time.
- Talk yourself through the analysis, journalizing, and posting of amounts.
- Maintain an awareness of where you are in the accounting cycle.

Suggested Abbreviations for Account Titles in Chapters 1–13

Because traditional accounting methods have called for the use of full account titles in journal entries and financial statements, the text and solutions keep abbreviations to a minimum. However, computerized accounting programs and working papers present significant space constraints, and students' handwriting differs considerably in size. As a result, many instructors have requested a list of suggested abbreviations for account titles. Please bear in mind that there is no standard list of abbreviations; these are suggestions only. Account titles that are not included in this list are generally short enough to be written out in full.

Accounts Payable	Accts. Pay. or A/P
Accounts Receivable	Accts. Rec. or A/R
Accumulated Depreciation, Equipment	Accum. Depr., Equip.
Depreciation Expense, Equipment	Depr. Exp., Equip.
R. P. Cline, Capital	R. P. Cline, Cap.
R. P. Cline, Drawing	R. P. Cline, Draw.
Employees' Bond Deduction Payable	Empl. Bond Ded. Pay.
Employees' Federal Income Tax Payable	Empl. Fed. Inc. Tax Pay.
Employees' Medical Insurance Payable	Empl. Med. Ins. Pay.
Employees' Union Dues Payable	Empl. Union Dues Pay.
Federal Unemployment Tax Payable	Fed. Unemp. Tax Pay.
FICA Tax Payable	FICA Tax Pay.
Interest Expense	Int. Exp.
Interest Income	Int. Inc.
Interest Payable	Int. Pay.
Merchandise Inventory	Merch. Inv.
Miscellaneous General Expense	Misc. Gen. Exp.
Miscellaneous Selling Expense	Misc. Sell. Exp.
Notes Payable	Notes Pay.
Notes Receivable	Notes Rec.
Prepaid Workers' Compensation Insurance	Prepaid Workers' Comp. Ins.
Purchases Discount	Purch. Disct.
Purchases Returns and Allowances	Purch. Ret. and Allow.
Sales Commissions Expense	Sales Comm. Exp.
Sales Discount	Sales Disct.
Sales Returns and Allowances	Sales Ret. and Allow.
State Unemployment Tax Payable	State Unemp. Tax Pay.
Workers' Compensation Insurance Expense	Workers' Comp. Ins. Exp.

Introduction

PERFORMANCE OBJECTIVES

1. Define *accounting*.
2. Explain the importance of accounting information.
3. Describe the various career opportunities in accounting.
4. Define *ethics*.

KEY TERMS

Accountant

Accounting

Economic unit

Ethics

Generally accepted accounting principles (GAAP)

Paraprofessional accountant

Transaction

---

1 | Asset, Liability, Owner's Equity, Revenue, and Expense Accounts

PERFORMANCE OBJECTIVES

1. Define and identify *asset*, *liability*, and *owner's equity* accounts.
2. Record a group of business transactions, in column form, involving changes in assets, liabilities, and owner's equity.
3. Define and identify *revenue* and *expense* accounts.
4. Record a group of business transactions, in column form, involving all five elements of the fundamental accounting equation.

KEY TERMS

Accounts

Accounts Payable

Accounts Receivable

Assets

Business entity

Capital

Chart of accounts

Creditor

Double-entry accounting

Equity

Expenses

Fair market value

Fundamental accounting equation
   (Assets = Liabilities + Owner's Equity)

Liabilities

Owner's equity

Revenues

Separate entity concept

Sole proprietorship

Withdrawal

STUDY GUIDE QUESTIONS

PART 1   True/False

For each of the following statements, indicate T if the statement is true and F if the statement is false.

T	F	1.	The term *owner's equity* means the owner's investment.
T	F	2.	When an asset is purchased for cash, the owner's equity account is decreased.
T	F	3.	People who loan money to a company are considered the company's debtors.
T	F	4.	A business entity is considered an economic unit.
(T)	F	5.	Equipment is considered an asset.
(T)	F	6.	Expenses have the effect of decreasing owner's equity.
T	F	7.	The amounts owed by charge customers are recorded in the Accounts Receivable account.
T	F	8.	Withdrawals by the owner decrease owner's equity.
T	F	9.	When a business receives a payment from a charge customer, the revenue account is not affected.
T	F	10.	An accountant keeps a separate record for each asset, liability, owner's equity, revenue, and expense account.

PART 2   Completion—Language of Business

Complete each of the following statements by writing the appropriate words in the spaces provided.

1. A one-owner business is called a(n) _____ .

2. Debts owed by a business are called _____ .

3. A person or business to whom money is owed is called a(n) _____ .

4. The categories listed under the classifications Assets, Liabilities, Owner's Equity, Revenues, and Expenses are called _____ .

5. An event affecting a business that can be expressed in terms of money and that must be recorded in the accounting records is called a(n) _____ .

6. The owner's investment or equity in an enterprise is called _____ .

7. The equation expressing the relationship of assets, liabilities, and owner's equity is called the _____ .

8. The _____ is the official list of account titles to be used to record the transactions of a business.

9. A financial interest in or claim to an asset is called _____ .

10. _____ represents the amount a business earns by providing or performing a service for a customer.

11. If the owner takes cash out of the business each month, this is called a(n) _____ .

12. The account used to record the amounts owed by charge customers is _____ .

13. _____ are the costs related to the earning of revenue.

PART 3   Classifying Accounts

The office of financial consultant S. Acevedo has the following accounts:

Income from Services	Wages Expense
Office Equipment	Mortgage Payable
Supplies Expense	Land
Accounts Payable	S. Acevedo, Capital
Building	Prepaid Insurance
Cash	Neon Sign
Rent Expense	S. Acevedo, Drawing

List each account under the appropriate heading.

Assets
_____
_____
_____
_____
_____

Liabilities
Acct Payable
Mortgage Payable

Owner's Equity
_____
_____

Revenue
_____

Expenses
_____
_____
_____

PART 4   Analyzing Transactions

Here are some typical transactions of Baber Insect Control Service. For each transaction, indicate the increase (+) or the decrease (–) in Assets (A), Liabilities (L), Owner's Equity (OE), Revenue (R), or Expenses (E) by placing the appropriate sign(s) in the appropriate column(s). The first transaction is given as an example.

	A	L	OE	R	E
0. *Example:* Owner invested cash	+		+		
1. Payment of rent					
2. Sales of services for cash					
3. Investment of equipment by owner					
4. Payment of insurance premium for two years					
5. Payment of wages					
6. Sales of services on account					
7. Withdrawal of cash by owner					
8. Purchase of supplies on account					
9. Collection from charge customer previously billed					
10. Payment made to creditor on account					

DEMONSTRATION PROBLEM

During November of this year, James Kirkland opened an accounting practice called James Kirkland, CPA. The following transactions were completed during the first month:

a. Deposited $13,500 in a bank account in the name of James Kirkland, CPA.
b. Paid rent for the month, $1,600 (Rent Expense).
c. Bought office equipment, including a computer and a printer, for $9,500 from Bingham Company. Paid $6,700 in cash, with the balance due in thirty days.
d. Purchased office supplies and announcements for $970 from City Stationers. Payment is due in thirty days.
e. Billed clients $5,500 for services rendered (Client Fees).
f. Paid $1,450 salary to secretary/assistant for the month.
g. Paid telephone bill of $210 (Telephone Expense).
h. Received cash from clients previously billed on account, $2,450.
i. Paid Bingham Company $970 to apply on account.
j. Paid $275 for continuing education course (Miscellaneous Expense).
k. Kirkland withdrew $2,200 for personal use.

Instructions

1. Record the transactions and the balance after each transaction, using the following headings:

Assets	=	Liabilities	+	Owner's Equity
Cash + Accts. Rec. + Equip.		Accounts Payable		J. Kirkland, + Revenue – Expenses Capital

2. Demonstrate that the total of one side of the equation equals the total of the other side of the equation.

NAME _____ DATE _____ CLASS _____

Problem 1-4A or 1-4B (concluded)

Left Side of Equals Sign	Amount	Right Side of Equals Sign	Amount
Cash		Accounts Payable	
Accounts Receivable		_____, Capital	
Prepaid Insurance		Revenue	_____
Truck		Subtotal	
Equipment	_____	Expenses	_____
Left Side Total	_____	Right Side Total	_____

T Accounts, Debits and Credits, Trial Balance, and Financial Statements

PERFORMANCE OBJECTIVES

1. Determine balances of T accounts having entries recorded on both sides of the accounts.
2. Present the fundamental accounting equation with the T account form, and label the plus and minus sides.
3. Present the fundamental accounting equation with the T account form, and label the debit and credit sides.
4. Record directly in T accounts a group of business transactions involving changes in asset, liability, owner's equity, revenue, and expense accounts for a service business.
5. Prepare a trial balance.
6. Prepare (a) an income statement, (b) a statement of owner's equity, and (c) a balance sheet.
7. Recognize the effect of transpositions and slides on account balances.

KEY TERMS

Balance sheet	Net loss
Compound entry	Normal balance
Credit	Report form
Debit	Slide
Financial position	Statement of owner's equity
Financial statement	T account form
Footings	Transposition
Income statement	Trial balance
Net income	

STUDY GUIDE QUESTIONS

PART 1   True/False

For each of the following statements, indicate T if the statement is true and F if the statement is false.

T (F)   1. Expenses have the effect of increasing owner's equity.

T   F   2. A summary of assets, liabilities, and owner's equity shows the financial position of an economic unit.

(T) F   3. The third line in the heading of a balance sheet indicates one specific date.

T (F)   4. The amounts owed by charge customers are recorded in the Accounts Payable account.

T   F   5. The net income for a given financial period is found on both the income statement and the statement of owner's equity.

T   F   6.   To prepare the financial statements for a business, you should prepare the balance sheet first, followed by the income ~~st~~ then the statement of owner's equity.

T   F   7.   The ~~in~~ ~~is the~~ connecting link between the income statement and the balance sheet.

T   F   8.   An income statement is prepared at the end of the financial period to show the results of operations.

T   F   9.   In the report form of the balance sheet, the elements in the accounting equation are presented one on top of the other.

T   F   10.   If the owner withdraws more than the amount of the net income, there will be an increase in owner's equity.

PART 2   Completion—Language of Business

Complete each of the following statements by writing the appropriate words in the spaces provided.

1. The left-hand side of any account is the _____ *debit* _____ side.

2. The small, penciled-in figures showing the totals of each side of a T account in a manual system are called _____ *footing* _____.

3. If the digits are switched around when you record a number, the error is called a(n) _____.

4. The report used to prove that the total of all the debit balances equals the total of all the credit balances is called a(n) _____.

5. A(n) _____ is used to record a transaction that has more than one debit and/or more than one credit.

6. The right-hand side of any account is called the _____ *Credit* _____ side.

PART 3   Accounting Entries

The following transactions were completed by C. R. Hendricks, Physical Therapist. Using appropriate account titles, record the transactions in pairs of T accounts, and show plus and minus signs with each T account. List accounts to be debited in the left-hand T account column and accounts to be credited in the right-hand T account column.

0. *Example:* Paid electric bill, $92.

Utilities Expense		Cash	
+	–	+	–
(0) 92			(0) 92

a. Bought professional equipment on account, $560.

b. Billed patients for services performed, $870.

c. Paid rent for the month, $1,000.

d. Bought supplies on account, $220.

e. Paid telephone bill, $110.

f. Collected $920 from patients previously billed.

g. Paid creditors on account, $700.

h. Paid salary of assistant, $900.

i. Bought office equipment for cash, $452.

DEMONSTRATION PROBLEM

Dr. Christy Russo maintains an office for the practice of veterinary medicine. The account balances as of September 1 are given below. All are normal balances.

Assets		**Revenue**	
Cash	$ 2,459	Professional Fees	$72,118
Accounts Receivable	18,120		
Prepaid Insurance	980	**Expenses**	
Automobile	20,650	Salary Expense	14,380
Furniture and Equipment	5,963	Rent Expense	10,320
		Gas and Oil Expense	859
Liabilities		Utilities Expense	1,213
Accounts Payable	1,590	Supplies Expense	840

Owner's Equity	
C. Russo, Capital	42,076
C. Russo, Drawing	40,000

The following transactions occurred during September of this year.

a. Paid rent for the month, $1,290.
b. Paid $1,800 for one year's coverage of liability insurance.
c. Bought medical equipment on account from Bennett Surgical Supply, $849, paying $200 down with the balance due in thirty days.
d. Billed patients for services performed, $9,015.
e. Paid employee salaries, $1,797.
f. Received and paid gas and electric bill, $112.
g. Received cash from patients previously billed, $11,060.
h. Received bill for gasoline for car, used only in the professional practice, from Garza Fuel Company, $116.
i. Paid creditors on account, $1,590.
j. Dr. Russo withdrew cash for personal use, $5,000.

Instructions

1. Correctly place plus and minus signs under each T account and label the sides of the T accounts as either debit or credit in the fundamental accounting equation. Record the account balances as of September 1.
2. Record the September transactions in the T accounts. Key each transaction to the letter that identifies the transaction.
3. Foot the columns.
4. Prepare a trial balance dated September 30.
5. Prepare an income statement for six months ended September 30, 20—.
6. Prepare a statement of owner's equity for six months ended September 30, 20—.
7. Prepare a balance sheet as of September 30, 20—.

SOLUTION

Assets

Cash

+ Debit		– Credit	
Bal.	2,459	(a)	1,290
(g)	11,060	(b)	1,800
	13,519	(c)	200
		(e)	1,797
		(f)	112
		(i)	1,590
		(j)	5,000
			11,789
Bal.	1,730		

Accounts Receivable

+ Debit		– Credit	
Bal.	18,120	(g)	11,060
(d)	9,015		
	27,135		
Bal.	16,075		

Prepaid Insurance

+ Debit		– Credit
Bal.	980	
(b)	1,800	
	2,780	
Bal.	2,780	

Automobile

+ Debit		– Credit
Bal.	20,650	

Furniture and Equipment

+ Debit		– Credit
Bal.	5,963	
(c)	849	
Bal.	6,812	

Liabilities =

Accounts Payable

– Debit		+ Credit	
(i)	1,590	Bal.	1,590
		(c)	649
		(h)	116
			2,355
		Bal.	765

Owner's Equity +

C. Russo, Capital

– Debit		+ Credit	
		Bal.	42,076

C. Russo, Drawing

+ Debit		– Credit
Bal.	40,000	
(j)	5,000	
Bal.	45,000	

Revenue +

Professional Fees

– Debit		+ Credit	
		Bal.	72,118
		(d)	9,015
		Bal.	81,133

Expenses –

Salary Expense

+ Debit		– Credit
Bal.	14,380	
(e)	1,797	
Bal.	16,177	

Rent Expense

+ Debit		– Credit
Bal.	10,320	
(a)	1,290	
Bal.	11,610	

Gas and Oil Expense

+ Debit		– Credit
Bal.	859	
(h)	116	
Bal.	975	

Utilities Expense

+ Debit		– Credit
Bal.	1,213	
(f)	112	
Bal.	1,325	

Supplies Expense

+ Debit		– Credit
Bal.	840	

Dr. Christy Russo
Trial Balance
September 30, 20–

ACCOUNT NAME	DEBIT	CREDIT
Cash	1,730.00	
Accounts Receivable	16,075.00	
Prepaid Insurance	2,780.00	
Automobile	20,650.00	
Furniture and Equipment	6,812.00	
Accounts Payable		765.00
C. Russo, Capital		42,076.00
C. Russo, Drawing	45,000.00	
Professional Fees		81,133.00
Salary Expense	16,177.00	
Rent Expense	11,610.00	
Gas and Oil Expense	975.00	
Utilities Expense	1,325.00	
Supplies Expense	840.00	
	123,974.00	123,974.00

SOLUTION (concluded)

Dr. Christy Russo
Income Statement
For Six Months Ended September 30, 20—

Revenue:		
Professional Fees		$81,133.00
Expenses:		
Salary Expense	$16,177.00	
Rent Expense	11,610.00	
Gas and Oil Expense	975.00	
Utilities Expense	1,325.00	
Supplies Expense	840.00	
Total Expenses		30,927.00
Net Income		$50,206.00

Dr. Christy Russo
Statement of Owner's Equity
For Two Months Ended September 30, 20—

C. Russo, Capital, April 1, 20—		$42,076.00
Net Income for April through September	$50,206.00	
Less Withdrawals for April through September	45,000.00	
Increase in Capital		5,206.00
C. Russo, Capital, September 30, 20—		$47,282.00

Dr. Christy Russo
Balance Sheet
September 30, 20—

Assets		
Cash	$ 1,730.00	
Accounts Receivable	16,075.00	
Prepaid Insurance	2,780.00	
Automobile	20,650.00	
Furniture and Equipment	6,812.00	
Total Assets		$48,047.00
Liabilities		
Accounts Payable		$ 765.00
Owner's Equity		
C. Russo, Capital		47,282.00
Total Liabilities and Owner's Equity		$48,047.00

EXERCISES

Exercise 2-1

a. _____
b. _____
c. _____
d. _____
e. _____
f. _____

g. _____

h. _____
i. _____
j. _____
k. _____

Exercise 2-2

Assets	=	Liabilities	+	Owner's Equity	+	Revenue	–	Expenses
+ –								
Dr. Cr.								

NAME _____ DATE _____ CLASS _____

Exercise 2-6 (concluded)

Exercise 2-7

		Amount of Difference	Debit or Credit Column of Trial Balance Understated or Overstated
0.	Example: A $149 debit to Accounts Receivable was not recorded.	$149	Debit column understated
a.	A $42 debit to Supplies Expense was recorded as $320.		
b.	A $155 debit to Accounts Payable was recorded twice.		
c.	A $179 debit to Prepaid Insurance was not recorded.		
d.	A $65 credit to Cash was not recorded.		
e.	A $190 debit to Equipment was recorded twice.		
f.	A $57 debit to Utilities Expense was recorded as $75.		

Exercise 2-8

a. _____

_____

_____

_____

b. _____

_____

_____

_____

c. _____

_____

_____

_____

d. _____

_____

_____

_____

Problem 2-1A or 2-1B

Assets = Liabilities + Owner's Equity + Revenues − Expenses

Assets	
+ −	

Cash

Debit	Credit
(a) 20000	(b) 1735
(a) 2110	125
7890	250
	2110

Shop Equipment

1735	2425
650	
2365	
2135	

Office Equipment

325	
700	
1225	

21050	2935

Liabilities
− +

Account Payable
− +

200	225
250	650
	200
	825

Asset

Owner's Equity
− +

	20,000
	700

Revenues
− +

Expenses
+ −

Supplies Expense

1735	
225	
650	

NAME _____

CLASS _____

DATE _____

Problem 2-2A or 2-2B

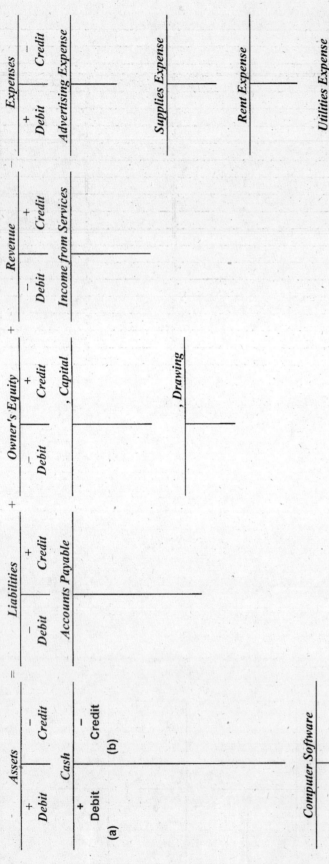

Assets = **Liabilities** + **Owner's Equity** + **Revenue** − **Expenses**

| + | − |
| Debit | Credit |

Cash

(a)

(b)

Computer Software

Office Equipment

Neon Sign

| − | + |
| Debit | Credit |

Accounts Payable

| − | + |
| Debit | Credit |

, Capital

, Drawing

| − | + |
| Debit | Credit |

Income from Services

| + | − |
| Debit | Credit |

Advertising Expense

Supplies Expense

Rent Expense

Utilities Expense

Wages Expense

Miscellaneous Expense

Problem 2-2A or 2-2B (concluded)

ACCOUNT NAME	DEBIT	CREDIT

Problem 2-3A or 2-3B

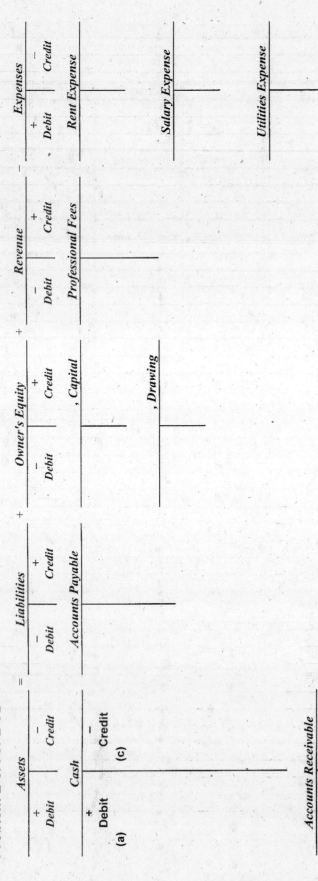

Assets

+	−
Debit	Credit

Cash

+	−
Debit	Credit
(a)	(c)

Accounts Receivable

Office Equipment

Office Furniture

= Liabilities +

−	+
Debit	Credit

Accounts Payable

Owner's Equity

−	+
Debit	Credit

, Capital

, Drawing

+ Revenue −

−	+
Debit	Credit

Professional Fees

− Expenses

+	−
Debit	Credit

Rent Expense

Salary Expense

Utilities Expense

Miscellaneous Expense

Problem 2-3A or 2-3B (continued)

ACCOUNT NAME	DEBIT	CREDIT	

Problem 2-3A or 2-3B (concluded)

Problem 2-4A or 2-4B

Cash	
+	**−**
Debit	**Credit**
(a)	(b)

Prepaid Insurance

Equipment

Furniture
and Fixtures

Accounts Payable

, Capital

, Drawing

Laundry Revenue

Wages Expense

Supplies Expense

Rent Expense

Utilities Expense

Miscellaneous
Expense

Problem 2-4A or 2-4B (continued)

ACCOUNT NAME	DEBIT	CREDIT

	DEBIT	CREDIT

Problem 2-4A or 2-4B (concluded)

The General Journal and the General Ledger

PERFORMANCE OBJECTIVES

1. Record a group of transactions pertaining to a service enterprise in a two-column general journal.
2. Post entries from a two-column general journal to general ledger accounts.
3. Prepare a trial balance from the ledger accounts.
4. Correct entries using the manual ruling method.
5. Correct entries using the manual or computerized correcting entry method.

KEY TERMS

Account numbers	Journalizing
Cost principle	Ledger account
Cross-reference	Posting
General ledger	Source documents
Journal	Two-column general journal

STUDY GUIDE QUESTIONS

PART 1   True/False

For each of the following statements, indicate T if the statement is true and F if the statement is false.

T	**F**	1.	The credit part of a journal entry always comes first.
T	**F**	2.	Dollar signs are required in all journal entries.
T	**F**	3.	A transaction must be posted before it is journalized.
T	F	4.	In a journal entry, if two accounts are debited, two accounts must be credited.
T	F	5.	The first step in the posting process is to write the date of the transaction.
T	F	6.	In the presentation of a general journal in the text, the title of the account credited is indented approximately one-half inch.
T	**F**	7.	A number in the Post. Ref. column in the ledger account indicates that the balance has been recorded in the trial balance.
T	F	8.	Failure to post an entire transaction from the journal to the ledger will cause an error in the trial balance.
T	F	9.	Having a running balance is an advantage of a four-column ledger account form.
T	**F**	10.	A trial balance is prepared directly from the journal.

PART 2   Completion—Language of Business

Complete each of the following statements by writing the appropriate words in the spaces provided.

1.   A book or file containing the accounts of a business is called a(n) ___ledger___ _____.

2.   The process of transferring information from the journal to the ledger is called ___Posting_____.

3.   Business papers that serve as evidence that a transaction took place are called ___Source documents_____.

4.   The ___Cost Principle_____ states that the purchase of an asset should be recorded at the agreed amount of the transaction.

5.   The process of recording a business transaction in a book of original entry is called ___Journalizing_____.

6.   A cross-reference exists when the journal page number is recorded in the Post. Ref. column of the ledger and the ledger account number is recorded in the ___Post Ref Column___ ___general journal___.

7.   The accounts in the ledger are listed according to ___the chart of accounts___.

PART 3   Completing a Journal Entry

Here are a partially completed journal entry and the Cash ledger account. Complete the entry, including the explanation, using the data given. The entry represents the first entry on page 33 and occurred during October of the current year.

GENERAL JOURNAL   PAGE ___33___

	DATE		DESCRIPTION	POST. REF.	DEBIT	CREDIT	
1	20 —						1
2	Oct.	29	Cash		1,100.00		2
3			Accounts Receivable	113	600		3
4			Income from Services	411		1,700.00	4
5							5
6							6

GENERAL LEDGER

ACCOUNT *Cash*   ACCOUNT NO.   *111*

DATE		ITEM	POST. REF.	DEBIT	CREDIT	BALANCE	
						DEBIT	CREDIT
20 —							
Oct.	1	Balance	√			2,900.00	
Nov	6		30	600.00		3,500.00	
Dec	6		30		700.00	2,800.00	
Jan	12		32	1,100.00		3,900.00	
Feb	14		32		400.00	3,500.00	
Mar	27		32		200.00	3,300.00	
Apr	29		33	1,100.00		4,400.00	
May							

1. What is the missing amount in the journal entry? __600__

2. What is the total cash received during October? __(1100)__

3. What is the total cash paid out during October? __1200__

4. The journal entry is an example of a(n) __Compound__ journal entry.

DEMONSTRATION PROBLEM

G. Bell, a fitness enthusiast, buys an existing exercise center, Body Firm. The following chart of accounts now applies:

Assets
111   Cash
124   Land
126   Building
128   Equipment

Liabilities
221   Accounts Payable
223   Mortgage Payable

Owner's Equity
311   G. Bell, Capital
312   G. Bell, Drawing

Revenue
411   Income from Services

Expenses
511   Wages Expense
512   Utilities Expense
513   Advertising Expense
514   Repair Expense
519   Miscellaneous Expense

Apr. 16   Bell deposited $100,000 in a bank account for the purpose of buying Body Firm.

17   Bought the assets of Body Firm for a total price of $188,000. The assets include equipment, $28,000; building, $96,000; and land, $64,000. Made a down payment of $89,000 and signed a mortgage note for the remainder.

17   Bought additional equipment from Fitness Supply Co. on account for $3,550, paying $710 down, with balance due in thirty days.

29   Celebrated the grand opening of Body Firm. Advertising expenses were paid in cash for the following:

Advertising in newspaper	314
Announcements mailed to local residents	85
Postage	125
Balloons, ribbons, flowers	126
Food and refreshments	58

30   Received fees for daily use of the facilities, $1,152.

30   Paid wages for the period April 17 through April 30, $833.

30   Received and paid electric bill, $129.

30   Received and paid repair bill, $96.

30   Bell withdrew $600 for personal use.

Instructions

1.   Record the transactions in the general journal.
2.   Post the transactions to the general ledger.
3.   Prepare a trial balance as of April 30.

SOLUTION

GENERAL JOURNAL   PAGE _____ *1* _____

	DATE		DESCRIPTION	POST. REF.	DEBIT	CREDIT	
1	20 —						1
2	Apr.	16	Cash	111	100,000.00		2
3			G. Bell, Capital	311		100,000.00	3
4			Invested cash in the business.				4
5							5
6		17	Equipment	128	28,000.00		6
7			Building	126	96,000.00		7
8			Land	124	64,000.00		8
9			Cash	111		89,000.00	9
10			Mortgage Payable	223		99,000.00	10
11			Bought Body Firm.				11
12							12
13		17	Equipment	128	3,550.00		13
14			Cash	111		710.00	14
15			Accounts Payable	221		2,840.00	15
16			Bought equipment on account from				16
17			Fitness Supply Co., with balance				17
18			due in 30 days.				18
19							19
20		29	Advertising Expense	513	708.00		20
21			Cash	111		708.00	21
22			Grand opening expenses.				22
23							23
24		30	Cash	111	1,152.00		24
25			Income from Services	411		1,152.00	25
26			Received fees.				26
27							27
28		30	Wages Expense	511	833.00		28
29			Cash	111		833.00	29
30			Paid wages for period				30
31			April 17 through April 30.				31
32							32
33		30	Utilities Expense	512	129.00		33
34			Cash	111		129.00	34
35			Paid electric bill.				35
36							36
37		30	Repair Expense	514	96.00		37
38			Cash	111		96.00	38
39			Paid repair bill.				39
40							40
41		30	G. Bell, Drawing	312	600.00		41
42			Cash	111		600.00	42
43			Withdrawal for personal use.				43
44							44

SOLUTION (continued)

GENERAL LEDGER

ACCOUNT **Cash**   ACCOUNT NO. **111**

DATE		ITEM	POST. REF.	DEBIT	CREDIT	BALANCE DEBIT	BALANCE CREDIT
20 —							
Apr.	16		1	100,000.00		100,000.00	
	17		1		89,000.00	11,000.00	
	17		1		710.00	10,290.00	
	29		1		708.00	9,582.00	
	30		1	1,152.00		10,734.00	
	30		1		833.00	9,901.00	
	30		1		129.00	9,772.00	
	30		1		96.00	9,676.00	
	30		1		600.00	9,076.00	

ACCOUNT **Land**   ACCOUNT NO. **124**

DATE		ITEM	POST. REF.	DEBIT	CREDIT	BALANCE DEBIT	BALANCE CREDIT
20 —							
Apr.	17		1	64,000.00		64,000.00	

ACCOUNT **Building**   ACCOUNT NO. **126**

DATE		ITEM	POST. REF.	DEBIT	CREDIT	BALANCE DEBIT	BALANCE CREDIT
20 —							
Apr.	17		1	96,000.00		96,000.00	

ACCOUNT **Equipment**   ACCOUNT NO. **128**

DATE		ITEM	POST. REF.	DEBIT	CREDIT	BALANCE DEBIT	BALANCE CREDIT
20 —							
Apr.	17		1	28,000.00		28,000.00	
	17		1	3,550.00		31,550.00	

SOLUTION *(continued)*

ACCOUNT   *Accounts Payable*   ACCOUNT NO. **221**

DATE		ITEM	POST. REF.	DEBIT	CREDIT	BALANCE	
						DEBIT	CREDIT
20 —							
Apr.	17		1		2,840.00		2,840.00

ACCOUNT   *Mortgage Payable*   ACCOUNT NO. **223**

DATE		ITEM	POST. REF.	DEBIT	CREDIT	BALANCE	
						DEBIT	CREDIT
20 —							
Apr.	17		1		99,000.00		99,000.00

ACCOUNT   *G. Bell, Capital*   ACCOUNT NO. **311**

DATE		ITEM	POST. REF.	DEBIT	CREDIT	BALANCE	
						DEBIT	CREDIT
20 —							
Apr.	16		1		100,000.00		100,000.00

ACCOUNT   *G. Bell, Drawing*   ACCOUNT NO. **312**

DATE		ITEM	POST. REF.	DEBIT	CREDIT	BALANCE	
						DEBIT	CREDIT
20 —							
Apr.	30		1	600.00		600.00	

ACCOUNT   *Income from Services*   ACCOUNT NO. **411**

DATE		ITEM	POST. REF.	DEBIT	CREDIT	BALANCE	
						DEBIT	CREDIT
20 —							
Apr.	30		1		1,152.00		1,152.00

SOLUTION (continued)

ACCOUNT   *Wages Expense*   ACCOUNT NO.   *511*

DATE		ITEM	POST. REF.	DEBIT	CREDIT	BALANCE DEBIT	BALANCE CREDIT
20 —							
Apr.	30		1	833.00		833.00	

ACCOUNT   *Utilities Expense*   ACCOUNT NO.   *512*

DATE		ITEM	POST. REF.	DEBIT	CREDIT	BALANCE DEBIT	BALANCE CREDIT
20 —							
Apr.	30		1	129.00		129.00	

ACCOUNT   *Advertising Expense*   ACCOUNT NO.   *513*

DATE		ITEM	POST. REF.	DEBIT	CREDIT	BALANCE DEBIT	BALANCE CREDIT
20 —							
Apr.	29		1	708.00		708.00	

ACCOUNT   *Repair Expense*   ACCOUNT NO.   *514*

DATE		ITEM	POST. REF.	DEBIT	CREDIT	BALANCE DEBIT	BALANCE CREDIT
20 —							
Apr.	30		1	96.00		96.00	

ACCOUNT   *Miscellaneous Expense*   ACCOUNT NO.   *519*

DATE		ITEM	POST. REF.	DEBIT	CREDIT	BALANCE DEBIT	BALANCE CREDIT

SOLUTION (concluded)

Body Firm
Trial Balance
April 30, 20—

ACCOUNT NAME	DEBIT	CREDIT
Cash	9,076.00	
Land	64,000.00	
Building	96,000.00	
Equipment	31,550.00	
Accounts Payable		2,840.00
Mortgage Payable		99,000.00
G. Bell, Capital		100,000.00
G. Bell, Drawing	600.00	
Income from Services		1,152.00
Wages Expense	833.00	
Utilities Expense	129.00	
Advertising Expense	708.00	
Repair Expense	96.00	
	202,992.00	202,992.00

EXERCISES

Exercise 3-1

1. _____
2. _____
3. _____
4. _____

5. _____
6. _____
7. _____
8. _____

Exercise 3-2

GENERAL JOURNAL   PAGE _____

	DATE	DESCRIPTION	POST. REF.	DEBIT	CREDIT	
1						1
2						2
3						3
4						4
5						5
6						6
7						7
8						8
9						9
10						10
11						11
12						12
13						13
14						14
15						15
16						16
17						17
18						18
19						19
20						20
21						21
22						22
23						23
24						24
25						25
26						26
27						27
28						28

Exercise 3-3

GENERAL JOURNAL

PAGE _____

	DATE		DESCRIPTION	POST. REF.	DEBIT	CREDIT	
1							1
2							2
3							3
4							4
5							5
6							6
7							7
8							8
9							9
10							10
11							11
12							12
13							13
14							14
15							15
16							16
17							17
18							18
19							19
20							20
21							21
22							22
23							23
24							24
25							25
26							26
27							27
28							28
29							29

Exercise 3-4

GENERAL LEDGER

ACCOUNT _Cash_ ACCOUNT NO. _111_

DATE		ITEM	POST. REF.	DEBIT	CREDIT	BALANCE	
						DEBIT	CREDIT

Exercise 3-5

_____

Exercise 3-6

Navarro Company
Trial Balance
June 30, 20--

ACCOUNT NAME	DEBIT	CREDIT
Cash		
Accounts Receivable		
Prepaid Insurance		
Equipment		
Accounts Payable		
M. Navarro, Capital		
M. Navarro, Drawing		
Professional Fees		
Supplies Expense		
Rent Expense		
Miscellaneous Expense		

Exercise 3-7

Transactions	Total Revenue	Total Expenses	Net Income
0. Example: A check for $325 was written to pay on account. The accountant debited Rent Expense for $325 and credited Cash for $325.	NA	O	U
a. $420 was received on account from customers. The accountant debited Cash for $420 and credited Professional Fees for $420.			
b. The owner withdrew $1,200 for personal use. The accountant debited Wages Expense for $1,200 and credited Cash for $1,200.			
c. A check was written for $1,250 to pay the rent. The accountant debited Rent Expense for $1,520 and credited Cash for $1,520.			
d. $1,800 was received on account from customers. The accountant debited Cash for $1,800 and credited the Capital account for $1,800.			
e. A check was written for $225 to pay the phone bill received and recorded earlier this month. The accountant debited Phone Expense for $225 and credited Cash for $225.			

NAME _____   DATE _____   CLASS _____

Exercise 3-8

GENERAL JOURNAL   PAGE _____

	DATE		DESCRIPTION	POST. REF.	DEBIT	CREDIT	
1							1
2							2
3							3
4							4
5							5
6							6
7							7
8							8
9							9
10							10
11							11
12							12
13							13
14							14
15							15
16							16
17							17
18							18
19							19
20							20
21							21
22							22
23							23
24							24
25							25
26							26
27							27
28							28
29							29
30							30
31							31
32							32
33							33
34							34
35							35
36							36
37							37
38							38
39							39
40							40
41							41
42							42
43							43
44							44

NAME _____ DATE _____ CLASS _____

Problem 3-1A or 3-1B

GENERAL JOURNAL   PAGE _____

	DATE		DESCRIPTION	POST. REF.	DEBIT	CREDIT	
1							1
2							2
3							3
4							4
5							5
6							6
7							7
8							8
9							9
10							10
11							11
12							12
13							13
14							14
15							15
16							16
17							17
18							18
19							19
20							20
21							21
22							22
23							23
24							24
25							25
26							26
27							27
28							28
29							29
30							30
31							31
32							32
33							33
34							34
35							35
36							36
37							37
38							38
39							39
40							40
41							41
42							42
43							43
44							44
45							45
46							46
47							47

Problem 3-1A or 3-1B (concluded)

GENERAL JOURNAL   PAGE _____

	DATE		DESCRIPTION	POST. REF.	DEBIT	CREDIT	
1							1
2							2
3							3
4							4
5							5
6							6
7							7
8							8
9							9
10							10
11							11
12							12
13							13
14							14
15							15
16							16
17							17
18							18
19							19
20							20
21							21
22							22
23							23
24							24
25							25
26							26
27							27
28							28
29							29
30							30
31							31
32							32
33							33
34							34
35							35
36							36
37							37
38							38
39							39

Problem 3-2A

GENERAL JOURNAL

PAGE ___5___

	DATE		DESCRIPTION	POST. REF.	DEBIT	CREDIT	
1	20--						1
2	Aug.	1	Rent Expense		1,000.00		2
3			Cash			1,000.00	3
4			Paid rent for August, Ck. No. 145.				4
5							5
6		5	Cash		27.00		6
7			Accounts Receivable			27.00	7
8			Bob's Deli, on account, Inv. No. 316.				8
9							9
10		8	Cash		3,241.00		10
11			Income from Services			3,241.00	11
12			Week of August 2.				12
13							13
14		10	Accounts Payable		512.00		14
15			Cash			512.00	15
16			Paid Osborne Equipment Co.,				16
17			on account, Ck. No. 146.				17
18							18
19		15	Cash		3,164.00		19
20			Income from Services			3,164.00	20
21			Week of August 9.				21
22							22
23		16	Wages Expense		1,286.00		23
24			Cash			1,286.00	24
25			Wages, August 1–15, Ck. No. 147.				25
26							26
27		18	Accounts Receivable		840.00		27
28			Income from Services			840.00	28
29			Metro Transit, for services				29
30			rendered, Inv. No. 317.				30
31							31
32		20	Supplies Expense		850.00		32
33			Accounts Payable			850.00	33
34			Bought supplies from Office Supply				34
35			Company, Inv. No. 6165.				35
36							36

Problem 3-2A (continued)

GENERAL JOURNAL   PAGE ____6____

	DATE		DESCRIPTION	POST. REF.	DEBIT	CREDIT	
1	20--						1
2	Aug.	22	Cash		3,020.00		2
3			Income from Services			3,020.00	3
4			Week of August 16.				4
5							5
6		24	Utilities Expense		320.00		6
7			Cash			320.00	7
8			Paid utilities bill, Ck. No. 148.				8
9							9
10		25	Accounts Payable		500.00		10
11			Cash			500.00	11
12			Office Supply Company on account,				12
13			Ck. No. 149.				13
14							14
15		29	Cash		2,067.00		15
16			Income from Services			2,067.00	16
17			Week of August 23.				17
18							18
19		31	Wages Expense		1,292.00		19
20			Cash			1,292.00	20
21			Wages, August 16–31,				21
22			Ck. No. 150.				22
23							23
24		31	Cash		300.00		24
25			Accounts Receivable			300.00	25
26			Metro Transit, on account,				26
27			Inv. No. 317.				27
28							28
29		31	Advertising Expense		568.00		29
30			Accounts Payable			568.00	30
31			Received advertising bill from				31
32			Community News, Inv. No. D1694.				32
33							33
34		31	M. Casey, Drawing		1,850.00		34
35			Cash			1,850.00	35
36			Withdrawal for personal use,				36
37			Ck. No. 151.				37
38							38
39							39

Problem 3-2A (continued)

GENERAL LEDGER

ACCOUNT   *Cash*   ACCOUNT NO.   *111*

DATE		ITEM	POST. REF.	DEBIT	CREDIT	BALANCE	
						DEBIT	CREDIT
20--							
July	31	Balance	✓			24,113.00	

ACCOUNT   *Accounts Receivable*   ACCOUNT NO.   *113*

DATE		ITEM	POST. REF.	DEBIT	CREDIT	BALANCE	
						DEBIT	CREDIT
20--							
July	31	Balance	✓			150.00	

ACCOUNT   *Prepaid Insurance*   ACCOUNT NO.   *117*

DATE		ITEM	POST. REF.	DEBIT	CREDIT	BALANCE	
						DEBIT	CREDIT
20--							
July	31	Balance	✓			840.00	

NAME _____ DATE _____ CLASS _____

Problem 3-2A (continued)

ACCOUNT _Equipment_   ACCOUNT NO. _124_

DATE		ITEM	POST. REF.	DEBIT	CREDIT	BALANCE DEBIT	BALANCE CREDIT
20--							
July	31	Balance	✓			18,950.00	

ACCOUNT _Accounts Payable_   ACCOUNT NO. _221_

DATE		ITEM	POST. REF.	DEBIT	CREDIT	BALANCE DEBIT	BALANCE CREDIT
20--							
July	31	Balance	✓				4,236.00

ACCOUNT _, Capital_   ACCOUNT NO. _311_

DATE		ITEM	POST. REF.	DEBIT	CREDIT	BALANCE DEBIT	BALANCE CREDIT
20--							
July	31	Balance	✓				42,000.00

ACCOUNT _, Drawing_   ACCOUNT NO. _312_

DATE		ITEM	POST. REF.	DEBIT	CREDIT	BALANCE DEBIT	BALANCE CREDIT
20--							
July	31	Balance	✓			4,500.00	

ACCOUNT _Income from Services_   ACCOUNT NO. _411_

DATE		ITEM	POST. REF.	DEBIT	CREDIT	BALANCE DEBIT	BALANCE CREDIT
20--							
July	31	Balance	✓				6,800.00

Problem 3-2A (continued)

ACCOUNT *Wages Expense*   ACCOUNT NO. *511*

DATE		ITEM	POST. REF.	DEBIT	CREDIT	BALANCE	
						DEBIT	CREDIT
20--							
July	31	Balance	✓			2,395.00	

ACCOUNT *Rent Expense*   ACCOUNT NO. *512*

DATE		ITEM	POST. REF.	DEBIT	CREDIT	BALANCE	
						DEBIT	CREDIT
20--							
July	31	Balance	✓			900.00	

ACCOUNT *Advertising Expense*   ACCOUNT NO. *513*

DATE		ITEM	POST. REF.	DEBIT	CREDIT	BALANCE	
						DEBIT	CREDIT
20--							
July	31	Balance	✓			487.00	

ACCOUNT *Utilities Expense*   ACCOUNT NO. *514*

DATE		ITEM	POST. REF.	DEBIT	CREDIT	BALANCE	
						DEBIT	CREDIT
20--							
July	31	Balance	✓			381.00	

ACCOUNT *Supplies Expense*   ACCOUNT NO. *515*

DATE		ITEM	POST. REF.	DEBIT	CREDIT	BALANCE	
						DEBIT	CREDIT
20--							
July	31	Balance	✓			320.00	

Problem 3-2A (continued)

ACCOUNT NAME	DEBIT	CREDIT

Problem 3-2A (concluded)

Problem 3-2B

GENERAL JOURNAL   PAGE ____4____

	DATE		DESCRIPTION	POST. REF.	DEBIT	CREDIT	
1	20--						1
2	May	1	Rent Expense		850.00		2
3			Cash			850.00	3
4			Paid rent for May, Ck. No. 148.				4
5							5
6		5	Cash		988.00		6
7			Accounts Receivable			988.00	7
8			Tay Company, on account,				8
9			Inv. No. 125.				9
10							10
11		7	Cash		1,548.00		11
12			Income from Services			1,548.00	12
13			Week of May 1.				13
14							14
15		8	Accounts Payable		346.00		15
16			Cash			346.00	16
17			Paid Tiffany Equipment Co.,				17
18			on account, Ck. No. 149.				18
19							19
20		14	Cash		1,655.00		20
21			Income from Services			1,655.00	21
22			Week of May 8.				22
23							23
24		15	Wages Expense		846.00		24
25			Cash			846.00	25
26			Paid wages, May 1–May 15,				26
27			Ck. No. 150.				27
28							28
29		17	Accounts Receivable		1,275.00		29
30			Income from Services			1,275.00	30
31			Le Company on account,				31
32			Inv. No. 126.				32
33							33
34		18	Supplies Expense		364.00		34
35			Accounts Payable			364.00	35
36			Bought supplies on account from				36
37			Vega Supply Company, Inv. No. 3160.				37
38							38

Problem 3-2B (continued)

GENERAL JOURNAL   PAGE ___5___

	DATE		DESCRIPTION	POST. REF.	DEBIT	CREDIT	
1	20--						1
2	May	21	Cash		1,679.00		2
3			Income from Services			1,679.00	3
4			Week of May 15.				4
5							5
6		23	Utilities Expense		435.00		6
7			Cash			435.00	7
8			Paid telephone bill, Ck. No. 151.				8
9							9
10		25	Accounts Payable		260.00		10
11			Cash			260.00	11
12			Paid Vega Supply Company on				12
13			account, Inv. No. 3160.				13
14							14
15		28	Cash		1,820.00		15
16			Income from Services			1,820.00	16
17			Week of May 22.				17
18							18
19		31	Wages Expense		1,276.00		19
20			Cash			1,276.00	20
21			Paid wages, May 16 – May 31.				21
22							22
23		31	Cash		250.00		23
24			Accounts Receivable			250.00	24
25			Le Company on account,				25
26			Inv. No. 126.				26
27							27
28		31	Advertising Expense		560.00		28
29			Accounts Payable			560.00	29
30			Received advertising bill from				30
31			Community News, Inv. No. 316.				31
32							32
33		31	R. Ochoa, Drawing		1,200.00		33
34			Cash			1,200.00	34
35			Withdrawal for personal use,				35
36			Ck. No. 152.				36
37							37

Problem 3-2B (continued)

GENERAL LEDGER

ACCOUNT *Cash*   ACCOUNT NO.   *111*

DATE		ITEM	POST. REF.	DEBIT	CREDIT	BALANCE	
						DEBIT	CREDIT
20--							
Apr.	30	Balance	✓			12,980.00	

ACCOUNT *Accounts Receivable*   ACCOUNT NO.   *113*

DATE		ITEM	POST. REF.	DEBIT	CREDIT	BALANCE	
						DEBIT	CREDIT
20--							
Apr.	30	Balance	✓			1,560.00	

ACCOUNT *Prepaid Insurance*   ACCOUNT NO.   *117*

DATE		ITEM	POST. REF.	DEBIT	CREDIT	BALANCE	
						DEBIT	CREDIT
20--							
Apr.	30	Balance	✓			460.00	

Problem 3-2B (continued)

ACCOUNT *Equipment* ACCOUNT NO. *124*

DATE		ITEM	POST. REF.	DEBIT	CREDIT	BALANCE	
						DEBIT	CREDIT
20--							
Apr.	30	Balance	✓			8,500.00	

ACCOUNT *Accounts Payable* ACCOUNT NO. *221*

DATE		ITEM	POST. REF.	DEBIT	CREDIT	BALANCE	
						DEBIT	CREDIT
20--							
Apr.	30	Balance	✓				2,080.00

ACCOUNT *, Capital* ACCOUNT NO. *311*

DATE		ITEM	POST. REF.	DEBIT	CREDIT	BALANCE	
						DEBIT	CREDIT
20--							
Apr.	30	Balance	✓				21,572.00

ACCOUNT *, Drawing* ACCOUNT NO. *312*

DATE		ITEM	POST. REF.	DEBIT	CREDIT	BALANCE	
						DEBIT	CREDIT
20--							
Apr.	30	Balance	✓			1,500.00	

ACCOUNT *Income from Services* ACCOUNT NO. *411*

DATE		ITEM	POST. REF.	DEBIT	CREDIT	BALANCE	
						DEBIT	CREDIT
20--							
Apr.	30	Balance	✓				4,236.00

Problem 3-2B (continued)

ACCOUNT   *Wages Expense*   ACCOUNT NO.   *511*

DATE		ITEM	POST. REF.	DEBIT	CREDIT	BALANCE	
						DEBIT	CREDIT
20--							
Apr.	30	Balance	✓			1,050.00	

ACCOUNT   *Rent Expense*   ACCOUNT NO.   *512*

DATE		ITEM	POST. REF.	DEBIT	CREDIT	BALANCE	
						DEBIT	CREDIT
20--							
Apr.	30	Balance	✓			850.00	

ACCOUNT   *Advertising Expense*   ACCOUNT NO.   *513*

DATE		ITEM	POST. REF.	DEBIT	CREDIT	BALANCE	
						DEBIT	CREDIT
20--							
Apr.	30	Balance	✓			423.00	

ACCOUNT   *Utilities Expense*   ACCOUNT NO.   *514*

DATE		ITEM	POST. REF.	DEBIT	CREDIT	BALANCE	
						DEBIT	CREDIT
20--							
Apr.	30	Balance	✓			385.00	

ACCOUNT   *Supplies Expense*   ACCOUNT NO.   *515*

DATE		ITEM	POST. REF.	DEBIT	CREDIT	BALANCE	
						DEBIT	CREDIT
20--							
Apr.	30	Balance	✓			180.00	

Problem 3-2B (continued)

ACCOUNT NAME	DEBIT	CREDIT

	DEBIT	CREDIT

Problem 3-2B (concluded)

Problem 3-3A

GENERAL JOURNAL   PAGE _____

	DATE		DESCRIPTION	POST. REF.	DEBIT	CREDIT	
1							1
2							2
3							3
4							4
5							5
6							6
7							7
8							8
9							9
10							10
11							11
12							12
13							13
14							14
15							15
16							16
17							17
18							18
19							19
20							20
21							21
22							22
23							23
24							24
25							25
26							26
27							27
28							28
29							29
30							30
31							31
32							32
33							33
34							34
35							35
36							36
37							37
38							38
39							39
40							40
41							41
42							42
43							43
44							44
45							45

Problem 3-3A (continued)

GENERAL JOURNAL   PAGE _____

	DATE		DESCRIPTION	POST. REF.	DEBIT	CREDIT	
1							1
2							2
3							3
4							4
5							5
6							6
7							7
8							8
9							9
10							10
11							11
12							12
13							13
14							14
15							15
16							16
17							17
18							18
19							19
20							20
21							21
22							22
23							23
24							24
25							25
26							26

Problem 3-3A (continued)

GENERAL LEDGER

ACCOUNT   *Cash*   ACCOUNT NO.   *111*

DATE		ITEM	POST. REF.	DEBIT	CREDIT	BALANCE	
						DEBIT	CREDIT
20--							
June	30	Balance	✓			25,312.00	

ACCOUNT   *Accounts Receivable*   ACCOUNT NO.   *113*

DATE		ITEM	POST. REF.	DEBIT	CREDIT	BALANCE	
						DEBIT	CREDIT
20--							
June	30	Balance	✓			560.00	

ACCOUNT   *Prepaid Insurance*   ACCOUNT NO.   *117*

DATE		ITEM	POST. REF.	DEBIT	CREDIT	BALANCE	
						DEBIT	CREDIT
20--							
June	30	Balance	✓			450.00	

ACCOUNT   *Equipment*   ACCOUNT NO.   *124*

DATE		ITEM	POST. REF.	DEBIT	CREDIT	BALANCE	
						DEBIT	CREDIT
20--							
June	30	Balance	✓			16,500.00	

ACCOUNT NAME _____ DATE _____ CLASS _____

Problem 3-3A (continued)

ACCOUNT *Accounts Payable*   ACCOUNT NO. ___221___

DATE		ITEM	POST. REF.	DEBIT	CREDIT	BALANCE DEBIT	BALANCE CREDIT
20--							
June	30	Balance	✓				2,976.00

ACCOUNT *, Capital*   ACCOUNT NO. ___311___

DATE		ITEM	POST. REF.	DEBIT	CREDIT	BALANCE DEBIT	BALANCE CREDIT
20--							
June	30	Balance	✓				39,846.00

ACCOUNT *, Drawing*   ACCOUNT NO. ___312___

DATE		ITEM	POST. REF.	DEBIT	CREDIT	BALANCE DEBIT	BALANCE CREDIT
20--							

ACCOUNT *Professional Fees*   ACCOUNT NO. ___411___

DATE		ITEM	POST. REF.	DEBIT	CREDIT	BALANCE DEBIT	BALANCE CREDIT
20--							

ACCOUNT *Salary Expense*   ACCOUNT NO. ___511___

DATE		ITEM	POST. REF.	DEBIT	CREDIT	BALANCE DEBIT	BALANCE CREDIT
20--							

Problem 3-3A (continued)

ACCOUNT __Rent Expense_____ ACCOUNT NO. _512_

DATE	ITEM	POST. REF.	DEBIT	CREDIT	BALANCE	
					DEBIT	CREDIT
20--						

ACCOUNT __Laboratory Expense_____ ACCOUNT NO. _513_

DATE	ITEM	POST. REF.	DEBIT	CREDIT	BALANCE	
					DEBIT	CREDIT
20--						

ACCOUNT __Utilities Expense_____ ACCOUNT NO. _514_

DATE	ITEM	POST. REF.	DEBIT	CREDIT	BALANCE	
					DEBIT	CREDIT
20--						

ACCOUNT __Supplies Expense_____ ACCOUNT NO. _515_

DATE	ITEM	POST. REF.	DEBIT	CREDIT	BALANCE	
					DEBIT	CREDIT
20--						

Problem 3-3A (concluded)

ACCOUNT NAME	DEBIT	CREDIT

Problem 3-3B

GENERAL JOURNAL   PAGE _____

	DATE		DESCRIPTION	POST. REF.	DEBIT	CREDIT	
1							1
2							2
3							3
4							4
5							5
6							6
7							7
8							8
9							9
10							10
11							11
12							12
13							13
14							14
15							15
16							16
17							17
18							18
19							19
20							20
21							21
22							22
23							23
24							24
25							25
26							26
27							27
28							28
29							29
30							30
31							31
32							32
33							33
34							34
35							35
36							36
37							37
38							38
39							39
40							40

Problem 3-3B (continued)

GENERAL JOURNAL   PAGE _____

	DATE		DESCRIPTION	POST. REF.	DEBIT	CREDIT	
1							1
2							2
3							3
4							4
5							5
6							6
7							7
8							8
9							9
10							10
11							11
12							12
13							13
14							14
15							15
16							16
17							17
18							18
19							19
20							20
21							21
22							22
23							23
24							24
25							25
26							26

Problem 3-3B (continued)

GENERAL LEDGER

ACCOUNT *Cash*   ACCOUNT NO. *111*

DATE		ITEM	POST. REF.	DEBIT	CREDIT	BALANCE	
						DEBIT	CREDIT
20--							
June	30	Balance	✓			4,568.00	

ACCOUNT *Accounts Receivable*   ACCOUNT NO. *113*

DATE		ITEM	POST. REF.	DEBIT	CREDIT	BALANCE	
						DEBIT	CREDIT
20--							
June	30	Balance	✓			3,045.00	

ACCOUNT *Prepaid Insurance*   ACCOUNT NO. *117*

DATE		ITEM	POST. REF.	DEBIT	CREDIT	BALANCE	
						DEBIT	CREDIT
20--							
June	30	Balance	✓			2,185.00	

ACCOUNT *Equipment*   ACCOUNT NO. *124*

DATE		ITEM	POST. REF.	DEBIT	CREDIT	BALANCE	
						DEBIT	CREDIT
20--							
June	30	Balance	✓			16,850.00	

Problem 3-3B (continued)

ACCOUNT *Accounts Payable*   ACCOUNT NO. _____ *221*

DATE		ITEM	POST. REF.	DEBIT	CREDIT	BALANCE	
						DEBIT	CREDIT
20--							
June	30	Balance	✓				2,804.00

ACCOUNT _____ *, Capital*   ACCOUNT NO. _____ *311*

DATE		ITEM	POST. REF.	DEBIT	CREDIT	BALANCE	
						DEBIT	CREDIT
20--							
June	30	Balance	✓				23,844.00

ACCOUNT _____ *, Drawing*   ACCOUNT NO. _____ *312*

DATE		ITEM	POST. REF.	DEBIT	CREDIT	BALANCE	
						DEBIT	CREDIT
20--							

ACCOUNT *Professional Fees*   ACCOUNT NO. _____ *411*

DATE		ITEM	POST. REF.	DEBIT	CREDIT	BALANCE	
						DEBIT	CREDIT
20--							

ACCOUNT *Salary Expense*   ACCOUNT NO. _____ *511*

DATE		ITEM	POST. REF.	DEBIT	CREDIT	BALANCE	
						DEBIT	CREDIT
20--							

Problem 3-3B (continued)

ACCOUNT _Rent Expense_____ ACCOUNT NO. _512_

DATE	ITEM	POST. REF.	DEBIT	CREDIT	BALANCE	
					DEBIT	CREDIT
20--						

ACCOUNT _Laboratory Expense_____ ACCOUNT NO. _513_

DATE	ITEM	POST. REF.	DEBIT	CREDIT	BALANCE	
					DEBIT	CREDIT
20--						

ACCOUNT _Utilities Expense_____ ACCOUNT NO. _514_

DATE	ITEM	POST. REF.	DEBIT	CREDIT	BALANCE	
					DEBIT	CREDIT
20--						

ACCOUNT _Supplies Expense_____ ACCOUNT NO. _515_

DATE	ITEM	POST. REF.	DEBIT	CREDIT	BALANCE	
					DEBIT	CREDIT
20--						

Problem 3-3B (concluded)

ACCOUNT NAME	DEBIT	CREDIT

NAME _____   DATE _____   CLASS _____

Problem 3-4A or 3-4B

GENERAL JOURNAL   PAGE _____

	DATE		DESCRIPTION	POST. REF.	DEBIT	CREDIT	
1							1
2							2
3							3
4							4
5							5
6							6
7							7
8							8
9							9
10							10
11							11
12							12
13							13
14							14
15							15
16							16
17							17
18							18
19							19
20							20
21							21
22							22
23							23
24							24
25							25
25							25
26							26
27							27
28							28
29							29
30							30
31							31
32							32
33							33
34							34
35							35
36							36
37							37
38							38
39							39
40							40
41							41
42							42
43							43
44							44
45							45

78

Problem 3-4A or 3-4B (continued)

GENERAL JOURNAL   PAGE _____

	DATE		DESCRIPTION	POST. REF.	DEBIT	CREDIT	
1							1
2							2
3							3
4							4
5							5
6							6
7							7
8							8
9							9
10							10
11							11
12							12
13							13
14							14
15							15
16							16
17							17
18							18
19							19
20							20
21							21
22							22
23							23
24							24
25							25
26							26
27							27
28							28
29							29
30							30
31							31
32							32
33							33
34							34
35							35
36							36
37							37
38							38
39							39
40							40
41							41
42							42
43							43
44							44
45							45

Problem 3-4A or 3-4B (continued)

GENERAL LEDGER

ACCOUNT _Cash_   ACCOUNT NO. _111_

DATE	ITEM	POST. REF.	DEBIT	CREDIT	BALANCE DEBIT	BALANCE CREDIT

ACCOUNT _Accounts Receivable_   ACCOUNT NO. _113_

DATE	ITEM	POST. REF.	DEBIT	CREDIT	BALANCE DEBIT	BALANCE CREDIT

ACCOUNT _Prepaid Insurance_   ACCOUNT NO. _117_

DATE	ITEM	POST. REF.	DEBIT	CREDIT	BALANCE DEBIT	BALANCE CREDIT

ACCOUNT _Equipment_   ACCOUNT NO. _124_

DATE	ITEM	POST. REF.	DEBIT	CREDIT	BALANCE DEBIT	BALANCE CREDIT

Problem 3-4A or 3-4B (continued)

ACCOUNT *Accounts Payable* ACCOUNT NO. _____ *221*

DATE	ITEM	POST. REF.	DEBIT	CREDIT	BALANCE	
					DEBIT	CREDIT

ACCOUNT *, Capital* ACCOUNT NO. _____ *311*

DATE	ITEM	POST. REF.	DEBIT	CREDIT	BALANCE	
					DEBIT	CREDIT

ACCOUNT *, Drawing* ACCOUNT NO. _____ *312*

DATE	ITEM	POST. REF.	DEBIT	CREDIT	BALANCE	
					DEBIT	CREDIT

ACCOUNT *Landscaping Income* ACCOUNT NO. _____ *411*

DATE	ITEM	POST. REF.	DEBIT	CREDIT	BALANCE	
					DEBIT	CREDIT

ACCOUNT *Salary Expense* ACCOUNT NO. _____ *511*

DATE	ITEM	POST. REF.	DEBIT	CREDIT	BALANCE	
					DEBIT	CREDIT

Problem 3-4A or 3-4B (continued)

ACCOUNT   *Rent Expense*   ACCOUNT NO.   *512*

DATE		ITEM	POST. REF.	DEBIT	CREDIT	BALANCE	
						DEBIT	CREDIT

ACCOUNT   *Gas and Oil Expense*   ACCOUNT NO.   *513*

DATE		ITEM	POST. REF.	DEBIT	CREDIT	BALANCE	
						DEBIT	CREDIT

ACCOUNT   *Utilities Expense*   ACCOUNT NO.   *514*

DATE		ITEM	POST. REF.	DEBIT	CREDIT	BALANCE	
						DEBIT	CREDIT

ACCOUNT   *Supplies Expense*   ACCOUNT NO.   *515*

DATE		ITEM	POST. REF.	DEBIT	CREDIT	BALANCE	
						DEBIT	CREDIT

NAME _____   DATE _____   CLASS _____

Problem 3-4A or 3-4B (concluded)

ACCOUNT NAME	DEBIT	CREDIT	

NAME _____ DATE _____ CLASS _____

Extra Form

GENERAL JOURNAL   PAGE _____

	DATE		DESCRIPTION	POST. REF.	DEBIT	CREDIT	
1							1
2							2
3							3
4							4
5							5
6							6
7							7
8							8
9							9
10							10
11							11
12							12
13							13
14							14
15							15
16							16
17							17
18							18
19							19
20							20
21							21
22							22
23							23
24							24
25							25
25							25
26							26
27							27
28							28
29							29
30							30
31							31
32							32
33							33
34							34
35							35
36							36
37							37
38							38
39							39
40							40
41							41
42							42
43							43
44							44
45							45

BEFORE A TEST CHECK: CHAPTERS 1–3

Part I: 1. ____   2. ____   3. ____   4. ____   5. ____   6. ____

Part II:

1.   GENERAL JOURNAL   PAGE _____

	DATE		DESCRIPTION	POST. REF.	DEBIT	CREDIT	
1							1
2							2
3							3
4							4
5							5
6							6
7							7
8							8
9							9
10							10
11							11
12							12
13							13
14							14
15							15
16							16
17							17
18							18
19							19
20							20
21							21
22							22
23							23
24							24
25							25
26							26
27							27
28							28
29							29
30							30
31							31
32							32
33							33
34							34

NAME _____

DATE _____ CLASS _____

BEFORE A TEST CHECK SOLUTIONS (continued)

Assets = **Liabilities** + **Owner's Equity** − **Revenue** − **Expenses**

| Dr. + | Cr. − | | Dr. − | Cr. + | | Dr. − | Cr. + | | Dr. − | Cr. + | | Dr. + | Cr. − |

2, 3, 4.

Cash (111)

Dr. + | Cr. −

Bal.

Bal.

86

BEFORE A TEST CHECK SOLUTIONS (continued)

5. _____

ACCOUNT NAME	DEBIT	CREDIT

6. _____

BEFORE A TEST CHECK SOLUTIONS (concluded)

7.

8.

4 Adjusting Entries and the Work Sheet

PERFORMANCE OBJECTIVES

1. Define *fiscal period* and *fiscal year*.
2. List the classifications of the accounts that occupy each column of a ten-column work sheet.
3. Complete a work sheet for a service enterprise, involving adjustments for expired insurance, depreciation, and accrued wages.
4. Prepare an income statement, a statement of owner's equity, and a balance sheet for a service business directly from the work sheet.
5. Journalize and post the adjusting entries.
6. Prepare (a) an income statement involving more than one revenue account and a net loss, (b) a statement of owner's equity with an additional investment and either a net income or a net loss, (c) a balance sheet for a business having more than one accumulated depreciation account, and (d) a balance sheet containing the statement of owner's equity information.

KEY TERMS

Accounting cycle	Depreciation
Accrual	Fiscal period
Accrued wages	Fiscal year
Adjusting entries	Matching principle
Adjustments	Mixed accounts
Book value or carrying value	Straight-line depreciation
Contra account	Work sheet
Contra asset account	

STUDY GUIDE QUESTIONS

PART 1   True/False

For each of the following statements, indicate T if the statement is true and F if the statement is false.

T F 1. Adjusting entries recorded on a work sheet must also be journalized.

T F 2. The book value of an asset is always equal to the asset's true market value.

T F 3. Each adjusting entry involves both an income statement account and a balance sheet account.

T F 4. The purpose of a work sheet is to enable the accountant to prepare the financial statements.

T F 5. The cost of insurance used will appear in the Adjustments Debit column, the Adjusted Trial Balance Debit column, and the Income Statement Debit column.

T F 6. The purpose of adjustments is to correct account amounts that do not reflect such things as depreciation, wages payable, or insurance expired.

T   F   7.   The purpose of depreciating an asset is to spread out the cost of the asset over its useful life.

T   F   8.   The normal balance of Accumulated Depreciation, Equipment, is on the credit side.

T   F   9.   If the total of the Income Statement Debit column is larger than the total of the Income Statement Credit column, the company must have a net loss.

T   F   10.   In a computerized system, a work sheet is as essential as it is in a manual system.

PART 2   Completion—Language of Business

Complete each of the following statements by writing the appropriate words in the spaces provided.

1.   The cost of an asset less the accumulated depreciation is called the _book value_ .

2.   The time span that covers a company's accounting cycle is called its _fiscal period_ .

3.   Since the plus and minus signs on Accumulated Depreciation, Equipment, are the opposite of the signs on Equipment, the Accumulated Depreciation, Equipment, account is called a(n) _Contra_ account.

4.   Internal transactions that are used to bring the ledger accounts up to date are called _Adjustments_ .

5.   The amount of unpaid wages owed to employees for the time between the last payday and the end of the fiscal period is called _Accrual_ .

6.   The _Acc. t cycle_ represents the steps in the accounting process that are completed during the fiscal period.

7.   The Prepaid Insurance account is called a(n) _Mixed Accts_ because its balance in the Trial Balance column of a work sheet consists partly of an income statement amount and partly of a balance sheet amount.

8.   The _Matching Principles_ requires that the expenses of one period must be related to the revenue of the same period.

9.   The term representing loss in usefulness of assets is _depreciation_ .

PART 3   Adjusting Entries

Record the adjusting entries directly in the T accounts, and label the other account.

1. Insurance expired, $510.

Prepaid Insurance		Insurance Exp.
Bal. 950	Adj 440	Adj 440

2. Additional depreciation, $2,500.

Accumulated Depreciation, Equipment		Depreciation Exp, Equipment
	Bal. 7,500 2500	2500

3. Accrued wages, $470.

Wages Expense		Wages Payable
Bal. 8,100 470		470

PART 4   Analyzing the Work Sheet

Carry the balances forward from the Trial Balance columns to the appropriate column. The first account is provided as an example.

ACCOUNT NAME	TRIAL BALANCE		ADJUSTMENTS		ADJ. TRIAL BAL.		INCOME STMT.		BALANCE SHEET	
	DEBIT	CREDIT	DEBIT	CREDIT	DEBIT	CREDIT	DEBIT	CREDIT	DEBIT	CREDIT
0. Equipment	X				X				X	
1. Cash	X				X				X	
2. C. Tumi, Capital		X				X				X
3. Advertising Expense	X				X		X			
4. Accounts Receivable	X				X				X	
5. Wages Expense	X				X		X			
6. Accumulated Depreciation, Equipment		X		X		X				X
7. Wages Payable		X		X		X				X
8. C. Tumi, Drawing	X				X				X	
9. Service Revenue		X				X		X		
10. Depreciation Expense, Equipment	X		X		X		X			

DEMONSTRATION PROBLEM

The general ledger of Ross Carpenters contains the following account balances for the year ended December 31.

Cash	$ 2,560	H. Ross, Drawing	$60,000
Accounts Receivable	7,428	Income from Services	89,845
Prepaid Insurance	960	Wages Expense	21,500
Equipment	4,270	Rent Expense	4,800
Accumulated Depreciation,		Supplies Expense	1,218
Equipment	1,230	Advertising Expense	1,216
Truck	21,550	Utilities Expense	1,344
Accumulated Depreciation, Truck	4,310	Insurance Expense	0
Accounts Payable	426	Depreciation Expense, Equipment	0
Wages Payable	0	Depreciation Expense, Truck	0
H. Ross, Capital	31,314	Miscellaneous Expense	279

Since the firm has been in operation for longer than a year, Accumulated Depreciation, Equipment, and Accumulated Depreciation, Truck, have balances that should be included on the trial balance.

    Data for the year-end adjustments are as follows:
    a.   Wages accrued at December 31, $448.
    b.   Insurance expired during the year, $768.
    c.   Depreciation of equipment during the year, $854.
    d.   Depreciation of truck during the year, $4,310.

Instructions

Complete the work sheet for the year.

SOLUTION

Ross Carpenters

Work Sheet

For Year Ended December 31, 20—

	ACCOUNT NAME	TRIAL BALANCE		ADJUSTMENTS	
		DEBIT	CREDIT	DEBIT	CREDIT
1	Cash	2,560.00			
2	Accounts Receivable	7,428.00			
3	Prepaid Insurance	960.00			(b) 768.00
4	Equipment	4,270.00			
5	Accumulated Depreciation,				
6	Equipment		1,230.00		(c) 854.00
7	Truck	21,550.00			
8	Accumulated Depreciation,				
9	Truck		4,310.00		(d) 4,310.00
10	Accounts Payable		426.00		
11	H. Ross, Capital		31,314.00		
12	H. Ross, Drawing	60,000.00			
13	Income from Services		89,845.00		
14	Wages Expense	21,500.00		(a) 448.00	
15	Rent Expense	4,800.00			
16	Supplies Expense	1,218.00			
17	Advertising Expense	1,216.00			
18	Utilities Expense	1,344.00			
19	Miscellaneous Expense	279.00			
20		127,125.00	127,125.00		
21	Wages Payable				(a) 448.00
22	Insurance Expense			(b) 768.00	
23	Depreciation Expense,				
24	Equipment			(c) 854.00	
25	Depreciation Expense,				
26	Truck			(d) 4,310.00	
27				6,380.00	6,380.00
28	Net Income				
29					
30					
31					
32					
33					
34					
35					
36					
37					
38					
39					
40					
41					

SOLUTION *(concluded)*

ADJUSTED TRIAL BALANCE		INCOME STATEMENT		BALANCE SHEET		
DEBIT	CREDIT	DEBIT	CREDIT	DEBIT	CREDIT	
2,560.00				2,560.00		1
7,428.00				7,428.00		2
192.00				192.00		3
4,270.00				4,270.00		4
						5
	2,084.00				2,084.00	6
21,550.00				21,550.00		7
						8
	8,620.00				8,620.00	9
	426.00				426.00	10
	31,314.00				31,314.00	11
60,000.00				60,000.00		12
	89,845.00		89,845.00			13
21,948.00		21,948.00				14
4,800.00		4,800.00				15
1,218.00		1,218.00				16
1,216.00		1,216.00				17
1,344.00		1,344.00				18
279.00		279.00				19
						20
	448.00				448.00	21
768.00		768.00				22
						23
854.00		854.00				24
						25
4,310.00		4,310.00				26
132,737.00	132,737.00	36,737.00	89,845.00	96,000.00	42,892.00	27
		53,108.00			53,108.00	28
		89,845.00	89,845.00	96,000.00	96,000.00	29

95

EXERCISES

Exercise 4-1

TRIAL BALANCE		ADJUSTED TRIAL BALANCE		INCOME STATEMENT		BALANCE SHEET	
DEBIT	CREDIT	DEBIT	CREDIT	DEBIT	CREDIT	DEBIT	CREDIT
Assets		Assets				Assets	

Exercise 4-2

	Account	Classification	Normal	Income Statement (IS) or Balance sheet (BS) Columns
0.	Example: Wages Expense	E	Debit	IS
a.	Prepaid Insurance			
b.	Accounts Payable			
c.	T. Robley, Capital			
d.	Accounts Receivable			
e.	Accumulated Depreciation, Building			
f.	T. Robley, Drawing			
g.	Rental Income			
h.	Equipment			
i.	Depreciation Expense, Equipment			
j.	Supplies Expense			

Exercise 4-3

✓	Account Name (in trial balance order)	Reason for Adjusting This Account
a.	Cash	
b.	Prepaid Insurance	
c.	Equipment	
d.	Accumulated Depreciation, Equipment	
e.	Accounts Payable	
f.	L. Lawson, Capital	
g.	L. Lawson, Drawing	
h.	Wages Expense	

Exercise 4-4

	ACCOUNT NAME	TRIAL BALANCE		ADJUSTMENTS	
		DEBIT	CREDIT	DEBIT	CREDIT
1	Cash	5,621.00			
2	Prepaid Insurance	900.00			
3	Equipment	4,680.00			
4	Accumulated Depreciation,				
5	Equipment		1,250.00		
6	Accounts Payable		2,649.00		
7	P. Ryan, Capital		4,624.00		
8	P. Ryan, Drawing	2,200.00			
9	Service Income		6,847.00		
10	Rent Expense	956.00			
11	Supplies Expense	385.00			
12	Wages Expense	560.00			
13	Miscellaneous Expense	68.00			
14		15,370.00	15,370.00		
15					
16					
17					
18					
19					
20					
21					
22					

NAME _____   DATE _____   CLASS _____

Exercise 4-5

	ACCOUNT NAME	TRIAL BALANCE		ADJUSTMENTS		ADJUSTED TRIAL BALANCE	
		DEBIT	CREDIT	DEBIT	CREDIT	DEBIT	CREDIT
1	Cash	4,620.00					
2	Prepaid Insurance	1,100.00					
3	Equipment	5,678.00					
4	Accumulated Depreciation,						
5	Equipment		1,456.00				
6	Accounts Payable		1,975.00				
7	D. Lee, Capital		6,126.00				
8	D. Lee, Drawing	1,800.00					
9	Service Fees		5,736.00				
10	Rent Expense	865.00					
11	Supplies Expense	367.00					
12	Wages Expense	785.00					
13	Miscellaneous Expense	78.00					
14		15,293.00	15,293.00				
15							
16							
17							
18							
19							
20							
21							
22							
23							
24							
25							
26							
27							
28							
29							
30							
31							
32							
33							
34							
35							
36							

Exercise 4-6

	DATE		DESCRIPTION	POST. REF.	DEBIT	CREDIT	
1							1
2							2
3							3
4							4
5							5
6							6
7							7
8							8
9							9
10							10
11							11
12							12
13							13
14							14
15							15
16							16
17							17

Exercise 4-7

	DATE		DESCRIPTION	POST. REF.	DEBIT	CREDIT	
1							1
2							2
3							3
4							4
5							5
6							6
7							7
8							8
9							9
10							10
11							11
12							12
13							13
14							14
15							15
16							16
17							17

Exercise 4-8

	DATE		DESCRIPTION	POST. REF.	DEBIT	CREDIT	
1							1
2							2
3							3
4							4
5							5
6							6
7							7
8							8
9							9
10							10
11							11
12							12
13							13
14							14
15							15
16							16
17							17

(_____ ÷ ____)   X ___ = _____

(_____ ÷ ____)   X ___ = _____

(_____ – _____)   = _____

NAME _____ DATE _____ CLASS _____

Extra Form

GENERAL JOURNAL

PAGE _____

	DATE		DESCRIPTION	POST. REF.	DEBIT	CREDIT	
1							1
2							2
3							3
4							4
5							5
6							6
7							7
8							8
9							9
10							10
11							11
12							12
13							13
14							14
15							15
16							16
17							17
18							18
19							19
20							20
21							21
22							22
23							23
24							24
25							25
26							26
27							27
28							28
29							29
30							30
31							31
32							32
33							33
34							34
35							35
36							36
37							37
38							38

Problem 4-1A or 4-1B

	ACCOUNT NAME	TRIAL BALANCE		ADJUSTMENTS	
		DEBIT	CREDIT	DEBIT	CREDIT
1	Cash				
2	Accounts Receivable				
3	Prepaid Insurance				
4	Office Equipment				
5	Accounts Payable				
6	, Capital				
7	, Drawing				
8	Commissions Earned				
9	Rent Expense				
10	Travel Expense				
11	Supplies Expense				
12	Utilities Expense				
13	Miscellaneous Expense				
14					
15					
16					
17					
18					
19					
20					
21					
22					
23					
24					
25					
26					
27					
28					
29					
30					
31					
32					
33					
34					
35					
36					
37					

Problem 4-1A or 4-1B (concluded)

ADJUSTED TRIAL BALANCE		INCOME STATEMENT		BALANCE SHEET		
DEBIT	CREDIT	DEBIT	CREDIT	DEBIT	CREDIT	
						1
						2
						3
						4
						5
						6
						7
						8
						9
						10
						11
						12
						13
						14
						15
						16
						17
						18
						19
						20
						21
						22
						23
						24
						25
						26
						27
						28
						29
						30
						31
						32
						33
						34
						35
						36
						37

NAME _____ DATE _____ CLASS _____

Problem 4-2A

	ACCOUNT NAME	TRIAL BALANCE DEBIT	TRIAL BALANCE CREDIT	ADJUSTMENTS DEBIT	ADJUSTMENTS CREDIT
1	Cash	6,229.00			
2	Prepaid Insurance	1,246.00			(a) 255.00
3	Equipment	6,288.00			
4	Accumulated Depreciation,				
5	Equipment		3,620.00		(b) 894.00
6	Office Furniture	3,580.00			
7	Accumulated Depreciation,				
8	Office Furniture		2,806.00		(c) 465.00
9	Truck	24,699.00			
10	Accumulated Depreciation, Truck		18,193.00		(d) 645.00
11	Accounts Payable		2,627.00		
12	J. Marquez, Capital		10,672.00		
13	J. Marquez, Drawing	3,200.00			
14	Professional Fees		12,176.00		
15	Salary Expense	2,055.00		(e) 477.00	
16	Rent Expense	1,025.00			
17	Travel Expense	348.00			
18	Utilities Expense	156.00			
19	Advertising Expense	496.00			
20	Supplies Expense	637.00			
21	Miscellaneous Expense	135.00			
22		50,094.00	50,094.00		
23	Insurance Expense			(a) 255.00	
24	Depreciation Expense, Equipment			(b) 894.00	
25	Depreciation Expense, Office				
26	Furniture			(c) 465.00	
27	Depreciation Expense, Truck			(d) 645.00	
28	Salaries Payable				(e) 477.00
29				2,736.00	2,736.00
30	Net Income				
31					
32					
33					
34					
35					
36					
37					
38					

Problem 4-2A (continued)

ADJUSTED TRIAL BALANCE		INCOME STATEMENT		BALANCE SHEET		
DEBIT	CREDIT	DEBIT	CREDIT	DEBIT	CREDIT	
6,229.00				6,229.00		1
991.00				991.00		2
6,288.00				6,288.00		3
						4
	4,514.00				4,514.00	5
3,580.00				3,580.00		6
						7
	3,271.00				3,271.00	8
24,699.00				24,699.00		9
	18,838.00				18,838.00	10
	2,627.00				2,627.00	11
	10,672.00				10,672.00	12
3,200.00				3,200.00		13
	12,176.00		12,176.00			14
2,532.00		2,532.00				15
1,025.00		1,025.00				16
348.00		348.00				17
156.00		156.00				18
496.00		496.00				19
637.00		637.00				20
135.00		135.00				21
						22
255.00		255.00				23
894.00		894.00				24
						25
465.00		465.00				26
645.00		645.00				27
	477.00				477.00	28
52,575.00	52,575.00	7,588.00	12,176.00	44,987.00	40,399.00	29
		4,588.00			4,588.00	30
		12,176.00	12,176.00	44,987.00	44,987.00	31
						32
						33
						34
						35
						36
						37
						38

Problem 4-2B

Delta Decorators
Work Sheet
For Month Ended March 31, 20--

	ACCOUNT NAME	TRIAL BALANCE DEBIT	TRIAL BALANCE CREDIT	ADJUSTMENTS DEBIT		ADJUSTMENTS CREDIT	
1	Cash	7,340.00					
2	Prepaid Insurance	1,136.00				(a)	354.00
3	Equipment	7,176.00					
4	Accumulated Depreciation,						
5	Equipment		2,512.00			(b)	490.00
6	Office Furniture	4,479.00					
7	Accumulated Depreciation,						
8	Office Furniture		1,795.00			(c)	368.00
9	Truck	20,874.00					
10	Accumulated Depreciation, Truck		14,367.00			(d)	985.00
11	Accounts Payable		1,584.00				
12	A. Ono, Capital		13,648.00				
13	A. Ono, Drawing	2,800.00					
14	Professional Fees		14,852.00				
15	Salary Expense	1,864.00		(e)	387.00		
16	Rent Expense	1,285.00					
17	Travel Expense	445.00					
18	Utilities Expense	168.00					
19	Advertising Expense	458.00					
20	Supplies Expense	548.00					
21	Miscellaneous Expense	185.00					
22		48,758.00	48,758.00				
23	Insurance Expense			(a)	354.00		
24	Depreciation Expense, Equipment			(b)	490.00		
25	Depreciation Expense, Office						
26	Furniture			(c)	368.00		
27	Depreciation Expense, Truck			(d)	985.00		
28	Salaries Payable					(e)	387.00
29					2,584.00		2,584.00
30	Net Income						
31							
32							
33							
34							
35							
36							
37							
38							

Problem 4-2B (continued)

ADJUSTED TRIAL BALANCE		INCOME STATEMENT		BALANCE SHEET		
DEBIT	CREDIT	DEBIT	CREDIT	DEBIT	CREDIT	
7,340.00				7,340.00		1
782.00				782.00		2
7,176.00				7,176.00		3
						4
	3,002.00				3,002.00	5
4,479.00				4,479.00		6
						7
	2,163.00				2,163.00	8
20,874.00				20,874.00		9
	15,352.00				15,352.00	10
	1,584.00				1,584.00	11
	13,648.00				13,648.00	12
2,800.00				2,800.00		13
	14,852.00		14,852.00			14
2,251.00		2,251.00				15
1,285.00		1,285.00				16
445.00		445.00				17
168.00		168.00				18
458.00		458.00				19
548.00		548.00				20
185.00		185.00				21
						22
354.00		354.00				23
490.00		490.00				24
						25
368.00		368.00				26
985.00		985.00				27
	387.00				387.00	28
50,988.00	50,988.00	7,537.00	14,852.00	43,451.00	36,136.00	29
		7,315.00			7,315.00	30
		14,852.00	14,852.00	43,451.00	43,451.00	31
						32
						33
						34
						35
						36
						37
						38

Problem 4-2A or 4-2B (continued)

Problem 4-2A or 4-2B (continued)

Problem 4-2A or 4-2B (continued)

Problem 4-2A or 4-2B (concluded)

GENERAL JOURNAL   PAGE _____

	DATE	DESCRIPTION	POST. REF.	DEBIT	CREDIT	
1						1
2						2
3						3
4						4
5						5
6						6
7						7
8						8
9						9
10						10
11						11
12						12
13						13
14						14
15						15
16						16
17						17
18						18
19						19
20						20
21						21
22						22
23						23
24						24
25						25
26						26
27						27
28						28
29						29
30						30
31						31
32						32
33						33
34						34
35						35
36						36
37						37

Problem 4-3A or 4-3B

	ACCOUNT NAME	TRIAL BALANCE		ADJUSTMENTS	
		DEBIT	CREDIT	DEBIT	CREDIT
1	Cash				
2	Prepaid Insurance				
3	Equipment				
4	Accumulated Depreciation,				
5	Equipment				
6	Accounts Payable				
7	, Capital				
8	, Drawing				
9	Income from Services				
10	Wages Expense				
11	Rent Expense				
12	Supplies Expense				
13	Utilities Expense				
14	Telephone Expense				
15	Miscellaneous Expense				
16					
17					
18					
19					
20					
21					
22					
23					
24					
25					
26					
27					
28					
29					
30					
31					
32					
33					
34					
35					
36					
37					

Problem 4-3A or 4-3B (continued)

ADJUSTED TRIAL BALANCE		INCOME STATEMENT		BALANCE SHEET		
DEBIT	CREDIT	DEBIT	CREDIT	DEBIT	CREDIT	
						1
						2
						3
						4
						5
						6
						7
						8
						9
						10
						11
						12
						13
						14
						15
						16
						17
						18
						19
						20
						21
						22
						23
						24
						25
						26
						27
						28
						29
						30
						31
						32
						33
						34
						35
						36
						37

NAME _____ DATE _____ CLASS _____

Problem 4-3A or 4-3B (concluded)

GENERAL JOURNAL   PAGE _____

	DATE		DESCRIPTION	POST. REF.	DEBIT	CREDIT	
1							1
2							2
3							3
4							4
5							5
6							6
7							7
8							8
9							9
10							10
11							11
12							12
13							13
14							14
15							15
16							16
17							17
18							18
19							19
20							20
21							21
22							22
23							23
24							24
25							25
26							26
27							27
28							28
29							29
30							30
31							31
32							32
33							33
34							34
35							35
36							36
37							37

NAME _____ DATE _____ CLASS _____

Extra Form

GENERAL JOURNAL   PAGE _____

	DATE		DESCRIPTION	POST. REF.	DEBIT	CREDIT	
1							1
2							2
3							3
4							4
5							5
6							6
7							7
8							8
9							9
10							10
11							11
12							12
13							13
14							14
15							15
16							16
17							17
18							18
19							19
20							20
21							21
22							22
23							23
24							24
25							25
26							26
27							27
28							28
29							29
30							30
31							31
32							32
33							33
34							34
35							35
36							36
37							37
38							38

Problem 4-4A or 4-4B

	ACCOUNT NAME	TRIAL BALANCE		ADJUSTMENTS	
		DEBIT	CREDIT	DEBIT	CREDIT
1	Cash				
2	Prepaid Insurance				
3	Equipment				
4	Accumulated Depreciation,				
5	Equipment				
6	Repair Equipment				
7	Accumulated Depreciation,				
8	Repair Equipment				
9	Accounts Payable				
10	, Capital				
11	, Drawing				
12	Golf Fees Income				
13	Concessions Income				
14	Wages Expense				
15	Rent Expense				
16	Utilities Expense				
17	Repair Expense				
18	Supplies Expense				
19	Miscellaneous Expense				
20					
21					
22					
23					
24					
25					
26					
27					
28					
29					
30					
31					
32					
33					
34					
35					

Problem 4-4A or 4-4B (continued)

ADJUSTED TRIAL BALANCE		INCOME STATEMENT		BALANCE SHEET		
DEBIT	CREDIT	DEBIT	CREDIT	DEBIT	CREDIT	
						1
						2
						3
						4
						5
						6
						7
						8
						9
						10
						11
						12
						13
						14
						15
						16
						17
						18
						19
						20
						21
						22
						23
						24
						25
						26
						27
						28
						29
						30
						31
						32
						33
						34
						35

Problem 4-4A or 4-4B (continued)

Problem 4-4A or 4-4B (continued)

Problem 4-4A or 4-4B (continued)

Problem 4-4A or 4-4B (concluded)

GENERAL JOURNAL   PAGE _____

	DATE		DESCRIPTION	POST. REF.	DEBIT	CREDIT	
1							1
2							2
3							3
4							4
5							5
6							6
7							7
8							8
9							9
10							10
11							11
12							12
13							13
14							14
15							15
16							16
17							17
18							18
19							19
20							20
21							21
22							22
23							23
24							24
25							25
26							26
27							27
28							28
29							29
30							30
31							31
32							32
33							33
34							34
35							35
36							36
37							37
38							38

Problem A-1

Year	Depreciation for the Year		Accumulated Depreciation		Book Value	

Problem A-2

Year	Depreciation for the Year		Accumulated Depreciation		Book Value	

Closing Entries and the Post-Closing Trial Balance

PERFORMANCE OBJECTIVES

1. List the steps in the accounting cycle.
2. Journalize and post closing entries for a service enterprise.
3. Prepare a post-closing trial balance.
4. Define the following methods of accounting: cash basis and accrual basis.
5. Prepare interim statements.

KEY TERMS

Accrual basis of accounting   Interim statements

Cash basis of accounting   Nominal or temporary-equity accounts

Closing entries   Post-closing trial balance

Income Summary account   Real or permanent accounts

STUDY GUIDE QUESTIONS

PART 1   True/False

For each of the following statements, indicate T if the statement is true and F if the statement is false.

T **(F)** 1. The first step in the closing procedure is to close the expense accounts into the Income Summary account.

(T) F 2. The post-closing trial balance is final proof that the total of the debit balances equals the total of the credit balances.

(T) F 3. After the closing entries have been posted, the final balance of the Capital account is the same as the amount recorded on the last line of the statement of owner's equity.

T **(F)** 4. Generally, the closing procedure is completed by making three entries.

T **(F)** 5. The purpose of the closing entries is to close the asset and liability accounts because their balances apply to only one fiscal period.

T **(F)** 6. The total of the expense accounts is recorded in Income Summary as a credit.

(T) F 7. The last step in the closing procedure is to close the Drawing account into the Capital account.

T **(F)** 8. If you have to debit Income Summary to close it, this indicates a net loss.

(T) F 9. Income Summary is an example of a nominal or temporary-equity account.

(T) F 10. The post-closing trial balance includes only the balances of real or permanent accounts.

PART 2   Completion—Language of Business

Complete each of the following statements by writing the appropriate words in the spaces provided.

1. After the closing entries have been journalized and posted, the ___*post closing trial bal*___ _____ is prepared as final proof that the accounts are in balance.

2. The accounts that have balances carried over to the next fiscal period are called ___*Real/Permanent*___ accounts.

3. Financial statements that are prepared during the fiscal period and cover a period of time less than the fiscal period are called ___*interim*___ statements.

4. The ___*Income Summary*___ account is used only during the closing procedure.

5. A journal entry that is made to clear an account or make the balance of that account equal to zero is called a(n) ___*Closing*___ entry.

6. The ___*Nominal*___ accounts apply to only one fiscal period and are closed at the end of the fiscal period.

7. An accounting basis under which revenue is recorded only when it is earned and expenses are recorded only when they are incurred is called the ___*accrual basis of acct*___.

8. The ___*Cash basis of acct*___ is an accounting basis under which revenue is recorded only when it is received in cash and most expenses are recorded only when they are paid in cash. Expenses to be counted that are not paid in cash include Depreciation Expense and Insurance Expense.

PART 3   Closing Entries

Using the following list of account titles, determine the account titles to be debited and credited for the closing entries below. Enter the letter for the account in the space provided.

a. Rent Expense   c. L. Drew, Drawing   e. L. Drew, Capital
b. Service Income   d. Income Summary   f. Wages Expense

		Debit	Credit
1.	Close out the balance of the revenue account.	*Service Inc.*	*Inc Summary*
2.	Close out the balances of the expense accounts.	*In Summary*	*Rent + Wages Exp*
3.	Close out the amount of the net income for the period.	*Income Summy*	*L Draw Cap*
4.	Close out the balance of the Drawing account.	*L Dr Cap*	*L Drew Drawing*

Dr + Cr

PART 4   Posting Closing Entries

After the first closing entries have been journalized and posted, the remaining accounts are shown below in T account form. Based on the T accounts, answer the following questions.

Income Summary		J. See, Capital		J. See, Drawing	
Debit	Credit	Debit	Credit	Debit	Credit
46,000	41,000		Bal. 150,000	Bal. 22,000	

1. The amount of the total revenue is $ *41,000* .
2. The amount of the total expenses is $ *46,000* .
3. The amount of the net income or net loss is $ *5,000* .
4. The amount of the total withdrawals is $ *22,000* .
5. The entry to close Income Summary is a debit to *J. See Cap* and a credit to *Income Summary* .
6. The entry to close J. See, Drawing, is a debit to *J. See Cap* and a credit to *J. C. Drawing* .
7. The amount of the increase or decrease in capital for the period is $ *27,000* .
8. The ending balance of J. See, Capital, is $ *123,000* .

DEMONSTRATION PROBLEM

After the adjusting entries have been posted, the ledger of C. Pitts, a financial planner, contains the following account balances as of December 31:

Cash	$ 3,064
Accounts Receivable	8,450
Equipment	10,500
Accumulated Depreciation, Equipment	4,200
Accounts Payable	756
C. Pitts, Capital	18,378
C. Pitts, Drawing	80,000
Income Summary	—
Commissions Earned	92,824
Income from Services	23,050
Salary Expense	21,600
Rent Expense	11,200
Supplies Expense	1,635
Depreciation Expense, Equipment	2,100
Miscellaneous Expense	659

Instructions

Record the closing entries in general journal form.

SOLUTION

GENERAL JOURNAL

PAGE _____

	DATE		DESCRIPTION	POST. REF.	DEBIT	CREDIT	
1	20—		*Closing Entries*				1
2	Dec.	31	Commissions Earned		92,824.00		2
3			Income from Services		23,050.00		3
4			Income Summary			115,874.00	4
5							5
6		31	Income Summary		37,194.00		6
7			Salary Expense			21,600.00	7
8			Rent Expense			11,200.00	8
9			Supplies Expense			1,635.00	9
10			Depreciation Expense, Equipment			2,100.00	10
11			Miscellaenous Expense			659.00	11
12							12
13		31	Income Summary		78,680.00		13
14			C. Pitts, Capital			78,680.00	14
15							15
16		31	C. Pitts, Capital		80,000.00		16
17			C. Pitts, Drawing			80,000.00	17
18							18

EXERCISES

Exercise 5-1

ACCOUNT TITLE	REAL	NOMINAL	CLOSED		INCOME STATEMENT	BALANCE SHEET
			YES	NO		
0. Example: Building	X			X		X
a. Prepaid Insurance						
b. Accounts Payable						
c. Wages Payable						
d. Services Income						
e. Rent Expense						
f. Supplies Expense						
g. Accumulated Depreciation, Equipment						

Exercise 5-2

GENERAL JOURNAL   PAGE _____

	DATE	DESCRIPTION	POST. REF.	DEBIT	CREDIT	
1						1
2						2
3						3
4						4
5						5
6						6
7						7
8						8
9						9
10						10
11						11
12						12
13						13
14						14
15						15
16						16

Exercise 5-3

GENERAL JOURNAL   PAGE _____

	DATE		DESCRIPTION	POST. REF.	DEBIT	CREDIT	
1							1
2							2
3							3
4							4
5							5
6							6
7							7
8							8
9							9
10							10
11							11
12							12
13							13
14							14
15							15
16							16
17							17
18							18
19							19
20							20

Exercise 5-4

GENERAL JOURNAL   PAGE _____

	DATE		DESCRIPTION	POST. REF.	DEBIT	CREDIT	
1							1
2							2
3							3
4							4
5							5
6							6
7							7
8							8
9							9
10							10
11							11
12							12
13							13
14							14
15							15
16							16
17							17
18							18
19							19
20							20

Exercise 5-5

GENERAL JOURNAL   PAGE _____

	DATE		DESCRIPTION	POST. REF.	DEBIT	CREDIT	
1							1
2							2
3							3
4							4
5							5
6							6
7							7
8							8
9							9
10							10
11							11
12							12
13							13
14							14
15							15
16							16
17							17
18							18
19							19
20							20

Exercise 5-6

a.

12							12
13							13
14							14
15							15
16							16
17							17

b. _____
_____
_____
_____

Exercise 5-7

ITEM	INCOME STATEMENT	STATEMENT OF OWNER'S EQUITY	BALANCE SHEET
0. Example: The total liabilities of the business at the end of the year.			X
a. The amount of the owner's Capital balance at the end of the year.			
b. The amount of depreciation expense on equipment during the year.			
c. The amount of the company's net income for the year.			
d. The book value of the equipment.			
e. Total insurance expired during the year.			
f. Total accounts receivable at the end of the year.			
g. Total withdrawals by the owner.			
h. The cost of utilities used during the year.			
i. The amount of the owner's Capital balance at the beginning of the year.			

Exercise 5-8

Problem 5-1A or 5-1B

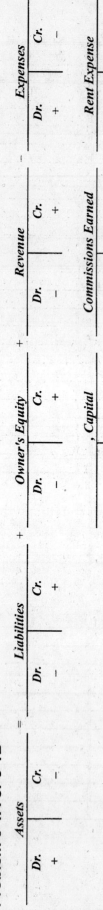

Assets

Dr.	Cr.
+	−

=

Liabilities

Dr.	Cr.
−	+

+

Owner's Equity

Dr.	Cr.
−	+

, Capital

, Drawing

Income Summary

+

Revenue

Dr.	Cr.
−	+

Commissions Earned

−

Expenses

Dr.	Cr.
+	−

Rent Expense

Supplies Expense

_Depreciation Expense,
Office Equipment_

Utilities Expense

Miscellaneous Expense

Problem 5-1A or 5-1B (concluded)

GENERAL JOURNAL   PAGE _____

	DATE		DESCRIPTION	POST. REF.	DEBIT	CREDIT	
1							1
2							2
3							3
4							4
5							5
6							6
7							7
8							8
9							9
10							10
11							11
12							12
13							13
14							14
15							15
16							16
17							17
18							18
19							19
20							20

Problem 5-2A or 5-2B

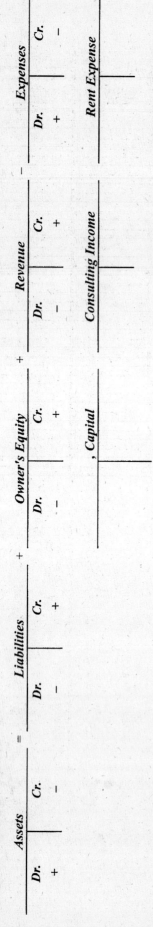

Assets = **Liabilities** + **Owner's Equity** + **Revenue** − **Expenses**

Assets	Liabilities	Owner's Equity	Revenue	Expenses
Dr.+ Cr.−	Dr.− Cr.+	Dr.− Cr.+	Dr.− Cr.+	Dr.+ Cr.−

, Capital

, Drawing

Income Summary

Consulting Income

Rent Expense

Wages Expense

Supplies Expense

Insurance Expense

Depreciation Expense, Equipment

Miscellaneous Expense

Problem 5-2A or 5-2B (concluded)

GENERAL JOURNAL   PAGE _____

	DATE	DESCRIPTION	POST. REF.	DEBIT	CREDIT	
1						1
2						2
3						3
4						4
5						5
6						6
7						7
8						8
9						9
10						10
11						11
12						12
13						13
14						14
15						15
16						16
17						17
18						18
19						19
20						20

Problem 5-3A

Ulmer Tour Company
Work Sheet
For Month Ended December 31, 20--

unadjusted

	ACCOUNT NAME	TRIAL BALANCE		ADJUSTMENTS			
		DEBIT	CREDIT	DEBIT		CREDIT	
1	Cash	3,948.00					
2	Office Equipment	3,460.00					
3	Accumulated Depreciation,						
4	Office Equipment		380.00		(a)		320.00
5	K. Ulmer, Capital		5,739.00				
6	K. Ulmer, Drawing	19,000.00					
7	Fees Earned		43,400.00				
8	Wages Expense	18,500.00		(b)	425.00		
9	Rent Expense	2,400.00					
10	Office Supplies Expense	328.00					
11	Telephone Expense	736.00					
12	Advertising Expense	926.00					
13	Miscellaneous Expense	221.00					
14		49,519.00	49,519.00				
15	Depreciation Expense, Office						
16	Equipment			(a)	320.00		
17	Wages Payable				(b)		425.00
18					745.00		745.00
19	Net Income						
20							
21							
22							
23							
24							
25							
26							
27							
28							
29							
30							
31							
32							
33							
34							

Problem 5-3A (continued)

ADJUSTED TRIAL BALANCE		INCOME STATEMENT		BALANCE SHEET		
DEBIT	CREDIT	DEBIT	CREDIT	DEBIT	CREDIT	
3,948.00				3,948.00		1
3,460.00				3,460.00		2
						3
	700.00				700.00	4
	5,739.00				5,739.00	5
19,000.00				19,000.00		6
	43,400.00		43,400.00			7
18,925.00		18,925.00				8
2,400.00		2,400.00				9
328.00		328.00				10
736.00		736.00				11
926.00		926.00				12
221.00		221.00				13
						14
						15
320.00		320.00				16
	425.00				425.00	17
50,264.00	50,264.00	23,856.00	43,400.00	26,408.00	6,864.00	18
		19,544.00			19,544.00	19
		43,400.00	43,400.00	26,408.00	26,408.00	20
						21
						22
						23
						24
						25
						26
						27
						28
						29
						30
						31
						32
						33
						34

Problem 5-3B

Valenti Insurance Agency
Work Sheet
For Year Ended December 31, 20--

	ACCOUNT NAME	TRIAL BALANCE		ADJUSTMENTS			
		DEBIT	CREDIT	DEBIT		CREDIT	
1	Cash	4,737.60					
2	Office Equipment	4,152.00					
3	Accumulated Depreciation, Office						
4	Equipment		456.00			(a)	384.00
5	M. Valenti, Capital		6,886.80				
6	M. Valenti, Drawing	22,800.00					
7	Fees Earned		52,080.00				
8	Wages Expense	22,200.00		(b)	510.00		
9	Rent Expense	2,880.00					
10	Office Supplies Expense	393.60					
11	Telephone Expense	883.20					
12	Advertising Expense	1,111.20					
13	Miscellaneous Expense	265.20					
14		59,422.80	59,422.80				
15	Depreciation Expense, Office						
16	Equipment			(a)	384.00		
17	Wages Payable					(b)	510.00
18					894.00		894.00
19	Net Income						
20							
21							
22							
23							
24							
25							
26							
27							
28							
29							
30							
31							
32							
33							
34							

Problem 5-3B (continued)

ADJUSTED TRIAL BALANCE		INCOME STATEMENT		BALANCE SHEET		
DEBIT	CREDIT	DEBIT	CREDIT	DEBIT	CREDIT	
4,737.60				4,737.60		1
4,152.00				4,152.00		2
						3
	840.00				840.00	4
	6,886.80				6,886.80	5
22,800.00				22,800.00		6
	52,080.00		52,080.00			7
22,710.00		22,710.00				8
2,880.00		2,880.00				9
393.60		393.60				10
883.20		883.20				11
1,111.20		1,111.20				12
265.20		265.20				13
						14
						15
384.00		384.00				16
	510.00				510.00	17
60,316.80	60,316.80	28,627.20	52,080.00	31,689.60	8,236.80	18
		23,452.80			23,452.80	19
		52,080.00	52,080.00	31,689.60	31,689.60	20
						21
						22
						23
						24
						25
						26
						27
						28
						29
						30
						31
						32
						33
						34

Problem 5-3A or 5-3B (continued)

GENERAL JOURNAL   PAGE ___17___

	DATE	DESCRIPTION	POST. REF.	DEBIT	CREDIT	
1						1
2						2
3						3
4						4
5						5
6						6
7						7
8						8
9						9
10						10
11						11
12						12
13						13
14						14
15						15
16						16
17						17
18						18
19						19
17						17
18						18
20						20
21						21
22						22
23						23
24						24
25						25
26						26
27						27
28						28
29						29

Problem 5-3A or 5-3B (continued)

GENERAL LEDGER

ACCOUNT _Cash_ _____ ACCOUNT NO. ____111____

DATE		ITEM	POST. REF.	DEBIT	CREDIT	BALANCE	
						DEBIT	CREDIT

ACCOUNT _Office Equipment_ _____ ACCOUNT NO. ____124____

DATE		ITEM	POST. REF.	DEBIT	CREDIT	BALANCE	
						DEBIT	CREDIT

ACCOUNT _Accumulated Depreciation, Office Equipment_ ___ ACCOUNT NO. ____125____

DATE		ITEM	POST. REF.	DEBIT	CREDIT	BALANCE	
						DEBIT	CREDIT

ACCOUNT _Wages Payable_ _____ ACCOUNT NO. ____222____

DATE		ITEM	POST. REF.	DEBIT	CREDIT	BALANCE	
						DEBIT	CREDIT

ACCOUNT _____, Capital_ _____ ACCOUNT NO. ____311____

DATE		ITEM	POST. REF.	DEBIT	CREDIT	BALANCE	
						DEBIT	CREDIT

ACCOUNT _____, Drawing_ _____ ACCOUNT NO. ____312____

DATE		ITEM	POST. REF.	DEBIT	CREDIT	BALANCE	
						DEBIT	CREDIT

Problem 5-3A or 5-3B (continued)

ACCOUNT _____ *Income Summary* _____ ACCOUNT NO. _____ *313*

DATE		ITEM	POST. REF.	DEBIT	CREDIT	BALANCE	
						DEBIT	CREDIT

ACCOUNT _____ *Fees Earned* _____ ACCOUNT NO. _____ *411*

DATE		ITEM	POST. REF.	DEBIT	CREDIT	BALANCE	
						DEBIT	CREDIT

ACCOUNT _____ *Wages Expense* _____ ACCOUNT NO. _____ *511*

DATE		ITEM	POST. REF.	DEBIT	CREDIT	BALANCE	
						DEBIT	CREDIT

ACCOUNT _____ *Rent Expense* _____ ACCOUNT NO. _____ *512*

DATE		ITEM	POST. REF.	DEBIT	CREDIT	BALANCE	
						DEBIT	CREDIT

ACCOUNT _____ *Office Supplies Expense* _____ ACCOUNT NO. _____ *513*

DATE		ITEM	POST. REF.	DEBIT	CREDIT	BALANCE	
						DEBIT	CREDIT

Problem 5-3A or 5-3B (concluded)

ACCOUNT **Depreciation Expense, Office Equipment**   ACCOUNT NO. _____ 514

DATE		ITEM	POST. REF.	DEBIT	CREDIT	BALANCE	
						DEBIT	CREDIT

ACCOUNT **Telephone Expense**   ACCOUNT NO. _____ 515

DATE		ITEM	POST. REF.	DEBIT	CREDIT	BALANCE	
						DEBIT	CREDIT

ACCOUNT **Advertising Expense**   ACCOUNT NO. _____ 516

DATE		ITEM	POST. REF.	DEBIT	CREDIT	BALANCE	
						DEBIT	CREDIT

ACCOUNT **Miscellaneous Expense**   ACCOUNT NO. _____ 519

DATE		ITEM	POST. REF.	DEBIT	CREDIT	BALANCE	
						DEBIT	CREDIT

ACCOUNT NAME	DEBIT	CREDIT

Problem 5-4A or 5-4B

	ACCOUNT NAME	TRIAL BALANCE		ADJUSTMENTS	
		DEBIT	CREDIT	DEBIT	CREDIT
1					
2					
3					
4					
5					
6					
7					
8					
9					
10					
11					
12					
13					
14					
15					
16					
17					
18					
19					
20					
21					
22					
23					
24					
25					
26					
27					
28					
29					
30					
31					
32					
33					
34					
35					
36					
37					
38					

Problem 5-4A or 5-4B (continued)

ADJUSTED TRIAL BALANCE		INCOME STATEMENT		BALANCE SHEET		
DEBIT	CREDIT	DEBIT	CREDIT	DEBIT	CREDIT	
						1
						2
						3
						4
						5
						6
						7
						8
						9
						10
						11
						12
						13
						14
						15
						16
						17
						18
						19
						20
						21
						22
						23
						24
						25
						26
						27
						28
						29
						30
						31
						32
						33
						34
						35
						36
						37
						38

Problem 5-4A or 5-4B (continued)

Problem 5-4A or 5-4B (continued)

Problem 5-4A or 5-4B (concluded)

GENERAL JOURNAL

PAGE _____

	DATE		DESCRIPTION	POST. REF.	DEBIT	CREDIT	
1							1
2							2
3							3
4							4
5							5
6							6
7							7
8							8
9							9
10							10
11							11
12							12
13							13
14							14
15							15
16							16
17							17
18							18
19							19
20							20
21							21
22							22
23							23
24							24
25							25
26							26
27							27
28							28
29							29
30							30
31							31
32							32
33							33
34							34
35							35
36							36

BEFORE A TEST CHECK SOLUTIONS: CHAPTERS 4–5

Part I: 1. ___ 2 ___ 3. ___ 4. ___ 5. ___ 6. ___

7. ___ 8. ___

Part II:

GENERAL JOURNAL   PAGE _____4_____

	DATE		DESCRIPTION	POST. REF.	DEBIT	CREDIT	
1							1
2							2
3							3
4							4
5							5
6							6
7							7
8							8
9							9
10							10
11							11
12							12
13							13
14							14
15							15
16							16
17							17
18							18
19							19

Part III: 1. ___ 2. ___ 3. ___ 4. ___ 5. ___ 6. ___

7. ___ 8. ___ 9. ___ 10. ___ 11. ___ 12. ___

13. ___ 14. ___ 15. ___ 16. ___ 17. ___ 18. ___

19. ___ 20. ___ 21. ___ 22. ___ 23. ___ 24. ___

25. ___

ACCOUNTING CYCLE REVIEW PROBLEM A

NAME _____   DATE _____   CLASS _____

ACCOUNTING CYCLE REVIEW PROBLEM A

GENERAL JOURNAL   PAGE _____1_____

	DATE		DESCRIPTION	POST. REF.	DEBIT	CREDIT	
1							1
2							2
3							3
4							4
5							5
6							6
7							7
8							8
9							9
10							10
11							11
12							12
13							13
14							14
15							15
16							16
17							17
18							18
19							19
20							20
21							21
22							22
23							23
24							24
25							25
26							26
27							27
28							28
29							29
30							30
31							31
32							32
33							33
34							34
35							35
36							36
37							37
38							38
39							39
40							40

ACCOUNTING CYCLE REVIEW PROBLEM A (continued)

GENERAL JOURNAL   PAGE ___2___

	DATE		DESCRIPTION	POST. REF.	DEBIT	CREDIT	
1							1
2							2
3							3
4							4
5							5
6							6
7							7
8							8
9							9
10							10
11							11
12							12
13							13
14							14
15							15
16							16
17							17
18							18
19							19
20							20
21							21
22							22
23							23
24							24
25							25
26							26
27							27
28							28
29							29
30							30
31							31
32							32
33							33
34							34
35							35
36							36
37							37
38							38
39							39
40							40

ACCOUNTING CYCLE REVIEW PROBLEM A (continued)

GENERAL JOURNAL   PAGE ___3___

	DATE		DESCRIPTION	POST. REF.	DEBIT	CREDIT	
1							1
2							2
3							3
4							4
5							5
6							6
7							7
8							8
9							9
10							10
11							11
12							12
13							13
14							14
15							15
16							16
17							17
18							18
19							19
20							20
21							21
22							22
23							23
24							24
25							25
26							26
27							27
28							28
29							29
30							30
31							31
32							32
33							33
34							34
35							35
36							36
37							37
38							38
39							39
40							40

ACCOUNTING CYCLE REVIEW PROBLEM A (continued)

GENERAL JOURNAL

PAGE 4

	DATE	DESCRIPTION	POST. REF.	DEBIT	CREDIT	
1						1
2						2
3						3
4						4
5						5
6						6
7						7
8						8
9						9
10						10
11						11
12						12
13						13
14						14
15						15
16						16
17						17
18						18
19						19
20						20
21						21
22						22
23						23
24						24
25						25
26						26
27						27
28						28
29						29
30						30
31						31
32						32
33						33
34						34
35						35
36						36
37						37
38						38
39						39
40						40

ACCOUNTING CYCLE REVIEW PROBLEM A (continued)

GENERAL JOURNAL   PAGE ___5___

	DATE	DESCRIPTION	POST. REF.	DEBIT	CREDIT	
1						1
2						2
3						3
4						4
5						5
6						6
7						7
8						8
9						9
10						10
11						11
12						12
13						13
14						14
15						15
16						16
17						17
18						18
19						19
20						20
21						21
22						22
23						23
24						24
25						25
26						26
27						27
28						28
29						29
30						30
31						31
32						32
33						33
34						34
35						35
36						36
37						37
38						38
39						39
40						40

ACCOUNTING CYCLE REVIEW PROBLEM A (continued)

GENERAL LEDGER

ACCOUNT _Cash_   ACCOUNT NO. _111_

DATE		ITEM	POST. REF.	DEBIT	CREDIT	BALANCE DEBIT	CREDIT

ACCOUNT _Accounts Receivable_   ACCOUNT NO. _112_

DATE		ITEM	POST. REF.	DEBIT	CREDIT	BALANCE DEBIT	CREDIT

ACCOUNT _Prepaid Insurance_   ACCOUNT NO. _114_

DATE		ITEM	POST. REF.	DEBIT	CREDIT	BALANCE DEBIT	CREDIT

ACCOUNTING CYCLE REVIEW PROBLEM A (continued)

ACCOUNT **Land**   ACCOUNT NO. *121*

DATE	ITEM	POST. REF.	DEBIT	CREDIT	BALANCE DEBIT	CREDIT

ACCOUNT **Building**   ACCOUNT NO. *122*

DATE	ITEM	POST. REF.	DEBIT	CREDIT	BALANCE DEBIT	CREDIT

ACCOUNT **Accumulated Depreciation, Building**   ACCOUNT NO. *123*

DATE	ITEM	POST. REF.	DEBIT	CREDIT	BALANCE DEBIT	CREDIT

ACCOUNT **Pool/Slide Facility**   ACCOUNT NO. *124*

DATE	ITEM	POST. REF.	DEBIT	CREDIT	BALANCE DEBIT	CREDIT

ACCOUNT **Accumulated Depreciation, Pool/Slide Facility**   ACCOUNT NO. *125*

DATE	ITEM	POST. REF.	DEBIT	CREDIT	BALANCE DEBIT	CREDIT

158

ACCOUNTING CYCLE REVIEW PROBLEM A (continued)

ACCOUNT *Pool Furniture*   ACCOUNT NO. _____ 126 _____

DATE	ITEM	POST. REF.	DEBIT	CREDIT	BALANCE DEBIT	BALANCE CREDIT

ACCOUNT *Accumulated Depreciation, Pool Furniture*   ACCOUNT NO. _____ 127 _____

DATE	ITEM	POST. REF.	DEBIT	CREDIT	BALANCE DEBIT	BALANCE CREDIT

ACCOUNT *Accounts Payable*   ACCOUNT NO. _____ 221 _____

DATE	ITEM	POST. REF.	DEBIT	CREDIT	BALANCE DEBIT	BALANCE CREDIT

ACCOUNT *Wages Payable*   ACCOUNT NO. _____ 222 _____

DATE	ITEM	POST. REF.	DEBIT	CREDIT	BALANCE DEBIT	BALANCE CREDIT

ACCOUNTING CYCLE REVIEW PROBLEM A (continued)

ACCOUNT *Mortgage Payable*   ACCOUNT NO.   *223*

DATE	ITEM	POST. REF.	DEBIT	CREDIT	BALANCE DEBIT	BALANCE CREDIT

ACCOUNT *W. Wong, Capital*   ACCOUNT NO.   *311*

DATE	ITEM	POST. REF.	DEBIT	CREDIT	BALANCE DEBIT	BALANCE CREDIT

ACCOUNT *W. Wong, Drawing*   ACCOUNT NO.   *312*

DATE	ITEM	POST. REF.	DEBIT	CREDIT	BALANCE DEBIT	BALANCE CREDIT

ACCOUNT *Income Summary*   ACCOUNT NO.   *313*

DATE	ITEM	POST. REF.	DEBIT	CREDIT	BALANCE DEBIT	BALANCE CREDIT

ACCOUNT *Income from Services*   ACCOUNT NO.   *411*

DATE	ITEM	POST. REF.	DEBIT	CREDIT	BALANCE DEBIT	BALANCE CREDIT

ACCOUNTING CYCLE REVIEW PROBLEM A (continued)

ACCOUNT *Concessions Income*   ACCOUNT NO. *412*

DATE	ITEM	POST. REF.	DEBIT	CREDIT	BALANCE	
					DEBIT	CREDIT

ACCOUNT *Pool Maintenance Expense*   ACCOUNT NO. *511*

DATE	ITEM	POST. REF.	DEBIT	CREDIT	BALANCE	
					DEBIT	CREDIT

ACCOUNT *Wages Expense*   ACCOUNT NO. *512*

DATE	ITEM	POST. REF.	DEBIT	CREDIT	BALANCE	
					DEBIT	CREDIT

ACCOUNT *Advertising Expense*   ACCOUNT NO. *513*

DATE	ITEM	POST. REF.	DEBIT	CREDIT	BALANCE	
					DEBIT	CREDIT

ACCOUNTING CYCLE REVIEW PROBLEM A (continued)

ACCOUNT *Utilities Expense*   ACCOUNT NO. *514*

DATE	ITEM	POST. REF.	DEBIT	CREDIT	BALANCE	
					DEBIT	CREDIT

ACCOUNT *Interest Expense*   ACCOUNT NO. *515*

DATE	ITEM	POST. REF.	DEBIT	CREDIT	BALANCE	
					DEBIT	CREDIT

ACCOUNT *Insurance Expense*   ACCOUNT NO. *517*

DATE	ITEM	POST. REF.	DEBIT	CREDIT	BALANCE	
					DEBIT	CREDIT

ACCOUNT *Depreciation Expense, Building*   ACCOUNT NO. *518*

DATE	ITEM	POST. REF.	DEBIT	CREDIT	BALANCE	
					DEBIT	CREDIT

ACCOUNT *Depreciation Expense, Pool/Slide Facility*   ACCOUNT NO. *519*

DATE	ITEM	POST. REF.	DEBIT	CREDIT	BALANCE	
					DEBIT	CREDIT

ACCOUNTING CYCLE REVIEW PROBLEM A (continued)

ACCOUNT _Depreciation Expense, Pool Furniture_   ACCOUNT NO. _520_

DATE		ITEM	POST. REF.	DEBIT	CREDIT	BALANCE	
						DEBIT	CREDIT

ACCOUNT _Miscellaneous Expense_   ACCOUNT NO. _522_

DATE		ITEM	POST. REF.	DEBIT	CREDIT	BALANCE	
						DEBIT	CREDIT

ACCOUNT _____   ACCOUNT NO. _____

DATE		ITEM	POST. REF.	DEBIT	CREDIT	BALANCE	
						DEBIT	CREDIT

ACCOUNT _____   ACCOUNT NO. _____

DATE		ITEM	POST. REF.	DEBIT	CREDIT	BALANCE	
						DEBIT	CREDIT

ACCOUNT _____   ACCOUNT NO. _____

DATE		ITEM	POST. REF.	DEBIT	CREDIT	BALANCE	
						DEBIT	CREDIT

ACCOUNTING CYCLE REVIEW PROBLEM A (continued)

	ACCOUNT NAME	TRIAL BALANCE		ADJUSTMENTS	
		DEBIT	CREDIT	DEBIT	CREDIT
1					
2					
3					
4					
5					
6					
7					
8					
9					
10					
11					
12					
13					
14					
15					
16					
17					
18					
19					
20					
21					
22					
23					
24					
25					
26					
27					
28					
29					
30					
31					
32					
33					
34					
35					
36					
37					
38					
39					
40					

ACCOUNTING CYCLE REVIEW PROBLEM A (continued)

ADJUSTED TRIAL BALANCE		INCOME STATEMENT		BALANCE SHEET		
DEBIT	CREDIT	DEBIT	CREDIT	DEBIT	CREDIT	
						1
						2
						3
						4
						5
						6
						7
						8
						9
						10
						11
						12
						13
						14
						15
						16
						17
						18
						19
						20
						21
						22
						23
						24
						25
						26
						27
						28
						29
						30
						31
						32
						33
						34
						35
						36
						37
						38
						39
						40

ACCOUNTING CYCLE REVIEW PROBLEM A (continued)

ACCOUNTING CYCLE REVIEW PROBLEM A (continued)

ACCOUNTING CYCLE REVIEW PROBLEM A (concluded)

ACCOUNT NAME	DEBIT	CREDIT	

ACCOUNTING CYCLE REVIEW PROBLEM B

NAME _____ DATE _____ CLASS _____

ACCOUNTING CYCLE REVIEW PROBLEM B

GENERAL JOURNAL   PAGE ___1___

	DATE		DESCRIPTION	POST. REF.	DEBIT	CREDIT	
1							1
2							2
3							3
4							4
5							5
6							6
7							7
8							8
9							9
10							10
11							11
12							12
13							13
14							14
15							15
16							16
17							17
18							18
19							19
20							20
21							21
22							22
23							23
24							24
25							25
26							26
27							27
28							28
29							29
30							30
31							31
32							32
33							33
34							34
35							35
36							36
37							37
38							38
39							39
40							40

ACCOUNTING CYCLE REVIEW PROBLEM B (continued)

GENERAL JOURNAL   PAGE ___2___

	DATE	DESCRIPTION	POST. REF.	DEBIT	CREDIT	
1						1
2						2
3						3
4						4
5						5
6						6
7						7
8						8
9						9
10						10
11						11
12						12
13						13
14						14
15						15
16						16
17						17
18						18
19						19
20						20
21						21
22						22
23						23
24						24
25						25
26						26
27						27
28						28
29						29
30						30
31						31
32						32
33						33
34						34
35						35
36						36
37						37
38						38
39						39

ACCOUNTING CYCLE REVIEW PROBLEM B (continued)

GENERAL JOURNAL

	DATE	DESCRIPTION	POST. REF.	DEBIT	CREDIT	
1						1
2						2
3						3
4						4
5						5
6						6
7						7
8						8
9						9
10						10
11						11
12						12
13						13
14						14
15						15
16						16
17						17
18						18
19						19
20						20
21						21
22						22
23						23
24						24
25						25
26						26
27						27
28						28
29						29
30						30
31						31
32						32
33						33
34						34
35						35
36						36
37						37
38						38
39						39
40						40
41						41

NAME _____ DATE _____ CLASS _____

ACCOUNTING CYCLE REVIEW PROBLEM B (continued)

GENERAL JOURNAL   PAGE ____4____

	DATE		DESCRIPTION	POST. REF.	DEBIT	CREDIT	
1							1
2							2
3							3
4							4
5							5
6							6
7							7
8							8
9							9
10							10
11							11
12							12
13							13
14							14
15							15
16							16
17							17
18							18
19							19
20							20
21							21
22							22
23							23
24							24
25							25
26							26
27							27
28							28
29							29
30							30
31							31
32							32
33							33
34							34
35							35
36							36
37							37
38							38
39							39
40							40
41							41
42							42

NAME _____ DATE _____ CLASS _____

ACCOUNTING CYCLE REVIEW PROBLEM B (continued)

GENERAL JOURNAL PAGE _____5_____

	DATE		DESCRIPTION	POST. REF.	DEBIT	CREDIT	
1							1
2							2
3							3
4							4
5							5
6							6
7							7
8							8
9							9
10							10
11							11
12							12
13							13
14							14
15							15
16							16
17							17
18							18
19							19
20							20
21							21
22							22
23							23
24							24
25							25
26							26
27							27
28							28
29							29
30							30
31							31
32							32
33							33
34							34
35							35
36							36
37							37
38							38
39							39
40							40
41							41

NAME _____ DATE _____ CLASS _____

ACCOUNTING CYCLE REVIEW PROBLEM B (continued)

GENERAL LEDGER

ACCOUNT   *Cash*   ACCOUNT NO.   *111*

DATE	ITEM	POST. REF.	DEBIT	CREDIT	BALANCE DEBIT	BALANCE CREDIT

ACCOUNT   *Accounts Receivable*   ACCOUNT NO.   *112*

DATE	ITEM	POST. REF.	DEBIT	CREDIT	BALANCE DEBIT	BALANCE CREDIT

ACCOUNT   *Prepaid Insurance*   ACCOUNT NO.   *114*

DATE	ITEM	POST. REF.	DEBIT	CREDIT	BALANCE DEBIT	BALANCE CREDIT

ACCOUNTING CYCLE REVIEW PROBLEM B (continued)

ACCOUNT *Land*   ACCOUNT NO. *121*

DATE	ITEM	POST. REF.	DEBIT	CREDIT	BALANCE	
					DEBIT	CREDIT

ACCOUNT *Pool Structure*   ACCOUNT NO. *125*

DATE	ITEM	POST. REF.	DEBIT	CREDIT	BALANCE	
					DEBIT	CREDIT

ACCOUNT *Accumulated Depreciation, Pool Structure*   ACCOUNT NO. *126*

DATE	ITEM	POST. REF.	DEBIT	CREDIT	BALANCE	
					DEBIT	CREDIT

ACCOUNT *Fan System*   ACCOUNT NO. *127*

DATE	ITEM	POST. REF.	DEBIT	CREDIT	BALANCE	
					DEBIT	CREDIT

ACCOUNT *Accumulated Depreciation, Fan System*   ACCOUNT NO. *128*

DATE	ITEM	POST. REF.	DEBIT	CREDIT	BALANCE	
					DEBIT	CREDIT

ACCOUNTING CYCLE REVIEW PROBLEM B (continued)

ACCOUNT   *Sailboats*   ACCOUNT NO.   *129*

DATE		ITEM	POST. REF.	DEBIT	CREDIT	BALANCE	
						DEBIT	CREDIT

ACCOUNT   *Accumulated Depreciation, Sailboats*   ACCOUNT NO.   *130*

DATE		ITEM	POST. REF.	DEBIT	CREDIT	BALANCE	
						DEBIT	CREDIT

ACCOUNT   *Accounts Payable*   ACCOUNT NO.   *221*

DATE		ITEM	POST. REF.	DEBIT	CREDIT	BALANCE	
						DEBIT	CREDIT

ACCOUNT   *Wages Payable*   ACCOUNT NO.   *222*

DATE		ITEM	POST. REF.	DEBIT	CREDIT	BALANCE	
						DEBIT	CREDIT

ACCOUNTING CYCLE REVIEW PROBLEM B (continued)

ACCOUNT _Mortgage Payable_ _____ ACCOUNT NO. _223_

DATE	ITEM	POST. REF.	DEBIT	CREDIT	BALANCE	
					DEBIT	CREDIT

ACCOUNT _R. Erdmon, Capital_ _____ ACCOUNT NO. _311_

DATE	ITEM	POST. REF.	DEBIT	CREDIT	BALANCE	
					DEBIT	CREDIT

ACCOUNT _R. Erdmon, Drawing_ _____ ACCOUNT NO. _312_

DATE	ITEM	POST. REF.	DEBIT	CREDIT	BALANCE	
					DEBIT	CREDIT

ACCOUNT _Income Summary_ _____ ACCOUNT NO. _313_

DATE	ITEM	POST. REF.	DEBIT	CREDIT	BALANCE	
					DEBIT	CREDIT

ACCOUNT _Income from Services_ _____ ACCOUNT NO. _411_

DATE	ITEM	POST. REF.	DEBIT	CREDIT	BALANCE	
					DEBIT	CREDIT

ACCOUNTING CYCLE REVIEW PROBLEM B (continued)

ACCOUNT *Concessions Income*   ACCOUNT NO. *412*

DATE	ITEM	POST. REF.	DEBIT	CREDIT	BALANCE DEBIT	BALANCE CREDIT

ACCOUNT *Sailboat Rental Expense*   ACCOUNT NO. *511*

DATE	ITEM	POST. REF.	DEBIT	CREDIT	BALANCE DEBIT	BALANCE CREDIT

ACCOUNT *Wages Expense*   ACCOUNT NO. *512*

DATE	ITEM	POST. REF.	DEBIT	CREDIT	BALANCE DEBIT	BALANCE CREDIT

ACCOUNT *Advertising Expense*   ACCOUNT NO. *513*

DATE	ITEM	POST. REF.	DEBIT	CREDIT	BALANCE DEBIT	BALANCE CREDIT

NAME _____ DATE _____ CLASS _____

ACCOUNTING CYCLE REVIEW PROBLEM B (continued)

ACCOUNT *Utilities Expense* ACCOUNT NO. *514*

DATE	ITEM	POST. REF.	DEBIT	CREDIT	BALANCE	
					DEBIT	CREDIT

ACCOUNT *Interest Expense* ACCOUNT NO. *515*

DATE	ITEM	POST. REF.	DEBIT	CREDIT	BALANCE	
					DEBIT	CREDIT

ACCOUNT *Insurance Expense* ACCOUNT NO. *516*

DATE	ITEM	POST. REF.	DEBIT	CREDIT	BALANCE	
					DEBIT	CREDIT

ACCOUNT *Depreciation Expense, Pool Structure* ACCOUNT NO. *517*

DATE	ITEM	POST. REF.	DEBIT	CREDIT	BALANCE	
					DEBIT	CREDIT

ACCOUNT *Depreciation Expense, Fan System* ACCOUNT NO. *518*

DATE	ITEM	POST. REF.	DEBIT	CREDIT	BALANCE	
					DEBIT	CREDIT

ACCOUNTING CYCLE REVIEW PROBLEM B (continued)

ACCOUNT _Depreciation Expense, Sailboats_   ACCOUNT NO. _519_

DATE	ITEM	POST. REF.	DEBIT	CREDIT	BALANCE	
					DEBIT	CREDIT

ACCOUNT _Miscellaneous Expense_   ACCOUNT NO. _522_

DATE	ITEM	POST. REF.	DEBIT	CREDIT	BALANCE	
					DEBIT	CREDIT

ACCOUNT _____   ACCOUNT NO. _____

DATE	ITEM	POST. REF.	DEBIT	CREDIT	BALANCE	
					DEBIT	CREDIT

ACCOUNT _____   ACCOUNT NO. _____

DATE	ITEM	POST. REF.	DEBIT	CREDIT	BALANCE	
					DEBIT	CREDIT

ACCOUNT _____   ACCOUNT NO. _____

DATE	ITEM	POST. REF.	DEBIT	CREDIT	BALANCE	
					DEBIT	CREDIT

ACCOUNTING CYCLE REVIEW PROBLEM B (continued)

	ACCOUNT NAME	TRIAL BALANCE		ADJUSTMENTS	
		DEBIT	CREDIT	DEBIT	CREDIT
1					
2					
3					
4					
5					
6					
7					
8					
9					
10					
11					
12					
13					
14					
15					
16					
17					
18					
19					
20					
21					
22					
23					
24					
25					
26					
27					
28					
29					
30					
31					
32					
33					
34					
35					
36					
37					
38					
39					
40					

ACCOUNTING CYCLE REVIEW PROBLEM B (continued)

ADJUSTED TRIAL BALANCE		INCOME STATEMENT		BALANCE SHEET		
DEBIT	CREDIT	DEBIT	CREDIT	DEBIT	CREDIT	
						1
						2
						3
						4
						5
						6
						7
						8
						9
						10
						11
						12
						13
						14
						15
						16
						17
						18
						19
						20
						21
						22
						23
						24
						25
						26
						27
						28
						29
						30
						31
						32
						33
						34
						35
						36
						37
						38
						39
						40

ACCOUNTING CYCLE REVIEW PROBLEM B (continued)

ACCOUNTING CYCLE REVIEW PROBLEM B (continued)

ACCOUNTING CYCLE REVIEW PROBLEM B (concluded)

ACCOUNT NAME	DEBIT	CREDIT

Accounting for Professional Enterprises: The Combined Journal (*Optional*)

PERFORMANCE OBJECTIVES

1. Describe the accounting records for a professional enterprise.
2. Record transactions for both a professional enterprise and a service enterprise in a combined journal.
3. Post from the combined journal and determine the cash balance.
4. Prepare a work sheet for a professional enterprise.
5. Prepare financial statements for a professional enterprise.
6. Record adjusting and closing entries in a combined journal.

KEY TERMS

Combined journal
Patient's ledger record
Professional enterprise
Special columns

STUDY GUIDE QUESTIONS

PART 1   True/False

For each of the following statements, indicate T if the statement is true and F if the statement is false.

T   F   1. When a patient sends in a payment, the receptionist records the amount on the patient's ledger record in the Debit column.

T   F   2. Explanations should be included in the combined journal.

T   F   3. In cases where the special columns in a combined journal can handle both the entire debit and credit amounts, it is not necessary to use the Account Name column except to write the name of the check payee.

T   F   4. In the Account Name column of a combined journal, accounts to be credited do not have to be indented.

T   F   5. The combined journal is used widely by professional and service-type enterprises.

T   F   6. The number of columns in a combined journal can vary from two to twenty.

T   F   7. Amounts in the Other Accounts Debit column of a combined journal are posted individually to the account shown in the Account Name column.

T   F   8. A dash in the Post. Ref. column of a combined journal indicates that individual amounts in the special columns are being posted as totals.

T   F   9. Combined journals with blank columns can be customized to meet the specific requirements of a given business.

T   F   10. When a combined journal is being used, the cash balance may be determined at any time during the month by taking the beginning balance of cash, adding the total cash credits so far during the month, and subtracting the total cash debits so far during the month.

PART 2   Chart of Accounts

L. Barrett, the owner of an electronics repair shop, has asked you to set up a tentative chart of accounts for his business. He rents space in a small shopping center and has one employee. He operates a service truck. Revenue is only in the form of cash. The firm does a considerable amount of advertising for the business.

Chart of Accounts

Assets

_____

_____

_____

_____

_____

_____

Liabilities

_____

_____

Owner's Equity

_____

_____

Revenue

_____

_____

Expenses

_____

_____

_____

_____

_____

_____

_____

PART 3 Combined Journal

L. Barrett decides to use a combined journal. Make a tentative list of the headings for the money columns for a combined journal.

_____

_____

_____

_____

_____

_____

DEMONSTRATION PROBLEM

Transactions for Heins' Cleaners are presented below.

June 1 N.L. Heins invests $40,000 cash in his new business.

2 Buys equipment from Craig Company costing $22,000, paying cash (Ck. No. 1).

2 Buys equipment costing $4,000 on credit from Drake Equipment Company.

5 Pays $1,000 to Drake Equipment Company to be applied against the firm's liability of $4,000 (Ck. No. 2).

5 Buys cleaning fluid and garment bags on account from Blair Supply Company for $400.

7 Cash revenue received for the first week, $960.

8 Pays rent for the month, $500 (Ck. No. 3).

10 Pays wages to a part-time employee, for the period June 1 through June 10, $440 (Ck. No. 4).

11 Pays $360 for a two-year liability insurance policy (Ck. No. 5).

14 Cash revenue received for the second week, $980.

14 Receives bill from the *City News* for newspaper advertising, $180.

15 Pays $1,800 to Drake Equipment Company as partial payment on account (Ck. No. 6).

15 Receives and pays bills for utilities, $220 (Ck. No. 7).

15 Pays $180 to *City News* for advertising (Ck. No. 8). (This bill has been previously recorded.)

21 Cash revenue received for the third week, $830.

23 Heins' Cleaners enters into a contract with Formal Rentals to clean formal garments on a credit basis. Heins' Cleaners bills Formal Rentals for services performed, $140.

24 Pays wages to part-time employee, $490, for June 11 through June 24 (Ck. No. 9).

26 Buys additional equipment for $940 from Drake Equipment Company, paying $140 down, with the remaining $800 on account (Ck. No. 10).

30 Cash received for the remainder of the month, $960.

30 Receives $90 from Formal Rentals to apply on amount previously billed.

30 Heins withdraws $1,200 in cash for personal use (Ck. No. 11).

Instructions

Record the June transactions in a combined journal, page 12.

SOLUTION

Notice the first transaction of June 5, involving payment to a creditor on account. The name of the creditor is recorded in the Account Name column. Likewise, in receiving cash from a customer on account (second entry of June 30), the name of the charge customer is recorded in the Account Name column.

Combined Journal (continued on next page)

	CASH		CK.	DATE		ACCOUNT NAME	POST. REF.	OTHER ACCOUNTS	
	DEBIT	CREDIT	NO.					DEBIT	CREDIT
1				20—					
2	40,000.00			June	1	N.L. Heins, Capital			40,000.00
3		22,000.00	1		2	Equipment, Craig Co.		22,000.00	
4					2	Equipment, Drake			
5						Equip. Co.		4,000.00	
6		1,000.00	2		5	Drake Equipment Co.	—		
7					5	Supplies Expense,			
8						Blair Supply Co.		400.00	
9	960.00				7	————————	—		
10		500.00	3		8	Rent Expense		500.00	
11		440.00	4		10	————————	—		
12		360.00	5		11	Prepaid Insurance		360.00	
13	980.00				14	————————	—		
14					14	Advertising Expense,			
15						City News		180.00	
16		1,800.00	6		15	Drake Equipment Co.	—		
17		220.00	7		15	Utilities Expense		220.00	
18		180.00	8		15	City News	—		
19	830.00				21	————————	—		
20					23	Formal Rentals	—		
21		490.00	9		24	————————	—		
22		140.00	10		26	Equipment, Drake			
23						Equip. Co.		940.00	
24	960.00				30	————————	—		
25	90.00				30	Formal Rentals	—		
26		1,200.00	11		30	N. L. Heins, Drawing		1,200.00	
27	43,820.00	28,330.00			30			29,800.00	40,000.00
28									
29									

Debits	$43,820		Credits	$28,330
	29,800			40,000
	140			90
	2,980			5,380
	930			3,870
	$77,670			$77,670

SOLUTION *(concluded)*

(continuation of Combined Journal)   PAGE ___12___

ACCOUNTS RECEIVABLE		ACCOUNTS PAYABLE		INCOME FROM SERVICES	WAGES EXPENSE	
DEBIT	CREDIT	DEBIT	CREDIT	CREDIT	DEBIT	
						1
						2
						3
						4
			4,000.00			5
		1,000.00				6
						7
			400.00			8
				960.00		9
						10
					440.00	11
						12
				980.00		13
						14
			180.00			15
		1,800.00				16
						17
		180.00				18
				830.00		19
140.00				140.00		20
					490.00	21
						22
			800.00			23
				960.00		24
	90.00					25
						26
140.00	90.00	2,980.00	5,380.00	3,870.00	930.00	27
						28
						29

EXERCISES

Exercise 6-1

GENERAL JOURNAL   PAGE _____

	DATE		DESCRIPTION	POST. REF.	DEBIT	CREDIT	
1							1
2							2
3							3
4							4
5							5
6							6

Exercise 6-2

a. _____

b. _____

c. _____

d. _____

Exercise 6-3

1. _____

2. _____

3. _____

4. _____

5. _____

6. _____

7. _____

8. _____

9. _____

Exercise 6-4

Combined Journal

| | CASH | | CK. NO. | DATE | ACCOUNT NAME | POST. REF. | OTHER ACCOUNTS | | PROFESSIONAL FEES | |
	DEPOSITS DEBIT	CHECKS CREDIT					DEBIT	CREDIT	CREDIT	
1										1
2										2
3										3

Exercise 6-5

_____

_____

_____

_____

_____

Exercise 6-6

_____

_____

_____

_____

_____

Exercise 6-7

_____

_____

_____

_____

_____

Exercise 6-8

Beginning balance (November 1) $ _____

Add cash debits   _____

Total $ _____

Less cash credits   _____

Ending balance (November 11) $ _____

Problem 6-1A or 6-1B

Combined Journal (continued on next page)

	CASH		CK. NO.	DATE	ACCOUNT NAME	POST. REF.	OTHER ACCOUNTS	
	DEBIT	CREDIT					DEBIT	CREDIT
1								
2								
3								
4								
5								
6								
7								
8								
9								
10								
11								
12								
13								
14								
15								
16								
17								
18								
19								
20								
21								
22								
23								
24								
25								
26								
27								
28								
29								
30								
31								
32								
33								
34								
35								
36								
37								

NAME _____ DATE _____ CLASS _____

Problem 6-1A or 6-1B (concluded)

PAGE _____

DRAWING	PROFESSIONAL FEES	MEDICAL SUPPLIES EXPENSE	LABORATORY EXPENSE	CLEANING EXPENSE	MISCELLANEOUS EXPENSE	
DEBIT	CREDIT	DEBIT	DEBIT	DEBIT	DEBIT	
						1
						2
						3
						4
						5
						6
						7
						8
						9
						10
						11
						12
						13
						14
						15
						16
						17
						18
						19
						20
						21
						22
						23
						24
						25
						26
						27
						28
						29
						30
						31
						32
						33
						34
						35
						36
						37

Problem 6-2A or 6-2B

Combined Journal (continued on next page)

	CASH		CK. NO.	DATE		ACCOUNT NAME	POST. REF.	OTHER ACCOUNTS	
	DEBIT	CREDIT						DEBIT	CREDIT
1									
2									
3									
4									
5									
6									
7									
8									
9									
10									
11									
12									
13									
14									
15									
16									
17									
18									
19									
20									
21									
22									
23									
24									
25									
26									
27									
28									
29									
30									
31									
32									
33									
34									
35									
36									
37									

Problem 6-2A or 6-2B (concluded)

PAGE _____

DRAWING	PROFESSIONAL FEES	ADVERTISING EXPENSE	TRAVEL EXPENSE	SUPPLIES EXPENSE	MISCELLANEOUS EXPENSE	
DEBIT	CREDIT	DEBIT	DEBIT	DEBIT	DEBIT	
						1
						2
						3
						4
						5
						6
						7
						8
						9
						10
						11
						12
						13
						14
						15
						16
						17
						18
						19
						20
						21
						22
						23
						24
						25
						26
						27
						28
						29
						30
						31
						32
						33
						34
						35
						36
						37

Problem 6-3A or 6-3B

Combined Journal (continued on next page)

	CASH		CK. NO.	DATE	ACCOUNT NAME	POST. REF.	OTHER ACCOUNTS	
	DEBIT	CREDIT					DEBIT	CREDIT
1								
2								
3								
4								
5								
6								
7								
8								
9								
10								
11								
12								
13								
14								
15								
16								
17								
18								
19								
20								
21								
22								
23								
24								
25								
26								
27								
28								
29								
30								
31								
32								
33								
34								
35								
36								
37								
38								

Problem 6-3A or 6-3B (continued)

PAGE _____

ACCOUNTS RECEIVABLE		PROFESSIONAL FEES	SALARY EXPENSE	UTILITIES EXPENSE	
DEBIT	CREDIT	CREDIT	DEBIT	DEBIT	
					1
					2
					3
					4
					5
					6
					7
					8
					9
					10
					11
					12
					13
					14
					15
					16
					17
					18
					19
					20
					21
					22
					23
					24
					25
					26
					27
					28
					29
					30
					31
					32
					33
					34
					35
					36
					37
					38

Problem 6-3A or 6-3B (continued)

GENERAL LEDGER

ACCOUNT *Cash* ACCOUNT NO. *111*

DATE		ITEM	POST. REF.	DEBIT	CREDIT	BALANCE	
						DEBIT	CREDIT
20--							
Aug.	31	Balance	✓			6,288.00	

ACCOUNT *Accounts Receivable* ACCOUNT NO. *112*

DATE		ITEM	POST. REF.	DEBIT	CREDIT	BALANCE	
						DEBIT	CREDIT
20--							
Aug.	31	Balance	✓			4,496.00	

ACCOUNT *Prepaid Insurance* ACCOUNT NO. *114*

DATE		ITEM	POST. REF.	DEBIT	CREDIT	BALANCE	
						DEBIT	CREDIT
20--							
Aug.	31	Balance	✓			3,600.00	

ACCOUNT *Equipment* ACCOUNT NO. *121*

DATE		ITEM	POST. REF.	DEBIT	CREDIT	BALANCE	
						DEBIT	CREDIT
20--							
Aug.	31	Balance	✓			18,920.00	

ACCOUNT *Accumulated Depreciation, Equipment* ACCOUNT NO. *122*

DATE		ITEM	POST. REF.	DEBIT	CREDIT	BALANCE	
						DEBIT	CREDIT
20--							
Aug.	31	Balance	✓				10,362.00

200

Problem 6-3A or 6-3B (continued)

ACCOUNT   *Accounts Payable* _____   ACCOUNT NO. ___221___

DATE		ITEM	POST. REF.	DEBIT	CREDIT	BALANCE	
						DEBIT	CREDIT
20--							
Aug.	31	Balance	✓				320.50

ACCOUNT   _____ *, Capital*   ACCOUNT NO. ___311___

DATE		ITEM	POST. REF.	DEBIT	CREDIT	BALANCE	
						DEBIT	CREDIT
20--							
Aug.	31	Balance	✓				40,115.00

ACCOUNT   _____ *, Drawing*   ACCOUNT NO. ___312___

DATE		ITEM	POST. REF.	DEBIT	CREDIT	BALANCE	
						DEBIT	CREDIT
20--							
Aug.	31	Balance	✓			16,750.00	

ACCOUNT   *Income Summary* _____   ACCOUNT NO. ___313___

DATE	ITEM	POST. REF.	DEBIT	CREDIT	BALANCE	
					DEBIT	CREDIT

ACCOUNT   *Professional Fees* _____   ACCOUNT NO. ___411___

DATE		ITEM	POST. REF.	DEBIT	CREDIT	BALANCE	
						DEBIT	CREDIT
20--							
Aug.	31	Balance	✓				33,100.00

Problem 6-3A or 6-3B (continued)

ACCOUNT **Salary Expense**   ACCOUNT NO. _511_

DATE		ITEM	POST. REF.	DEBIT	CREDIT	BALANCE	
						DEBIT	CREDIT
20--							
Aug.	31	Balance	✓			17,350.00	

ACCOUNT **Rent Expense**   ACCOUNT NO. _512_

DATE		ITEM	POST. REF.	DEBIT	CREDIT	BALANCE	
						DEBIT	CREDIT
20--							
Aug.	31	Balance	✓			7,200.00	

ACCOUNT **Laboratory Expense**   ACCOUNT NO. _513_

DATE		ITEM	POST. REF.	DEBIT	CREDIT	BALANCE	
						DEBIT	CREDIT
20--							
Aug.	31	Balance	✓			4,250.00	

ACCOUNT **Utilities Expense**   ACCOUNT NO. _514_

DATE		ITEM	POST. REF.	DEBIT	CREDIT	BALANCE	
						DEBIT	CREDIT
20--							
Aug.	31	Balance	✓			1,765.50	

ACCOUNT **Depreciation Expense, Equipment**   ACCOUNT NO. _515_

DATE		ITEM	POST. REF.	DEBIT	CREDIT	BALANCE	
						DEBIT	CREDIT

Problem 6-3A or 6-3B (continued)

ACCOUNT *Supplies Expense*   ACCOUNT NO. *516*

DATE		ITEM	POST. REF.	DEBIT	CREDIT	BALANCE DEBIT	BALANCE CREDIT
20--							
Aug.	31	Balance	✓			2,280.00	

ACCOUNT *Miscellaneous Expense*   ACCOUNT NO. *517*

DATE		ITEM	POST. REF.	DEBIT	CREDIT	BALANCE DEBIT	BALANCE CREDIT
20--							
Aug.	31	Balance	✓			998.00	

Problem 6-3A or 6-3B (concluded)

ACCOUNT NAME	DEBIT	CREDIT	

Problem 6-4A or 6-4B

Chart of Accounts

Assets		Revenue	
		Expenses	
Liabilities			
Owner's Equity			

Problem 6-4A or 6-4B (continued)

Combined Journal (continued on next page)

	CASH		CK. NO.	DATE	ACCOUNT NAME	POST. REF.	OTHER ACCOUNTS	
	DEBIT	CREDIT					DEBIT	CREDIT
1								
2								
3								
4								
5								
6								
7								
8								
9								
10								
11								
12								
13								
14								
15								
16								
17								
18								
19								
20								
21								
22								
23								
24								
25								
26								
27								
28								
29								
30								
31								
32								
33								
34								
35								
36								
37								
38								

Problem 6-4A or 6-4B (concluded)

PAGE _____

ACCOUNTS PAYABLE		INCOME FROM SERVICES	WAGES EXPENSE	
DEBIT	CREDIT	CREDIT	DEBIT	
				1
				2
				3
				4
				5
				6
				7
				8
				9
				10
				11
				12
				13
				14
				15
				16
				17
				18
				19
				20
				21
				22
				23
				24
				25
				26
				27
				28
				29
				30
				31
				32
				33
				34
				35
				36
				37
				38

Bank Accounts and Cash Funds

PERFORMANCE OBJECTIVES

1. Describe the procedure for depositing checks.
2. Reconcile a bank statement.
3. Record the required journal entries directly from the bank reconciliation.
4. Record journal entries to establish and reimburse a Petty Cash Fund.
5. Complete petty cash vouchers and petty cash payments records.
6. Record the journal entries to establish a Change Fund.
7. Record journal entries for transactions involving Cash Short and Over.

KEY TERMS

ABA number
ATM (automated teller machine)
Bank reconciliation
Bank statement
Blank endorsement
Canceled checks
Cash funds
Change Fund
Collections
Denominations
Deposit in transit
Deposit slips
Drawer
Electronic Funds Transfer (EFT)
Endorsement

Interest income
Internal control
Ledger balance of cash
MICR
NSF (not sufficient funds) checks
Outstanding checks
Payee
Petty Cash Fund
Petty cash payments record
Petty cash voucher
Promissory note
Qualified endorsement
Restrictive endorsement
Service charge
Signature card

STUDY GUIDE QUESTIONS

PART 1   True/False

For each of the following statements, indicate T if the statement is true and F if the statement is false.

T   F   1. Cash receipts, deposits, and bank reconciliations should always be handled by the same person.

T   F   2. Each petty cash payment is entered separately in the petty cash payments record, not the general journal.

T   F   3. The amount set aside for change will vary by the type and size of the business.

T   F   4. Before recording an amount in the Cash Short and Over account, one must deduct the amount of the change fund and then compare the actual cash and the amount sold for cash.

T   F   5. On a bank reconciliation, outstanding checks are deducted from the bank statement balance.

T   F   6. Payments made from the petty cash fund are journalized by account when the petty cash fund is reimbursed.

T   F   7. A credit memo increases the depositor's bank balance.

T   F   8. The entry to reimburse the Petty Cash Fund involves a debit to Petty Cash Fund and a credit to Cash.

T   F   9. The entry for an NSF check involves a debit to Accounts Receivable and a credit to Cash.

T   F   10. A credit balance in the Cash Short and Over account is listed on the income statement under Miscellaneous Expense.

PART 2   Completion—Language of Business

Complete each of the following statements by writing the appropriate word(s) in the spaces provided.

1. The party that writes a check is called the _____.

2. The amount that the bank charges a depositor for handling checks and collections is called a(n) _____.

3. The method used to transfer title of a check is known as a(n) _____.

4. Varieties of coins and currency are called _____.

5. Checks issued by the depositor that have been paid by the bank and included with the bank statement are called _____.

6. An endorsement that prevents further circulation of a check is called a(n) _____ _____.

7. The party who receives the check is called the _____.

8. On a bank reconciliation, the balance of the Cash account in the general ledger is called the _____.

9. A deposit not recorded on the bank statement because the deposit was made between the bank's cut-off date and the time the statement is received is called a(n) _____.

10. The _____ is a cash fund used to handle transactions where customers pay cash for goods and services.

11. An endorsement of a check that contains the words "without recourse" is called a(n) _____.

12. The procedure used to determine why there is a difference between the balance of Cash in the company's general ledger and in the company's bank records is called a(n) _____ _____.

13. _____ are checks that have been written by the depositor and deducted on the depositor's records but have not yet reached the bank for payment.

14. In a(n) _____, the holder (payee) of a check simply signs her or his name on the back of the check.

PART 3 Reimbursing the Petty Cash Fund

Quality Bakery has the petty cash payments record shown on the next page. The amount of the debit balance of the Petty Cash Fund account is _____ . Record the entry in general journal form to reimburse the Petty Cash Fund.

GENERAL JOURNAL   PAGE _____

	DATE		DESCRIPTION	POST. REF.	DEBIT	CREDIT	
1							1
2							2
3							3
4							4
5							5
6							6
7							7
8							8
9							9
10							10
11							11
12							12
13							13
14							14

PETTY CASH PAYMENTS RECORD

PERIOD OF TIME *June 20—* PAGE *37*

	DATE	VOU. NO.	EXPLANATION	PAYMENTS	REPAIR EXPENSE	DELIVERY EXPENSE	MISC. EXPENSE	OTHER ACCOUNTS ACCOUNT	AMOUNT	
1	*20—*									1
2	*June* 3	1	H. Ball	7.00				H. Ball,		2
3								Drawing	7.00	3
4	7	2	Marking pens	5.16			5.16			4
5	9	3	Ben's Delivery	4.20		4.20				5
6	12	4	Lightbulbs	6.32			6.32			6
7	17	5	Postage stamps	5.00			5.00			7
8	21	6	Repair fuses	7.10	7.10					8
9	29	7	H. Ball	4.50				H. Ball,		9
10								Drawing	4.50	10
11	30		Totals	39.28	7.10	4.20	16.48		11.50	11
12										12
13										13
14			Balance in Fund	$20.72						14
15			Reimbursed Ck.							15
16			No. 711	-39.28						16
17			Total	$60.00						17
18										18

DEMONSTRATION PROBLEM

The Reading Company made the following transactions during June of this year involving its Petty Cash Fund, its Change Fund, its Cash Short and Over, and its Income from Services accounts:

June	1	Established a Change Fund, $200.
	3	Established a Petty Cash Fund, $100.
	14	Recorded cash revenue for period June 1 through 14: cash register tape, $4,980.21; cash count, $5,175.39.
	30	Reimbursed the Petty Cash Fund, $94. The petty cash payments record indicated the following expenditures: Supplies Expense, $32; Delivery Expense, $16; Advertising Expense, $35; Miscellaneous Expense, $11.
	30	Recorded cash revenue for period June 15 through 30: cash register tape, $5,239.16; cash count, $5,441.09.
	30	Recorded an NSF check received from J. Blakely listed on the bank reconciliation, $157.

Instructions

Record the transactions in general journal form.

SOLUTION

GENERAL JOURNAL   PAGE _____

	DATE		DESCRIPTION	POST. REF.	DEBIT	CREDIT	
1	20—						1
2	June	1	Change Fund		200.00		2
3			Cash			200.00	3
4			Established a Change Fund.				4
5							5
6		3	Petty Cash Fund		100.00		6
7			Cash			100.00	7
8			Established a Petty Cash Fund.				8
9							9
10		14	Cash		4,975.39		10
11			Cash Short and Over		4.82		11
12			Income from Services			4,980.21	12
13			To record cash revenue for period				13
14			June 1 through 14 involving a				14
15			cash shortage of $4.82.				15
16							16
17		30	Supplies Expense		32.00		17
18			Delivery Expense		16.00		18
19			Advertising Expense		35.00		19
20			Miscellaneous Expense		11.00		20
21			Cash			94.00	21
22			Reimbursed the Petty Cash Fund.				22
23							23
24		30	Cash		5,241.09		24
25			Income from Services			5,239.16	25
26			Cash Short and Over			1.93	26
27			To record cash revenue for period				27
28			June 15 through 30 involving a				28
29			cash overage of $1.93.				29
30							30
31		30	Accounts Receivable		157.00		31
32			Cash			157.00	32
33			To record an NSF check received				33
34			from J. Blakely.				34
35							35

EXERCISES

Exercise 7-1

Bank Statement Balance			$3,754.00
Add:	Deposit in transit	*(a)*	
Deduct:	Outstanding checks		$3,754.00
	No. 210	$210.00	
	No. 224	*(b)*	
	No. 227	320.00	851.00
Adjusted Bank Statement Balance		*(c)*	
Ledger Balance of Cash			$2,840.00
Add:	Note collected by bank		427.00
		(d)	
Deduct:	Bank service and collection charge	*(e)*	
	NSF check from customer	85.00	97.00
Adjusted Ledger Balance of Cash		*(f)*	

Exercise 7-2

GENERAL JOURNAL   PAGE _____

	DATE	DESCRIPTION	POST. REF.	DEBIT	CREDIT	
1						1
2						2
3						3
4						4
5						5
6						6
7						7
8						8
9						9
10						10
11						11
12						12
13						13
14						14
15						15
16						16
17						17
18						18
19						19
20						20
21						21
22						22

Exercise 7-3

Bank Statement Balance
Add:
                                    _____

Deduct: _____   _____ - _____ = _____

Adjusted Bank Statement Balance   _____

Exercise 7-4

ITEM	ADD TO BANK STATEMENT BALANCE	SUBTRACT FROM BANK STATEMENT BALANCE	ADD TO LEDGER BALANCE OF CASH	SUBTRACT FROM LEDGER BALANCE OF CASH
a. A check-printing charge				
b. An outstanding check				
c. A deposit for $187 listed incorrectly on the bank statement as $178				
d. A collection charge the bank made for a note it collected for its depositor				
e. A check written for $40.73 and recorded incorrectly in the checkbook as $40.37				
f. A deposit in transit				
g. An NSF check received from a customer				
h. A check written for $72.39 and recorded incorrectly in the checkbook as $720.39				

Exercise 7-5

Bank Reconciliation

Bank Statement Balance	$
Add:	
	$
Deduct:	$
Adjusted Bank Statement Balance	$
Ledger Balance of Cash	$
Add:	
Deduct:	$
Adjusted Ledger Balance of Cash	$

Exercise 7-6

GENERAL JOURNAL   PAGE _____

	DATE	DESCRIPTION	POST. REF.	DEBIT	CREDIT	
1						1
2						2
3						3
4						4
5						5
6						6
7						7
8						8
9						9
10						10
11						11
12						12
13						13
14						14
15						15
16						16
17						17
18						18
19						19
20						20
21						21
22						22
23						23
24						24

Exercise 7-7

GENERAL JOURNAL   PAGE _____

	DATE	DESCRIPTION	POST. REF.	DEBIT	CREDIT	
1						1
2						2
3						3
4						4
5						5
6						6
7						7

Exercise 7-8

a. _____

_____

_____

_____

_____

_____

_____

_____

_____

_____

_____

b. _____

_____

_____

_____

_____

_____

_____

_____

_____

Problem 7-1A or 7-1B

Bank Reconciliation

Bank Statement Balance $ _____
Add: _____
     $ _____

Deduct: _____
_____ $ _____
_____
_____
_____

Adjusted Bank Statement Balance $ _____

Ledger Balance of Cash $ _____
Add: _____ $ _____
_____
_____ $ _____

Deduct: _____
Adjusted Ledger Balance of Cash $ _____

GENERAL JOURNAL   PAGE _____

	DATE	DESCRIPTION	POST. REF.	DEBIT	CREDIT	
1						1
2						2
3						3
4						4
5						5
6						6
7						7
8						8
9						9
10						10
11						11
12						12
13						13
14						14
15						15

NAME _____   DATE _____   CLASS _____

Problem 7-2A or 7-2B

GENERAL JOURNAL   PAGE _____ *1*_____

	DATE	DESCRIPTION	POST. REF.	DEBIT	CREDIT	
1						1
2						2
3						3
4						4
5						5
6						6
7						7
8						8
9						9
10						10
11						11
12						12
13						13
14						14
15						15
16						16
17						17
18						18
19						19
20						20
21						21
22						22
23						23
24						24
25						25
26						26
27						27
28						28
29						29
30						30
31						31
32						32
33						33
34						34
35						35
36						36
37						37
38						38

NAME _____   DATE _____   CLASS _____

Problem 7-2A or 7-2B (concluded)

PETTY CASH PAYMENTS RECORD   PAGE _____1_____

	DATE	VOUCHER NO.	EXPLANATION	PAYMENTS	DISTRIBUTION OF PAYMENTS					
					OFFICE SUPPLIES EXPENSE	DELIVERY EXPENSE	MISC. EXPENSE	OTHER ACCOUNTS		
								ACCOUNT	AMOUNT	
1										1
2										2
3										3
4										4
5										5
6										6
7										7
8										8
9										9
10										10
11										11
12										12
13										13
14										14
15										15
16										16
17										17
18										18
19										19
20										20
21										21
22										22
23										23

Problem 7-3A or 7-3B

GENERAL JOURNAL   PAGE _____

	DATE	DESCRIPTION	POST. REF.	DEBIT	CREDIT	
1						1
2						2
3						3
4						4
5						5
6						6
7						7
8						8
9						9
10						10
11						11
12						12
13						13
14						14
15						15
16						16
17						17
18						18
19						19
20						20
21						21
22						22
23						23
24						24
25						25
26						26
27						27
28						28
29						29
30						30
31						31
32						32
33						33
34						34
35						35
36						36
37						37

Problem 7-4A or 7-4B

Bank Reconciliation

Bank Statement Balance		$
Add: _____		
		$ _____
Deduct: _____		
_____	$	
_____		
_____		
Adjusted Bank Statement Balance	_____	$ _____
Ledger Balance of Cash		$
Add: _____		
_____		
		$ _____
Deduct: _____	$	
_____		
_____		
_____	_____	
Adjusted Ledger Balance of Cash		$ _____

GENERAL JOURNAL   PAGE _____

	DATE	DESCRIPTION	POST. REF.	DEBIT	CREDIT	
1						1
2						2
3						3
4						4
5						5
6						6
7						7
8						8
9						9
10						10
11						11
12						12
13						13
14						14
15						15

Problem 7-4A or 7-4B (concluded)

THIS FORM IS PROVIDED TO HELP YOU BALANCE
YOUR BANK STATEMENT

CHECKS OUTSTANDING NOT CHARGED TO ACCOUNT

No.	$
TOTAL	$

BEFORE YOU START

PLEASE BE SURE YOU HAVE ENTERED IN YOUR CHECK-
BOOK ALL AUTOMATIC TRANSACTIONS SHOWN ON
THE FRONT OF YOUR STATEMENT.

YOU SHOULD HAVE ADDED IF ANY OCCURRED:	YOU SHOULD HAVE SUB-TRACTED IF ANY OCCURRED:
1. Loan advances.	1. Automatic loan payments.
2. Credit memos.	2. Automatic savings transfers.
3. Other automatic deposits.	3. Service charges.
	4. Debit memos.
	5. Other automatic deductions and payments.

BANK BALANCE SHOWN
ON THIS STATEMENT $ _____

ADD

DEPOSITS NOT SHOWN
ON THIS STATEMENT
(IF ANY) $ _____

$ _____

TOTAL $ _____

SUBTRACT

CHECKS OUTSTANDING $ _____

BALANCE $ _____

SHOULD AGREE WITH YOUR CHECKBOOK BALANCE
AFTER DEDUCTING SERVICE CHARGES (IF ANY)
SHOWN ON THIS STATEMENT.

Please examine immediately and report if incorrect. If no reply is received within 10 days, the account will be considered correct.

IN CASE OF ERRORS OR INQUIRIES ABOUT YOUR BILL

Send your inquiry in writing on a separate sheet so that the creditor receives it within 60 days after the bill was mailed to you. Your written inquiry must include:

1. Your name and account number;
2. A description of the error and why (to the extent you can explain) you believe it is an error; and
3. The dollar amount of the suspected error.

If you have authorized your creditor to automatically pay your bill from your checking or savings account, you can stop or re-verse payment on any amount you think is wrong by mailing your notice so that the creditor receives it within 11 days after the bill was sent to you.

You remain obligated to pay the parts of your bill not in dispute, but you do not have to pay any amount in dispute during the time the creditor is resolving the dispute. During that same time, the creditor may not take any action to collect disputed amounts or report disputed amounts as delinquent.

This is a summary of your rights; a full statement of your rights and the creditor's responsibilities under the Federal Fair Credit Billing Act will be sent to you both upon request and in response to a billing error notice.

NAME _____ DATE _____ CLASS _____

Problem B-1

GENERAL JOURNAL

PAGE _____

	DATE	DESCRIPTION	POST. REF.	DEBIT	CREDIT	
1						1
2						2
3						3
4						4
5						5
6						6
7						7
8						8
9						9
10						10
11						11
12						12
13						13
14						14
15						15
16						16
17						17

Problem B-2

GENERAL JOURNAL

PAGE _____

	DATE	DESCRIPTION	POST. REF.	DEBIT	CREDIT	
1						1
2						2
3						3
4						4
5						5
6						6
7						7
8						8
9						9
10						10
11						11
12						12
13						13
14						14
15						15
16						16
17						17
18						18
19						19
20						20
21						21

224

Problem B-3

GENERAL JOURNAL   PAGE _____

	DATE		DESCRIPTION	POST. REF.	DEBIT	CREDIT	
1							1
2							2
3							3
4							4
5							5
6							6
7							7
8							8
9							9
10							10
11							11
12							12
13							13
14							14
15							15
16							16
17							17
18							18
19							19
20							20
21							21
22							22
23							23
24							24
25							25
26							26
27							27
28							28
29							29
30							30
31							31
32							32
33							33
34							34
35							35
36							36
37							37

8 Employee Earnings and Deductions

PERFORMANCE OBJECTIVES

1. Understand the role of laws that affect payroll deductions and contributions.
2. Calculate total earnings based on an hourly, piece-rate, or commission basis.
3. Determine deductions using tables of employees' income tax withholding.
4. Complete a payroll register.
5. Journalize the payroll entry from a payroll register.
6. Maintain employees' individual earnings records.

KEY TERMS

Calendar year	Medicare taxes
Current Tax Payment Act	Net pay
Employee	Payroll bank account
Employee's individual earnings record	Payroll register
Employee's Withholding Allowance Certificate (Form W-4)	Social Security Act of 1935
	Social Security taxes
Exemption	Taxable earnings
Fair Labor Standards Act (FLSA)	Wage-bracket tax tables
FICA taxes	Withholding allowance
Gross pay	Workers' compensation laws
Independent contractor	

STUDY GUIDE QUESTIONS

PART 1   True/False

For each of the following statements, indicate T if the statement is true and F if the statement is false.

T F 1. Social Security and Medicare taxes are paid by both the employer and the employee.

T F 2. The difference between an employee's net pay and take-home pay is the amount of personal deductions.

T F 3. Information for an employee's individual earnings record is taken directly from the general journal.

T F 4. The payroll register is considered to be a book of original entry.

T F 5. On a payroll register, an employee's net amount paid equals total earnings minus total individual deductions.

T F 6. Some businesses use a special payroll bank account.

T F 7. Individual earnings records need not be kept for salaried employees.

T F 8. The basis for the payroll register is the payroll journal entry.

T F 9. Employees (with a few exceptions) are required by law to participate in the Social Security program provided by the Federal Insurance Contributions Act.

T F 10. There is a tax ceiling or limit to the amount of earnings taxable under both Social Security and Medicare.

PART 2   Completion—Language of Business

Complete each of the following statements by writing the appropriate word(s) in the spaces provided.

1. Total earnings for an employee are called the employee's _____ .

2. A(n) _____ is one who works for compensation under the direction or control of an employer.

3. Another term having the same meaning as withholding allowance is _____ _____ .

4. Another term having the same meaning as take-home pay is _____ _____ .

5. Someone who is engaged for a definite job and who chooses his or her own means of doing the work is a(n) _____ .

6. Each employee's personal payroll information for the year is listed in the employee's

    _____ .

PART 3   Calculation of Earnings

Herschel Company pays its employees time-and-a-half for all hours worked in excess of forty per week. For the first week of October, determine the total earnings for each of the following employees.

Employee's Name	Hours Worked	Regular Hourly Rate	Total Earnings
A.L. Gordon	43	$ 7.60	_____
L.A. Larson	47	9.40	_____
C.W. Neilson	49	11.20	_____

PART 4   Payroll Entry

Using the column totals for the week ended March 14 as listed in the payroll register, give the entry in general journal form to record the payroll. Number the page 79.

Total Earnings	$93,640.00
Federal Income Tax Deduction	9,300.00
Social Security Tax Deduction	5,805.68 359.95
Medicare Tax Deduction	1,357.78
U.S. Savings Bonds Deduction	900.00
Union Dues Deduction	1,200.00
Medical Insurance Deduction	2,000.00
Net Amount	73,076.54
Sales Salary Expense	72,000.00
Office Salary Expense	21,640.00

DEMONSTRATION PROBLEM

Kelsey Company's payroll register reveals the following information concerning its two employees for the month ended July 31 of this year:

D. C. Garcia		T. C. Bennett	
Total earnings	$2,000.00	Total earnings	$1,800.00
Federal income tax withheld	400.00	Federal income tax withheld	360.00
Social Security tax withheld	124.00	Social Security tax withheld	111.60
Medicare tax withheld	29.00	Medicare tax withheld	26.10
Medical insurance withheld	129.00	Medical insurance withheld	125.00
Net amount (Ck. No. 6701)	1,318.00	Net amount (Ck. No. 6702)	1,177.30

The employees are paid by checks issued on the firm's regular bank account.

Instructions

Prepare the entry to record and pay the payroll in a general journal.

SOLUTION

GENERAL JOURNAL   PAGE _____

	DATE		DESCRIPTION	POST. REF.	DEBIT	CREDIT	
1	20—						1
2	July	31	Salary Expens		3,800.00		2
3			Employees' Federal Income Tax Payable			760.00	3
4			FICA Tax Payable			290.70	4
5			Employees' Medical Insurance Payable			254.00	5
6			Cash			2,495.30	6
7			Paid salaries for the month				7
8			(D. C. Garcia, $1,318, Ck. No.				8
9			6701; T. C. Bennett, $1,177.30,				9
10			Ck. No. 6702).				10
11							11

EXERCISES

Exercise 8-1

a.   Forty hours at straight time × $10.80 per hour $ _____
      Four hours overtime × $16.20 per hour
      Total gross pay $ _____

b.   Forty hours at straight time × $12.50 per hour $ _____
      Ten hours overtime × $18.75 per hour
      Total gross pay $ _____

c. $10,885 × 0.08 $ _____

d. $40,800 ÷ 52 weeks = $784.62 per week $ _____
      $784.62 per week ÷ 40 hours = $19.62 per regular hour
      Forty hours at straight time × $19.62 per hour
      Three hours overtime × $29.43 per hour

                                                         $ _____

Exercise 8-2

a.   _____ hours at straight time   × _____ per hour $ _____
b.   _____ hours overtime   × _____ per hour
c.   Total gross pay $ _____
d.   Federal income tax withholding $ _____
e.   Social Security tax withholding at 6.2 percent
f.   Medicare tax withholding at 1.45 percent   _____
g.   Total withholding
h.   Net pay $ _____

Exercise 8-3

	EMPLOYEE	ALLOW-ANCES	TOTAL EARNINGS	SOCIAL SECURITY TAX WITHHELD	MEDICARE TAX WITHHELD	FEDERAL INCOME TAX WITHHELD	UNION DUES WITHHELD	MEDICAL INSURANCE WITHHELD	NET PAY
a.	Aston, F. B.	1	$ 900.00				$ 25.00	$ 35.00	
b.	Dwyer, S. J.	2	920.00				25.00	35.00	
c.	Flynn, K. A.	3	1,110.00				25.00	40.00	
d.	Harden, J. L.	0	1,025.00				25.00	40.00	
e.	Nguyen, H.	2	925.00				25.00	35.00	
	Totals		$4,880.00				$125.00	$185.00	

Exercise 8-4

1. **_____**

2. **_____**

3. **_____**

4. **_____**

5. **_____**

6. **_____**

Exercise 8-5

EMPLOYEE	BEGINNING CUMULATIVE EARNINGS	TOTAL EARNINGS	ENDING CUMULATIVE EARNINGS	TAXABLE EARNINGS		
				UNEMPLOY-MENT	SOCIAL SECURITY	MEDICARE
Axton, C.	94,000.00	7,691.00	101,691.00			
Edgar, E.	45,465.00	3,680.00	49,145.00			
Gorman, L.	36,879.00	3,064.00	39,943.00			
Jolson, R.	24,634.00	2,325.00	26,959.00			
Nixel, P.	6,850.00	2,463.00	9,313.00			

Exercise 8-6

GENERAL JOURNAL   PAGE _____

	DATE		DESCRIPTION	POST. REF.	DEBIT	CREDIT	
1							1
2							2
3							3
4							4
5							5
6							6
7							7
8							8
9							9
10							10
11							11
12							12
13							13

Exercise 8-7

	BARTON	RINGNESS	TOTAL	
Regular earnings	$1,750.00			
Overtime earnings		120.00		
Total earnings	$1,860.00			
Federal income tax withheld	$ 335.00			
State income tax withheld		92.00		
Social Security tax withheld	115.32	111.60		
Medicare tax withheld	26.97	26.10		
Medical insurance withheld	106.00	97.00		
Total deductions	$ 688.88	$ 554.70		
Net pay		$1,245.30		

Exercise 8-8

GENERAL JOURNAL   PAGE _____

	DATE	DESCRIPTION	POST. REF.	DEBIT	CREDIT	
1						1
2						2
3						3
4						4
5						5
6						6
7						7
8						8
9						9
10						10
11						11
12						12
13						13
14						14

Problem 8-1A or 8-1B

REGULAR PAY	OVERTIME PAY	GROSS PAY	NET PAY
hours x ___ ___ per hour = _____	hours x ___ ___ per hour = _____	Regular pay Overtime pay _____ Gross pay _____	Gross pay Less Federal income tax _____ _____ _____ _____ _____ Total deductions Net Pay _____

Problem 8-2A or 8-2B

PAYROLL REGISTER FOR WEEK ENDED _____

	NAME	TOTAL HOURS	BEGINNING CUMULATIVE EARNINGS	EARNINGS			ENDING CUMULATIVE EARNINGS
				REGULAR	OVERTIME	TOTAL	
1							
2							
3							
4							
5							
6							
7							
8							

Problem 8-2A or 8-2B (concluded)

(continuation of PAYROLL REGISTER)   PAGE _____

TAXABLE EARNINGS			DEDUCTIONS				PAYMENTS			
UNEMPLOY- MENT	SOCIAL SECURITY	MEDICARE	FEDERAL INCOME TAX	SOCIAL SECURITY TAX	MEDI- CARE TAX	TOTAL	NET AMOUNT	CK. NO.	WAGES EXPENSE DEBIT	
										1
										2
										3
										4
										5
										6
										7
										8

GENERAL JOURNAL   PAGE _____

	DATE	DESCRIPTION	POST. REF.	DEBIT	CREDIT	
1						1
2						2
3						3
4						4
5						5
6						6
7						7
8						8
9						9
10						10
11						11
12						12
13						13
14						14
15						15
16						16
17						17
18						18
19						19
20						20
21						21
22						22
23						23

Problem 8-3A or 8-3B

PAYROLL REGISTER FOR WEEK ENDED _____

	NAME	TOTAL HOURS	BEGINNING CUMULATIVE EARNINGS	EARNINGS			ENDING CUMULATIVE EARNINGS
				REGULAR	OVERTIME	TOTAL	
1							
2							
3							
4							
5							
6							
7							
8							
9							
10							

Problem 8-3A or 8-3B (concluded)

(continuation of PAYROLL REGISTER)   PAGE _____

TAXABLE EARNINGS			DEDUCTIONS				PAYMENTS		WAGES EXPENSE DEBIT	
UNEMPLOY-MENT	SOCIAL SECURITY	MEDICARE	FEDERAL INCOME TAX	SOCIAL SECURITY TAX	MEDI-CARE TAX	TOTAL	NET AMOUNT	CK. NO.		
										1
										2
										3
										4
										5
										6
										7
										8
										9
										10

GENERAL JOURNAL   PAGE _____

	DATE	DESCRIPTION	POST. REF.	DEBIT	CREDIT	
1						1
2						2
3						3
4						4
5						5
6						6
7						7
8						8
9						9
10						10
11						11
12						12
13						13
14						14
15						15
16						16
17						17
18						18
19						19
20						20

Problem 8-4A or 8-4B

PAYROLL REGISTER FOR WEEK ENDED _____

	NAME	TOTAL HOURS	BEGINNING CUMULATIVE EARNINGS	TOTAL EARNINGS	ENDING CUMULATIVE EARNINGS	TAXABLE EARNINGS		
						UNEMPLOY-MENT	SOCIAL SECURITY	MEDICARE
1								
2								
3								
4								
5								
6								
7								
8								
9								
10								
11								
12								

Problem 8-4A or 8-4B (concluded)

(continuation of PAYROLL REGISTER)   PAGE _____

	DEDUCTIONS						PAYMENTS		EXPENSE ACCOUNT DEBITED		
FEDERAL INCOME TAX	SOCIAL SECURITY TAX	MEDI-CARE TAX	OTHER		TOTAL	NET AMOUNT	CK. NO.	SALES SALARY EXPENSE	OFFICE SALARY EXPENSE		
			CODE	AMOUNT							
											1
											2
											3
											4
											5
											6
											7
											8
											9
											10
											11
											12

GENERAL JOURNAL   PAGE _____

	DATE		DESCRIPTION	POST. REF.	DEBIT	CREDIT	
1							1
2							2
3							3
4							4
5							5
6							6
7							7
8							8
9							9
10							10
11							11
12							12
13							13
14							14
15							15
16							16
17							17
18							18
19							19
20							20
21							21

9

Employer Taxes, Payments, and Reports

PERFORMANCE OBJECTIVES

1. Calculate the amount of payroll tax expense and journalize the entry.
2. Journalize the entry for the deposit of employees' federal income taxes withheld and FICA taxes (both employees' withheld and employer's matching share) and prepare the deposit coupon.
3. Journalize the entries for the payment of employer's state and federal unemployment taxes.
4. Journalize the entry for the deposit of employees' state income taxes withheld.
5. Complete Employer's Quarterly Federal Tax Return, Form 941.
6. Prepare W-2 and W-3 forms and Form 940.
7. Calculate the premium for workers' compensation insurance, and prepare the entry for payment in advance.
8. Determine the amount of the end-of-the-year adjustments for (a) workers' compensation insurance and (b) accrued salaries and wages, and record the adjustments.

KEY TERMS

Employer identification number
Federal unemployment tax (FUTA)
Form 940
Form 941
Form W-2

Form W-3
Payroll Tax Expense
Quarters
State unemployment tax (SUTA)
Workers' compensation insurance

STUDY GUIDE QUESTIONS

PART 1   True/False

For each of the following statements, indicate T if the statement is true and F if the statement is false.

T   F   1. Companies must furnish their employees with W-2 forms by April 15.
T   F   2. The Payroll Tax Expense account handles the unemployment taxes as well as the employer's and employee's FICA taxes and employee income taxes.
T   F   3. The purpose of Form 941 is to report employee income taxes and employer and employee Social Security and Medicare taxes.
T   F   4. The times for making deposits of FICA taxes and employees' income taxes withheld depend strictly on the number of employees involved.
T   F   5. Form 940 is an annual tax return that relates to federal unemployment tax.
T   F   6. A premium for workers' compensation insurance is paid at the beginning of the year.

T   F   7.   The state unemployment tax is determined by multiplying the net amount as shown in the payroll register by the state unemployment tax rate.

T   F   8.   The federal unemployment tax is usually paid by the employer only.

T   F   9.   If the Unemployment Taxable Earnings column of the payroll register is blank, this indicates that the employee has cumulative earnings for the calendar year of more than the maximum unemployment taxable income.

T   F   10.   Form W-4 is submitted to the Internal Revenue Service along with copies of the employees' W-2 forms.

PART 2   Completion—Language of Business

Complete each of the following statements by writing the appropriate word(s) in the spaces provided.

1.   The second _____ of the year consists of the months of April, May, and June.

2.   _____ provides an employee with his or her total earnings and tax deductions for the year.

3.   Employers' reports submitted to the Internal Revenue Service all must contain the _____.

4.   The _____ account is used to record the employees' and employer's matching portion of the FICA tax, the federal unemployment tax, and the state unemployment tax.

5.   _____ is used to provide benefits for employees injured on the job.

6.   Form _____ is submitted to the Social Security Administration accompanied by copies of W-2 forms.

7.   _____ is the Employer's Quarterly Federal Tax Return.

PART 3   Completing Form W-2

Complete the facsimile Form W-2 provided for Jane C. Parker. Parker is employed by Benson Company, 1620 Hampton Place, Boston, Massachusetts 02116. Benson Company's federal employer identification number is 72-1162127, and its state identification number is 42-6916. The following information is taken from Parker's Individual Earnings Record. Her address is 2219 Henderson Street, Boston, Massachusetts 02121. Her Social Security number is 562-25-6329. During the year, Parker earned $34,218.42. Her withholdings were as follows: federal income tax, $3,716.22; state income tax, $1,780.04; Social Security tax withheld, $2,121.54; Medicare tax withheld, $496.17.

a Control number	**22222**	OMB No. 1545-0008		
b Employer identification number (EIN)			**1** Wages, tips, other compensation	**2** Federal income tax withheld
c Employer's name, address, and ZIP code			**3** Social security wages	**4** Social security tax withheld
			5 Medicare wages and tips	**6** Medicare tax withheld
			7 Social security tips	**8** Allocated tips
d Employee's social security number			**9** Advance EIC payment	**10** Dependent care benefits
e Employee's first name and initial / Last name / Suff.			**11** Nonqualified plans	**12a**
			13 Statutory employee / Retirement plan / Third-party sick pay	**12b**
			14 Other	**12c**
				12d
f Employee's address and ZIP code				

15 State Employer's state ID number	16 State wages, tips, etc.	17 State income tax	18 Local wages, tips, etc.	19 Local income tax	20 Locality name

Form **W-2** Wage and Tax Statement   **20___**   Department of the Treasury—Internal Revenue Service

Copy 1—For State, City, or Local Tax Department

DEMONSTRATION PROBLEM

The totals of the payroll register for all employees of Point-to-Point Moving are given below. Assume the employment taxes are as follows:

State Unemployment, 5.4 percent	Social Security, 6.2 percent
Federal Unemployment, 0.8 percent	Medicare, 1.45 percent
Total Earnings	$96,345
State Unemployment Taxable Earnings	21,200
Federal Unemployment Taxable Earnings	21,200
Social Security Taxable Earnings	84,500
Medicare Taxable Earnings	96,345
Federal Income Tax Deduction	26,964
Social Security Tax Deduction	5,239
Medicare Tax Deduction	1,397
Union Dues Deduction	1,560
Medical Insurance Deduction	4,250

Instructions

Journalize the following entries:

a. To record the payroll, assuming the use of a payroll bank account.
b. To record the payroll tax expense.
c. To pay the payroll.
d. To record the deposit of federal taxes that will be reported on the Employer's Quarterly Federal Tax Return (Form 941): employees' income taxes withheld, employees' FICA taxes withheld, and employer's share of FICA tax.
e. To record payment of state unemployment insurance that will be reported on the state unemployment insurance tax form.
f. To record the deposit of federal unemployment insurance that will be reported on the Employer's Annual Federal Unemployment Tax Return (Form 940).
g. To record payment of employees' union dues withheld.
h. To record payment of employees' medical insurance withheld.

SOLUTION

GENERAL JOURNAL   PAGE _____

	DATE		DESCRIPTION	POST. REF.	DEBIT	CREDIT	
1		a.	*Wages Expense*		96,345.00		1
2			*Employees' Federal Income Tax Payable*			26,964.00	2
3			*FICA Tax Payable*			6,636.00	3
4			*Employees' Union Dues Payable*			1,560.00	4
5			*Employees' Medical Insurance Payable*			4,250.00	5
6			*Wages Payable*			56,935.00	6
7			*To record wages as listed in the payroll*				7
8			*register.*				8
9							9

SOLUTION *(concluded)*

GENERAL JOURNAL   PAGE _____

	DATE	DESCRIPTION	POST. REF.	DEBIT	CREDIT	
1	b.	Payroll Tax Expense		7,950.40		1
2		FICA Tax Payable			6,636.00	2
3		State Unemployment Tax Payable			1,144.80	3
4		Federal Unemployment Tax Payable			169.60	4
5		To record employer's share of FICA tax				5
6		and federal and state unemployment taxes.				6
7		(FICA tax = Social Security tax +				7
8		Medicare tax; Social Security tax =				8
9		$84,500 X 0.062 = $5,239				9
10		Medicare tax = $96,345 X 0.0145				10
11		= $1,397				11
12		FICA tax = $5,239 + $1,397				12
13		= $6,636)				13
14		SUTA tax = $21,200 X 0.054				14
15		= $1,144.80				15
16		FUTA tax = $21,200 X 0.008				16
17		= $169.60				17
18						18
19	c.	Wages Payable		56,935.00		19
20		Cash--Payroll Bank Account			56,935.00	20
21		Paid wages.				21
22						22
23	d.	Employees' Federal Income Tax Payable		26,964.00		23
24		FICA Tax Payable		13,272.00		24
25		Cash			40,236.00	25
26		Issued check to record deposit of federal				26
27		taxes.				27
28						28
29	e.	State Unemployment Tax Payable		1,144.80		29
30		Cash			1,144.80	30
31		To record payment of state unemployment				31
32		tax.				32
33						33
34	f.	Federal Unemployment Tax Payable		169.60		34
35		Cash			169.60	35
36		To record deposit of federal				36
37		unemployment tax.				37
38						38
39	g.	Employees' Union Dues Payable		1,560.00		39
40		Cash			1,560.00	40
41		To record payment of employees' union				41
42		dues withheld.				42
43						43
44	h.	Employees' Medical Insurance Payable		4,250.00		44
45		Cash			4,250.00	45
46		To record payment of employees'				46
47		medical insurance premiums withheld.				47
48						48

EXERCISES

Exercise 9-1

GENERAL JOURNAL   PAGE _____

	DATE		DESCRIPTION	POST. REF.	DEBIT	CREDIT	
1							1
2							2
3							3
4							4
5							5
6							6
7							7
8							8
9							9
10							10

Exercise 9-2

a. _____

_____

b. _____

_____

GENERAL JOURNAL   PAGE _____

	DATE		DESCRIPTION	POST. REF.	DEBIT	CREDIT	
1							1
2							2
3							3
4							4
5							5
6							6
7							7
8							8
9							9
10							10
11							11
12							12
13							13
14							14
15							15
16							16
17							17
18							18
19							19
20							20

Exercise 9-3

GENERAL JOURNAL   PAGE _____

a.

	DATE		DESCRIPTION	POST. REF.	DEBIT	CREDIT	
1							1
2							2
3							3
4							4
5							5
6							6
7							7
8							8
9							9
10							10

GENERAL JOURNAL   PAGE _____

b.

	DATE		DESCRIPTION	POST. REF.	DEBIT	CREDIT	
1							1
2							2
3							3
4							4
5							5
6							6
7							7
8							8
9							9
10							10
11							11
12							12
13							13

Exercise 9-4

	NAME	BEGINNING CUMULATIVE EARNINGS	TOTAL EARNINGS	ENDING CUMULATIVE EARNINGS	TAXABLE EARNINGS			
					UNEMPLOY-MENT	SOCIAL SECURITY	MEDICARE	
1								1
2								2
3								3
4								4
5								5
6								6
7								7
8								8

GENERAL JOURNAL   PAGE _____

	DATE	DESCRIPTION	POST. REF.	DEBIT	CREDIT	
1						1
2						2
3						3
4						4
5						5
6						6
7						7
8						8
9						9
10						10
11						11
12						12
13						13
14						14
15						15
16						16
17						17

Exercise 9-5

GENERAL JOURNAL   PAGE _____

	DATE	DESCRIPTION	POST. REF.	DEBIT	CREDIT	
1						1
2						2
3						3
4						4
5						5
6						6
7						7

Exercise 9-6

GENERAL JOURNAL   PAGE _____

	DATE	DESCRIPTION	POST. REF.	DEBIT	CREDIT	
1						1
2						2
3						3
4						4
5						5
6						6
7						7
8						8
9						9
10						10
11						11
12						12
13						13
14						14
15						15
16						16
17						17

Exercise 9-7

GENERAL JOURNAL PAGE _____

	DATE		DESCRIPTION	POST. REF.	DEBIT	CREDIT	
1							1
2							2
3							3
4							4
5							5
6							6
7							7
8							8
9							9
10							10
11							11
12							12
13							13
14							14
15							15
16							16
17							17

Exercise 9-8

GENERAL JOURNAL   PAGE _____

a.

	DATE		DESCRIPTION	POST. REF.	DEBIT	CREDIT	
1							1
2							2
3							3
4							4
5							5
6							6
7							7
8							8

GENERAL JOURNAL   PAGE _____

b.

	DATE		DESCRIPTION	POST. REF.	DEBIT	CREDIT	
1							1
2							2
3							3
4							4
5							5
6							6
7							7
8							8

Problem 9-1A or 9-1B

GENERAL JOURNAL   PAGE _____

	DATE	DESCRIPTION	POST. REF.	DEBIT	CREDIT	
1						1
2						2
3						3
4						4
5						5
6						6
7						7
8						8
9						9
10						10
11						11
12						12
13						13
14						14
15						15
16						16
17						17
18						18
19						19
20						20
21						21
22						22
23						23
24						24
25						25
26						26
27						27
28						28
29						29
30						30
31						31
32						32
33						33
34						34
35						35
36						36
37						37
38						38

Problem 9-2A or 9-2B

PAYROLL REGISTER FOR WEEK ENDED _____

	NAME	BEGINNING CUMULATIVE EARNINGS	TOTAL EARNINGS	ENDING CUMULATIVE EARNINGS	TAXABLE EARNINGS		
					UNEMPLOY-MENT	SOCIAL SECURITY	MEDICARE
1							
2							
3							
4							
5							
6							
7							
8							
9							
10							
11							
12							
13							
14							
15							
16							
17							
18							
19							
20							
21							
22							
23							
24							
25							
26							
27							
28							
29							
30							
31							
32							
33							

Problem 9-2A or 9-2B (continued)

(continuation of PAYROLL REGISTER)   PAGE ___72___

| DEDUCTIONS | | | | | PAYMENTS | | | |
FEDERAL INCOME TAX	STATE INCOME TAX	SOCIAL SECURITY TAX	MEDICARE TAX	TOTAL	NET AMOUNT	CK. NO.	SALARY EXPENSE DEBIT	
								1
								2
								3
								4
								5
								6
								7
								8
								9
								10
								11
								12
								13
								14
								15
								16
								17
								18
								19
								20
								21
								22
								23
								24
								25
								26
								27
								28
								29
								30
								31
								32
								33

Problem 9-2A or 9-2B (concluded)

GENERAL JOURNAL   PAGE _____

	DATE		DESCRIPTION	POST. REF.	DEBIT	CREDIT	
1							1
2							2
3							3
4							4
5							5
6							6
7							7
8							8
9							9
10							10
11							11
12							12
13							13
14							14
15							15
16							16
17							17
18							18
19							19
20							20
21							21
22							22
23							23
24							24
25							25
26							26
27							27
28							28
29							29
30							30
31							31
32							32
33							33
34							34

254

Problem 9-3A or 9-3B

Form **941 for 2006:** **Employer's QUARTERLY Federal Tax Return**
(Rev. January 2006)

Department of the Treasury — Internal Revenue Service

990106

OMB No. 1545-0029

(EIN)
Employer identification number ☐☐ – ☐☐☐☐☐☐☐

Name *(not your trade name)*

Trade name *(if any)*

Address
Number   Street   Suite or room number
City   State   ZIP code

Report for this Quarter ...
(Check one.)

☐ 1: January, February, March

☐ 2: April, May, June

☐ 3: July, August, September

☐ 4: October, November, December

Read the separate instructions before you fill out this form. Please type or print within the boxes.

Part 1: Answer these questions for this quarter.

1 Number of employees who received wages, tips, or other compensation for the pay period including: *Mar. 12 (Quarter 1), June 12 (Quarter 2), Sept. 12 (Quarter 3), Dec. 12 (Quarter 4)*   **1** ☐

2 Wages, tips, and other compensation . . . .   **2** ☐

3 Total income tax withheld from wages, tips, and other compensation . . . .   **3** ☐

4 If no wages, tips, and other compensation are subject to social security or Medicare tax .   ☐ Check and go to line 6.

5 Taxable social security and Medicare wages and tips:

	Column 1		Column 2
5a Taxable social security wages	☐	× .124 =	☐
5b Taxable social security tips	☐	× .124 =	☐
5c Taxable Medicare wages & tips	☐	× .029 =	☐

5d Total social security and Medicare taxes (*Column 2*, lines 5a + 5b + 5c = line 5d) .   **5d** ☐

6 Total taxes before adjustments (lines 3 + 5d = line 6) . . . .   **6** ☐

7 TAX ADJUSTMENTS (Read the instructions for line 7 before completing lines 7a through 7h.):

7a Current quarter's fractions of cents . . . .   ☐

7b Current quarter's sick pay . . . .   ☐

7c Current quarter's adjustments for tips and group-term life insurance   ☐

7d Current year's income tax withholding (attach Form 941c) . . .   ☐

7e Prior quarters' social security and Medicare taxes (attach Form 941c)   ☐

7f Special additions to federal income tax (attach Form 941c) . . .   ☐

7g Special additions to social security and Medicare (attach Form 941c)   ☐

7h TOTAL ADJUSTMENTS (Combine all amounts: lines 7a through 7g.) . . . . . .   **7h** ☐

8 Total taxes after adjustments (Combine lines 6 and 7h.) . . . .   **8** ☐

9 Advance earned income credit (EIC) payments made to employees . . . .   **9** ☐

10 Total taxes after adjustment for advance EIC (line 8 – line 9 = line 10) . . . .   **10** ☐

11 Total deposits for this quarter, including overpayment applied from a prior quarter . . . .   **11** ☐

12 Balance due (If line 10 is more than line 11, write the difference here.) . . . .   **12** ☐
Make checks payable to *United States Treasury.*

13 Overpayment (If line 11 is more than line 10, write the difference here.)   ☐   Check one ☐ Apply to next return.
☐ Send a refund.

▶ You **MUST** fill out both pages of this form and **SIGN** it.

Next ➡

For Privacy Act and Paperwork Reduction Act Notice, see the back of the Payment Voucher.   Cat. No. 17001Z   Form **941** (Rev. 1-2006)

Problem 9-4A or 9-4B

GENERAL JOURNAL   PAGE ___77___

	DATE	DESCRIPTION	POST. REF.	DEBIT	CREDIT	
1						1
2						2
3						3
4						4
5						5
6						6
7						7
8						8
9						9
10						10
11						11
12						12
13						13
14						14
15						15
16						16
17						17
18						18
19						19
20						20
21						21
22						22
23						23
24						24
25						25
26						26
27						27
28						28
29						29
30						30
31						31
32						32
33						33
34						34
35						35

NAME _____ DATE _____ CLASS _____

Problem 9-4A or 9-4B (concluded)

GENERAL JOURNAL PAGE ___78___

	DATE		DESCRIPTION	POST. REF.	DEBIT	CREDIT	
1							1
2							2
3							3
4							4
5							5
6							6
7							7
8							8
9							9
10							10
11							11
12							12
13							13
14							14
15							15
16							16
17							17
18							18
19							19
20							20
21							21
22							22
23							23
24							24
25							25
26							26
27							27
28							28
29							29
30							30
31							31
32							32
33							33
34							34
35							35
36							36
37							37
38							38
39							39
40							40

BEFORE A TEST CHECK SOLUTIONS: CHAPTERS 7–9

Part I: 1. _____ 2. _____

3. _____   4. _____ 5. _____

Part II: 1. _____

_____

_____

_____

Earnings for 45 hours:

_____ $ _____

_____ $ _____

2.   GENERAL JOURNAL   PAGE _____

	DATE		DESCRIPTION	POST. REF.	DEBIT	CREDIT	
1							1
2							2
3							3
4							4
5							5
6							6
7							7
8							8
9							9
10							10
11							11

3.   GENERAL JOURNAL   PAGE _____

	DATE		DESCRIPTION	POST. REF.	DEBIT	CREDIT	
1							1
2							2
3							3
4							4
5							5
6							6
7							7
8							8
9							9
10							10
11							11

Part III: 1. ___ 2. ___ 3. ___ 4. ___ 5. ___

10 The Sales Journal and the Purchases Journal

PERFORMANCE OBJECTIVES

1. Describe the specific accounts used by a merchandising firm.
2. Journalize transactions in a sales journal.
3. Post sales journal transactions to an accounts receivable ledger and a general ledger.
4. Prepare a schedule of accounts receivable.
5. Journalize sales returns and allowances, including credit memorandums and returns involving sales tax, in a general journal, and post to the accounts receivable ledger and general ledger.
6. Journalize transactions in a three-column purchases journal.
7. Post purchases journal transactions to an accounts payable ledger and a general ledger.
8. Prepare a schedule of accounts payable.
9. Journalize transactions involving purchases returns and allowance in a general journal, and post to the accounts payable ledger and general ledger.
10. Describe the procedures for handling freight charges on merchandise and other goods.

KEY TERMS

Accounts payable ledger
Accounts receivable ledger
Controlling account
Credit memorandum
FOB destination
FOB shipping point
Freight In account
Invoices
Merchandise inventory
Merchandising business
Purchase order
Purchase requisition
Purchase accounts

Purchases Discounts account
Purchases journal
Purchases Returns and Allowances account
Retail business
Sales account
Sales Discounts account
Sales journal
Sales Returns and Allowances account
Sales Tax Payable account
Special journals
Subsidiary ledger
Summarizing entry
Wholesale business

STUDY GUIDE QUESTIONS—SALES JOURNAL

PART 1   True/False

For each of the following statements, indicate T if the statement is true and F if the statement is false.

T   F   1.   Posting from the sales journal to the accounts receivable ledger accounts should take place after each entry.

T   F   2.   The sales journal is used to record all sales.

T   F   3.   A business can list customer accounts in alphabetical order in its accounts receivable ledger.

T   F   4.   Increases in Sales Returns and Allowances are recorded on the credit side.

T   F   5.   Check marks in the Post. Ref. column of the sales journal indicate that the amounts are not to be posted.

T   F   6.   At the end of the month, after all posting is completed, the total of the schedule of accounts receivable should equal the balance of the Sales account in the general ledger.

(T)   F   7.   The Accounts Receivable account in the general ledger contains a separate account for each customer.

T   F   8.   When using a sales journal, you do not have to post to any accounts in the general ledger.

T   F   9.   The schedule of accounts receivable lists the balances of all the charge customer accounts at the end of the month.

T   F   10. Each sale is supposed to be posted monthly to the individual customer accounts.

PART 2   Completion—Language of Business

Complete each of the following statements by writing the appropriate word(s) in the spaces provided.

1.   The book of original entry used to record sales of merchandise on account is called a(n)

_____ .

2.   A stock of ready-made goods that a company buys and intends to resell at a profit is called

_____ .

3.   Books of original entry used to record specialized types of transactions are referred to as

_____special journal_____ .

4.   The Accounts Receivable account in the general ledger is called a(n)   _controlling acct_ .

5.   The accounts receivable ledger may be called a special ledger or a(n)   _subsidiary acct_

_____ .

6.   A document issued by the seller to a customer allowing a reduction from the price at which the goods were originally sold is called a(n)   _____ .

STUDY GUIDE QUESTIONS—PURCHASES JOURNAL

PART 1   True/False

For each of the following statements, indicate T if the statement is true and F if the statement is false.

(T) F   1.   The purchase requisition is sent to the supplier.

T   F   2.   The Purchases account is used to record the buying of merchandise for resale only.

T   F   3.   Increases in the Purchases Returns and Allowances account are recorded on the debit side.

T   F   4.   If the freight charges are FOB shipping point, the buyer pays the transportation charges.

T   F   5.   Each purchase is posted daily to the Accounts Payable account.

(T) F   6.   The purchases journal is used for the buying of merchandise for cash and on account.

(T) F   7.   At the end of the month, the total of the schedule of accounts payable should equal the balance of the Purchases account.

T   (F)   8.   The purchases journal contains an Accounts Payable Debit column, a Freight In Debit column, and a Purchases Credit column.

(T) F   9.   Check marks in the Post. Ref. column of the purchases journal indicate that the amounts in the Accounts Payable column have been posted to the accounts payable ledger.

T   F   10.   If the transportation terms are FOB destination, the cost of the freight charge is included in the selling price.

PART 2   Completion—Language of Business

Complete each of the following statements by writing the appropriate word(s) in the spaces provided.

1.   The form sent to the supplier of merchandise is called a(n) *purchas requistion* .

2.   When the buyer pays the transportation charges on incoming merchandise, the shipping terms are called FOB .

3.   Plans and procedures built into the accounting system to promote efficiency and prevent fraud and waste are called _____.

4.   From the buyer's viewpoint, the form prepared by the seller listing the items shipped, their costs, and the mode of shipment is called a(n) _____.

5.   A document sent by the seller to the buyer, indicating that the Accounts Receivable account is being reduced on the seller's books, is known as a(n) _____.

6.   A transportation arrangement in which the seller retains title to the goods in transit is called _____.

DEMONSTRATION PROBLEM—SALES JOURNAL

The following selected transactions were competed by Adams Company:

Sept. 16   Sold merchandise on account to Foster Company, sales invoice no. 1032, $3,742.
20   Sold merchandise on account to King Company, sales invoice no. 1033, $8,950.
25   Sold merchandise on account to Zimmer Company, sales invoice no. 1034; $173.
27   King Company returned $982 of merchandise relating to sales invoice no. 1033; Adams Company issued credit memo no. 131.

Instructions

1. Record the transactions in either the sales journal or the general journal, as appropriate.
2. Immediately after recording each transaction, post to the accounts receivable ledger.
3. Post the entries from the general journal and the total of the sales journal to the general ledger.
4. Prepare a schedule of accounts receivable.
5. Compare the total of the schedule of accounts receivable with the September 30 balance of the Accounts Receivable (controlling) account.

SOLUTION

SALES JOURNAL   PAGE ___134___

	DATE	INV. NO.	CUSTOMER'S NAME	POST. REF.	ACCOUNTS RECEIVABLE DR. SALES CREDIT	
1	20--					1
2	Sept. 16	1032	Foster Company	✓	3,742.00	2
3	20	1033	King Company	✓	8,950.00	3
4	25	1034	Zimmer Company	✓	173.00	4
5	30				12,865.00	5
6					(113) (411)	6
7						7

GENERAL JOURNAL   PAGE ___159___

	DATE	DESCRIPTION	POST. REF.	DEBIT	CREDIT	
1	20--					1
2	Sept. 27	Sales Returns and Allowances	412	982.00		2
3		Accounts Receiviable, King Company	113/ ✓		982.00	3
4		Credit memo no. 131 relating to				4
5		invoice no. 1033.				5
6						6

SOLUTION *(continued)*

GENERAL LEDGER

ACCOUNT *Accounts Receivable*   ACCOUNT NO ___113___

DATE		ITEM	POST. REF.	DEBIT	CREDIT	BALANCE DEBIT	BALANCE CREDIT
20--							
Sept.	1	Balance	✓			5,390.00	
	27		J159		982.00	4,408.00	
	30		S134	12,865.00		17,273.00	

ACCOUNT *Sales*   ACCOUNT NO ___411___

DATE		ITEM	POST. REF.	DEBIT	CREDIT	BALANCE DEBIT	BALANCE CREDIT
20--							
Sept.	1	Balance	✓				51,597.00
	30		S134		12,865.00		64,462.00

ACCOUNT *Sales Returns and Allowances*   ACCOUNT NO ___412___

DATE		ITEM	POST. REF.	DEBIT	CREDIT	BALANCE DEBIT	BALANCE CREDIT
20--							
Sept.	1	Balance	✓			2,777.00	
	27		J159	982.00		3,759.00	

SOLUTION *(concluded)*

ACCOUNTS RECEIVABLE LEDGER

NAME   *Foster Company*

ADDRESS   *330 Wexler Road, S.W.*

Atlanta, GA 30305

DATE		ITEM	POST. REF.	DEBIT	CREDIT	BALANCE
20--						
Sept.	1		✓			5,390.00
	16		S134	3,742.00		9,132.00

NAME   *King Company*

ADDRESS   *1450 Myron Avenue, S.W.*

Atlanta, GA 30307

DATE		ITEM	POST. REF.	DEBIT	CREDIT	BALANCE
20--						
Sept.	20		S134	8,950.00		8,950.00
	27		J159		982.00	7,968.00

NAME   *Zimmer Company*

ADDRESS   *1226 Euclid Avenue, S.W.*

Atlanta, GA 30309

DATE		ITEM	POST. REF.	DEBIT	CREDIT	BALANCE
20--						
Sept.	25		S134	173.00		173.00

Adams Company

Schedule of Accounts Receivable

September 30, 20--

Foster Company	$ 9,132.00
King Company	7,968.00
Zimmer Company	173.00
	$17,273.00

DEMONSTRATION PROBLEM—PURCHASES JOURNAL

Brownfield Company, which is located in San Diego, California, completed the following transactions in August:

Aug.   3   Bought merchandise on account from Keller Company, invoice no. 1998, $5,544; terms 2/10, n/30; dated August 1; FOB Los Angeles, freight prepaid and added to the invoice, $554 (total $6,098).

       10   Bought supplies on account from Nichols Company, invoice no. A1120, $572; terms net 30 days; dated August 10; FOB San Diego.

       12   Received credit memo no. 170 from Keller Company, $640, for merchandise returned.

       15   Bought merchandise on account from Lopez Company, invoice no. 3567C, $3,977; terms 1/10, n/30; dated August 12; FOB Reno; freight prepaid and added to the invoice, $380 (total $4,357).

       17   Received credit memo no. 435 from Nichols Company, $52, for allowance on damaged supplies purchased August 10.

Instructions

1. Record the transactions in either the three-column purchases journal or the general journal, as appropriate.
2. Post the entries to the accounts payable ledger daily.
3. Post the entries in the general journal immediately after you make each entry.
4. Post the totals from the three-column purchases journal at the end of the month.
5. Prepare a schedule of accounts payable.
6. Compare the total of the schedule of accounts payable with the balance of the controlling account.

SOLUTION

PURCHASES JOURNAL   PAGE   *81*

	DATE		SUPPLIER'S NAME	INVOICE NUMBER	INVOICE DATE	TERMS	POST. REF.	ACCOUNTS PAYABLE CREDIT	FREIGHT IN DEBIT	PURCHASES DEBIT	
1	20--										1
2	Aug.	3	Keller Company	1998	8/1	2/10, n/30	✓	6,098.00	554.00	5,544.00	2
3		15	Lopez Company	3567C	8/12	1/10, n/30	✓	4,357.00	380.00	3,977.00	3
4		31						10,455.00	934.00	9,521.00	4
5								(212)	(514)	(511)	5
6											6

SOLUTION (continued)

GENERAL JOURNAL   PAGE __105__

	DATE		DESCRIPTION	POST. REF.	DEBIT	CREDIT	
1	20--						1
2	Aug.	10	Supplies Expense	613	572.00		2
3			Accounts Payable, Nichols Company	212/ ✓		572.00	3
4			Bought supplies on account, invoice				4
5			no. A1120, dated August 10, net				5
6			30 days.				6
7							7
8		12	Accounts Payable, Keller Company	212/ ✓	640.00		8
9			Purchases Returns and Allowances	512		640.00	9
10			Credit memo no. 170 for merchandise				10
11			returned.				11
12							12
13		17	Accounts Payable, Nichols Company	212/ ✓	52.00		13
14			Supplies	112		52.00	14
15			Credit memo no. 435 for allowance				15
16			on damaged supplies.				16
17							17

GENERAL LEDGER

ACCOUNT __Accounts Payable__   ACCOUNT NO __212__

DATE		ITEM	POST. REF.	DEBIT	CREDIT	BALANCE	
						DEBIT	CREDIT
20--							
Aug.	1	Balance	✓				3,780.00
	10		J105		572.00		4,352.00
	12		J105	640.00			3,712.00
	17		J105	52.00			3,660.00
	31		P81		10,455.00		14,115.00

ACCOUNT __Purchases__   ACCOUNT NO __511__

DATE		ITEM	POST. REF.	DEBIT	CREDIT	BALANCE	
						DEBIT	CREDIT
20--							
Aug.	1	Balance	✓			73,185.00	
	31		P81	9,521.00		82,706.00	

SOLUTION (continued)

ACCOUNT *Purchases Returns and Allowances*   ACCOUNT NO ____512____

DATE		ITEM	POST. REF.	DEBIT	CREDIT	BALANCE	
						DEBIT	CREDIT
20--							
Aug.	1	Balance	✓				2,035.00
	12		J105		640.00		2,675.00

ACCOUNT *Freight In*   ACCOUNT NO ____514____

DATE		ITEM	POST. REF.	DEBIT	CREDIT	BALANCE	
						DEBIT	CREDIT
20--							
Aug.	1	Balance	✓			7,459.00	
	31		P81	934.00		8,393.00	

ACCOUNT *Supplies Expense*   ACCOUNT NO ____613____

DATE		ITEM	POST. REF.	DEBIT	CREDIT	BALANCE	
						DEBIT	CREDIT
20--							
Aug.	1	Balance	✓			5,790.00	
	10		J105	572.00		6,362.00	
	17		J105		52.00	6,310.00	

SOLUTION *(concluded)*

ACCOUNTS PAYABLE LEDGER

NAME *Keller Company*
ADDRESS *679 Gurnard Ave.*
Des Moines, IA 50371

DATE		ITEM	POST. REF.	DEBIT	CREDIT	BALANCE
20--						
Aug.	1	Balance	✓			1,970.00
	3		P81		6,098.00	8,068.00
	12		J105	640.00		7,428.00

NAME *Lopez Company*
ADDRESS *482 Jeffries Way*
Des Moines, IA 50372

DATE		ITEM	POST. REF.	DEBIT	CREDIT	BALANCE
20--						
Aug.	1	Balance	✓			1,810.00
	15		P81		4,357.00	6,167.00

NAME *Nichols Company*
ADDRESS *3864 Silva Ave.*
Des Moines, IA 50372

DATE		ITEM	POST. REF.	DEBIT	CREDIT	BALANCE
20--						
Aug.	10		J105		572.00	572.00
	17		J105	52.00		520.00

Brownfield Company
Schedule of Accounts Payable
August 31, 20--

Keller Company	$ 7,428.00
Lopez Company	6,167.00
Nichols Company	520.00
Total Accounts Payable	$14,115.00

NAME _____ DATE _____ CLASS _____

EXERCISES

Exercise 10-1

SALES JOURNAL   PAGE ___18___

	DATE		INV. NO.	CUSTOMER'S NAME	POST. REF.	ACCOUNTS RECEIVABLE DR. SALES CREDIT	
1	20--						1
2	Oct.	3	414	Anderson Company		443.24	2
3		4	415	R. T. Holcomb		1,426.90	3
4		7	416	Gray and Malo		1,647.00	4
5		11	417	Mercer Mobil		3,112.16	5
6		16	418	J. L. Anthony		2,130.00	6
7		22	419	C. A. Goldschmidt		1,944.05	7
8		31	420	F. A. Baumann		2,791.00	8
9		31					9
10						( ) ( )	10
11							11

PURCHASES JOURNAL   PAGE ___10___

	DATE		SUPPLIER'S NAME	INVOICE NUMBER	INVOICE DATE	TERMS	POST. REF.	ACCOUNTS PAYABLE CREDIT	FREIGHT IN DEBIT	PURCHASES DEBIT	
1	20--										1
2	Oct.	2	Colter, Inc.	2706	7/31	2/10, n/30		759.00	49.00	710.00	2
3		3	Thomas and Son	982	8/2	n/30		829.00	57.00	772.00	3
4		5	Archer Mfg. Co.	10611	8/3	2/10, n/30		564.00		564.00	4
5		9	Spence Products Co.	B643	8/6	1/10, n/30		165.00	10.00	155.00	5
6		18	L. C. Walter	46812	8/17	n/60		228.00		228.00	6
7		25	Delaney and Cox	1024	8/23	2/10, n/30		376.00	14.00	362.00	7
8		26	Colter, Inc.	2801	8/25	2/10, n/30		406.00	22.00	384.00	8
9		31									9
10								( )	( )	( )	10
11											11

Exercise 10-1 (continued)

ACCOUNTS RECEIVABLE LEDGER

Anderson Company		J. L. Anthony		F. A. Baumann	
+	−	+	−	+	−

C. A. Goldschmidt		Gray and Malo		R. T. Holcomb		Mercer Mobil	
+	−	+	−	+	−	+	−

GENERAL LEDGER

Accounts Receivable 113		Accounts Payable 212		Sales 411	
+	−	−	+	−	+

Purchases 511		Freight In 514	
+	−	+	−

ACCOUNTS PAYABLE LEDGER

Archer Mfg. Co.		Colter, Inc.		Delaney and Cox	
−	+	−	+	−	+

Spence Products Co.		Thomas and Son		L. C. Walter	
−	+	−	+	−	+

Exercise 10-1 (concluded)

Exercise 10-2

a. _____

b. _____

c. _____

NAME _____   DATE _____   CLASS _____

Exercise 10-3

GENERAL JOURNAL   PAGE _____

	DATE	DESCRIPTION	POST. REF.	DEBIT	CREDIT	
1						1
2						2
3						3
4						4
5						5
6						6
7						7
8						8
9						9
10						10
11						11
12						12
13						13
14						14
15						15
16						16
17						17
18						18
19						19
20						20
21						21

272

Exercise 10-4

GENERAL JOURNAL   PAGE ___52___

	DATE		DESCRIPTION	POST. REF.	DEBIT	CREDIT	
1	20--						1
2	June	16	Sales Returns and Allowances		241.27		2
3			Accounts Receiviable, R. D. Moen			241.27	3
4			Issued credit memo no. 131.				4
5							5

GENERAL LEDGER

ACCOUNT   *Accounts Receivable*   ACCOUNT NO. ___113___

DATE		ITEM	POST. REF.	DEBIT	CREDIT	BALANCE DEBIT	BALANCE CREDIT
20--							
June	1	Balance	✓			6,511.19	

ACCOUNT   *Sales Returns and Allowances*   ACCOUNT NO. ___412___

DATE		ITEM	POST. REF.	DEBIT	CREDIT	BALANCE DEBIT	BALANCE CREDIT
20--							
June	1	Balance	✓			314.60	

ACCOUNTS RECEIVABLE LEDGER

NAME   **R. D. Moen**
ADDRESS   *416 Fifth Avenue*
Dallas, Texas 75204

DATE		ITEM	POST. REF.	DEBIT	CREDIT	BALANCE
20--						
May	31		S26	312.60		312.60

Exercise 10-5

COMPANY: _____

GENERAL JOURNAL   PAGE _____

	DATE		DESCRIPTION	POST. REF.	DEBIT	CREDIT	
1	20--						1
2							2
3							3
4							4
5							5
6							6

COMPANY: _____

GENERAL JOURNAL   PAGE _____

	DATE		DESCRIPTION	POST. REF.	DEBIT	CREDIT	
1	20--						1
2							2
3							3
4							4
5							5
6							6
7							7

Exercise 10-6

a. _____

_____

b. _____

_____

c. _____

_____

Exercise 10-7

GENERAL JOURNAL   PAGE _____

	DATE	DESCRIPTION	POST. REF.	DEBIT	CREDIT	
1						1
2						2
3						3
4						4
5						5
6						6
7						7
8						8
9						9
10						10
11						11
12						12
13						13
14						14

Exercise 10-8

GENERAL JOURNAL   PAGE ___92___

	DATE		DESCRIPTION	POST. REF.	DEBIT	CREDIT	
1	20--						1
2	July	14	Accounts Payable, Bullock and				2
3			Hendricks		192.30		3
4			Purchases Returns and Allowances			192.30	4
5			Credit memo no. 942 for return				5
6			of merchandise.				6
7							7

GENERAL LEDGER

ACCOUNT   **Accounts Payable**   ACCOUNT NO. ___212___

DATE		ITEM	POST. REF.	DEBIT	CREDIT	BALANCE DEBIT	BALANCE CREDIT	
20--								
July	1	Balance	✓				2,761.24	

ACCOUNT   **Purchases Returns and Allowances**   ACCOUNT NO. ___512___

DATE		ITEM	POST. REF.	DEBIT	CREDIT	BALANCE DEBIT	BALANCE CREDIT	
20--								
July	1	Balance	✓				230.16	

ACCOUNTS PAYABLE LEDGER

NAME   **Bullock and Hendricks**
ADDRESS   **542 Roselle Blvd.**
Richmond, CA 94879

DATE		ITEM	POST. REF.	DEBIT	CREDIT	BALANCE
20--						
June	13		P73		218.00	218.00

Problem 10-1A or 10-1B

SALES JOURNAL   PAGE _____

	DATE	INV. NO.	CUSTOMER'S NAME	POST. REF.	ACCOUNTS RECEIVABLE DEBIT, SALES CREDIT	
1						1
2						2
3						3
4						4
5						5
6						6
7						7
8						8
9						9
10						10
11						11

GENERAL JOURNAL   PAGE _____

	DATE	DESCRIPTION	POST. REF.	DEBIT	CREDIT	
1						1
2						2
3						3
4						4
5						5
6						6
7						7
8						8
9						9
10						10
11						11
12						12
13						13
14						14
15						15
16						16

Problem 10-1A or 10-1B (continued)

GENERAL LEDGER

ACCOUNT *Accounts Receivable*   ACCOUNT NO. *113*

DATE		ITEM	POST. REF.	DEBIT	CREDIT	BALANCE	
						DEBIT	CREDIT
20--							
Apr.	1	Balance	✓			1,169.42	

ACCOUNT *Sales*   ACCOUNT NO. *411*

DATE		ITEM	POST. REF.	DEBIT	CREDIT	BALANCE	
						DEBIT	CREDIT
20--							
Apr.	1	Balance	✓				11,260.44

ACCOUNT *Sales Returns and Allowances*   ACCOUNT NO. *412*

DATE		ITEM	POST. REF.	DEBIT	CREDIT	BALANCE	
						DEBIT	CREDIT
20--							
Apr.	1	Balance	✓			396.42	

ACCOUNTS RECEIVABLE LEDGER

NAME *Blair and Barnes*

ADDRESS _____

DATE		ITEM	POST. REF.	DEBIT	CREDIT	BALANCE
20--						
Apr.	1	Balance	✓			927.76

Problem 10-1A or 10-1B (continued)

NAME *Danton Hardware*
ADDRESS

DATE		ITEM	POST. REF.	DEBIT	CREDIT	BALANCE

NAME *L. R. Feldman Company*
ADDRESS

DATE		ITEM	POST. REF.	DEBIT	CREDIT	BALANCE

NAME *Meyer Company*
ADDRESS

DATE		ITEM	POST. REF.	DEBIT	CREDIT	BALANCE
20--						
Apr.	1	Balance	✓			241.66

NAME *Oberman Company*
ADDRESS

DATE		ITEM	POST. REF.	DEBIT	CREDIT	BALANCE

Problem 10-1A or 10-1B (concluded)

NAME   *Pope and Rogers* _____

ADDRESS _____

DATE		ITEM	POST. REF.	DEBIT	CREDIT	BALANCE

Problem 10-2A or 10-2B

SALES JOURNAL   PAGE _____

	DATE	INV. NO.	CUSTOMER'S NAME	POST. REF.	ACCOUNTS RECEIVABLE DEBIT	SALES TAX PAYABLE CREDIT	SALES CREDIT	
1								1
2								2
3								3
4								4
5								5
6								6
7								7
8								8
9								9
10								10
11								11

GENERAL JOURNAL   PAGE _____

	DATE	DESCRIPTION	POST. REF.	DEBIT	CREDIT	
1						1
2						2
3						3
4						4
5						5
6						6
7						7
8						8
9						9
10						10
11						11
12						12
13						13
14						14
15						15

Problem 10-2A or 10-2B (continued)

GENERAL LEDGER

ACCOUNT _Accounts Receivable_   ACCOUNT NO. ___113___

DATE		ITEM	POST. REF.	DEBIT	CREDIT	BALANCE	
						DEBIT	CREDIT
20--							
Mar.	1	Balance	✓			111.22	

ACCOUNT _Sales Tax Payable_   ACCOUNT NO. ___214___

DATE		ITEM	POST. REF.	DEBIT	CREDIT	BALANCE	
						DEBIT	CREDIT
20--							
Mar.	1	Balance	✓				72.84

ACCOUNT _Sales_   ACCOUNT NO. ___411___

DATE		ITEM	POST. REF.	DEBIT	CREDIT	BALANCE	
						DEBIT	CREDIT

ACCOUNT _Sales Returns and Allowances_   ACCOUNT NO. ___412___

DATE		ITEM	POST. REF.	DEBIT	CREDIT	BALANCE	
						DEBIT	CREDIT

Problem 10-2A or 10-2B (continued)

ACCOUNTS RECEIVABLE LEDGER

NAME *American Legion*
ADDRESS

DATE		ITEM	POST. REF.	DEBIT	CREDIT	BALANCE
20--						
Mar.	1	Balance	✓			34.22

NAME *B. Carter*
ADDRESS

DATE		ITEM	POST. REF.	DEBIT	CREDIT	BALANCE

NAME *R. Dresher*
ADDRESS

DATE		ITEM	POST. REF.	DEBIT	CREDIT	BALANCE

NAME *C. Marlo*
ADDRESS

DATE		ITEM	POST. REF.	DEBIT	CREDIT	BALANCE
20--						
Mar.	1	Balance	✓			19.50

Problem 10-2A or 10-2B (concluded)

NAME   *Ponderosa Savings and Loan Association* _____
ADDRESS _____

DATE		ITEM	POST. REF.	DEBIT	CREDIT	BALANCE
20--						
Mar.	1	Balance	✓			57.50

NAME   *Turner Funeral Home* _____
ADDRESS _____

DATE		ITEM	POST. REF.	DEBIT	CREDIT	BALANCE

Problem 10-3A or 10-3B

PURCHASES JOURNAL

PAGE _____

	DATE	SUPPLIER'S NAME	INV. NO.	INV. DATE	TERMS	POST. REF.	ACCOUNTS PAYABLE CREDIT	FREIGHT IN DEBIT	PURCHASES DEBIT	
1										1
2										2
3										3
4										4
5										5
6										6
7										7
8										8
9										9
10										10
11										11
12										12
13										13

GENERAL LEDGER

ACCOUNT *Accounts Payable*   ACCOUNT NO. 212

DATE	ITEM	POST. REF.	DEBIT	CREDIT	BALANCE DEBIT	BALANCE CREDIT

ACCOUNT *Purchases*   ACCOUNT NO. 511

DATE	ITEM	POST. REF.	DEBIT	CREDIT	BALANCE DEBIT	BALANCE CREDIT

ACCOUNT *Freight In*   ACCOUNT NO. 514

DATE	ITEM	POST. REF.	DEBIT	CREDIT	BALANCE DEBIT	BALANCE CREDIT

Problem 10-3A or 10-3B (continued)

ACCOUNTS PAYABLE LEDGER

NAME _____

ADDRESS _____

	DATE	ITEM	POST. REF.	DEBIT	CREDIT	BALANCE	

NAME _____

ADDRESS _____

	DATE	ITEM	POST. REF.	DEBIT	CREDIT	BALANCE	

NAME _____

ADDRESS _____

	DATE	ITEM	POST. REF.	DEBIT	CREDIT	BALANCE	

NAME _____

ADDRESS _____

	DATE	ITEM	POST. REF.	DEBIT	CREDIT	BALANCE	

Problem 10-3A or 10-3B (concluded)

NAME _____

ADDRESS _____

DATE		ITEM	POST. REF.	DEBIT	CREDIT	BALANCE	

NAME _____

ADDRESS _____

DATE		ITEM	POST. REF.	DEBIT	CREDIT	BALANCE	

Problem 10-4A or 10-4B

SALES JOURNAL   PAGE _____ 24 _____

	DATE	INV. NO.	CUSTOMER'S NAME	POST. REF.	ACCOUNTS RECEIVABLE DEBIT SALES CREDIT	
1						1
2						2
3						3
4						4
5						5
6						6
7						7
8						8
9						9
10						10
11						11
12						12
13						13
14						14
15						15
16						16

PURCHASES JOURNAL   PAGE _____ 18 _____

	DATE	SUPPLIER'S NAME	INV. NO.	INV. DATE	TERMS	POST. REF.	ACCOUNTS PAYABLE CREDIT	FREIGHT IN DEBIT	PURCHASES DEBIT	
1										1
2										2
3										3
4										4
5										5
6										6
7										7
8										8
9										9
10										10
11										11
12										12
13										13
14										14
15										15
16										16
17										17
18										18

NAME _____ DATE _____ CLASS _____

Problem 10-4A or 10-4B (continued)

GENERAL JOURNAL 68

	DATE	DESCRIPTION	POST. REF.	DEBIT	CREDIT	
1						1
2						2
3						3
4						4
5						5
6						6
7						7
8						8
9						9
10						10
11						11
12						12
13						13
14						14
15						15
16						16
17						17
18						18
19						19
20						20
21						21
22						22
23						23

ACCOUNTS RECEIVABLE LEDGER

NAME _____

ADDRESS _____

DATE	ITEM	POST. REF.	DEBIT	CREDIT	BALANCE

NAME _____ DATE _____ CLASS _____

Problem 10-4A or 10-4B (continued)

NAME _____
ADDRESS _____

DATE	ITEM	POST. REF.	DEBIT	CREDIT	BALANCE

NAME _____
ADDRESS _____

DATE	ITEM	POST. REF.	DEBIT	CREDIT	BALANCE

NAME _____
ADDRESS _____

DATE	ITEM	POST. REF.	DEBIT	CREDIT	BALANCE

ACCOUNTS PAYABLE LEDGER

NAME _____
ADDRESS _____

DATE	ITEM	POST. REF.	DEBIT	CREDIT	BALANCE

Problem 10-4A or 10-4B (continued)

NAME _____
ADDRESS _____

DATE		ITEM	POST. REF.	DEBIT	CREDIT	BALANCE

NAME _____
ADDRESS _____

DATE		ITEM	POST. REF.	DEBIT	CREDIT	BALANCE

NAME _____
ADDRESS _____

DATE		ITEM	POST. REF.	DEBIT	CREDIT	BALANCE

NAME _____
ADDRESS _____

DATE		ITEM	POST. REF.	DEBIT	CREDIT	BALANCE

Problem 10-4A or 10-4B (continued)

GENERAL LEDGER

ACCOUNT **Accounts Receivable** ACCOUNT NO. _113_

DATE		ITEM	POST. REF.	DEBIT	CREDIT	BALANCE	
						DEBIT	CREDIT
20--							
Apr.	1	Balance	✓			1,400.00	

ACCOUNT **Accounts Payable** ACCOUNT NO. _212_

DATE		ITEM	POST. REF.	DEBIT	CREDIT	BALANCE	
						DEBIT	CREDIT
20--							
Apr.	1	Balance	✓				378.00

ACCOUNT **Sales** ACCOUNT NO. _411_

DATE		ITEM	POST. REF.	DEBIT	CREDIT	BALANCE	
						DEBIT	CREDIT
20--							
Apr.	1	Balance	✓				11,000.00

ACCOUNT **Sales Returns and Allowances** ACCOUNT NO. _412_

DATE		ITEM	POST. REF.	DEBIT	CREDIT	BALANCE	
						DEBIT	CREDIT
20--							
Apr.	1	Balance	✓			410.00	

Problem 10-4A or 10-4B (continued)

ACCOUNT _Purchases_   ACCOUNT NO. _511_

DATE		ITEM	POST. REF.	DEBIT	CREDIT	BALANCE DEBIT	BALANCE CREDIT
20--							
Apr.	1	Balance	✓			9,600.00	

ACCOUNT _Purchases Returns and Allowances_   ACCOUNT NO. _512_

DATE		ITEM	POST. REF.	DEBIT	CREDIT	BALANCE DEBIT	BALANCE CREDIT
20--							
Apr.	1	Balance	✓				60.00

ACCOUNT _Freight In_   ACCOUNT NO. _514_

DATE		ITEM	POST. REF.	DEBIT	CREDIT	BALANCE DEBIT	BALANCE CREDIT
20--							
Apr.	1	Balance	✓			712.00	

ACCOUNT _Office Supplies Expense_   ACCOUNT NO. _613_

DATE		ITEM	POST. REF.	DEBIT	CREDIT	BALANCE DEBIT	BALANCE CREDIT
20--							
Apr.	1	Balance	✓			220.00	

Problem 10-4A or 10-4B (concluded)

Problem C-1A

GENERAL JOURNAL   PAGE _____

	DATE		DESCRIPTION	POST. REF.	DEBIT	CREDIT	
1							1
2							2
3							3
4							4
5							5
6							6
7							7
8							8
9							9
10							10
11							11
12							12
13							13
14							14
15							15
16							16
17							17
18							18
19							19
20							20
21							21
22							22
23							23
24							24
25							25
26							26
27							27
28							28
29							29
30							30
31							31
32							32
33							33
34							34
35							35
36							36
37							37
38							38
39							39
40							40
41							41
42							42
43							43
44							44
45							45

NAME _____ DATE _____ CLASS _____

Problem C-1A (continued)

GENERAL JOURNAL   PAGE _____

	DATE		DESCRIPTION	POST. REF.	DEBIT	CREDIT	
1							1
2							2
3							3
4							4
5							5
6							6
7							7
8							8
9							9
10							10
11							11
12							12
13							13
14							14
15							15
16							16
17							17
18							18
19							19
20							20
21							21
22							22
23							23
24							24
25							25
26							26
27							27
28							28
29							29
30							30
31							31
32							32
33							33
34							34
35							35
36							36
37							37
38							38
39							39
40							40
41							41
42							42
43							43
44							44
45							45

296

Problem C-1A (continued)

GENERAL LEDGER

ACCOUNT   *Accounts Receivable*   ACCOUNT NO.   113

DATE		ITEM	POST. REF.	DEBIT	CREDIT	BALANCE DEBIT	BALANCE CREDIT
20--							
Apr.	1	Balance	✓			1,400.00	

ACCOUNT   *Accounts Payable*   ACCOUNT NO.   212

DATE		ITEM	POST. REF.	DEBIT	CREDIT	BALANCE DEBIT	BALANCE CREDIT
20--							
Apr.	1	Balance	✓				378.00

ACCOUNT   *Sales*   ACCOUNT NO.   411

DATE		ITEM	POST. REF.	DEBIT	CREDIT	BALANCE DEBIT	BALANCE CREDIT
20--							
Apr.	1	Balance	✓				11,000.00

ACCOUNT   *Sales Returns and Allowances*   ACCOUNT NO.   412

DATE		ITEM	POST. REF.	DEBIT	CREDIT	BALANCE DEBIT	BALANCE CREDIT
20--							
Apr.	1	Balance	✓			410.00	

Problem C-1A (continued)

ACCOUNT _Purchases_ _____ ACCOUNT NO. _511_

DATE		ITEM	POST. REF.	DEBIT	CREDIT	BALANCE	
						DEBIT	CREDIT
20--							
Apr.	1	Balance	✓			9,600.00	

ACCOUNT _Purchases Returns and Allowances_ _____ ACCOUNT NO. _512_

DATE		ITEM	POST. REF.	DEBIT	CREDIT	BALANCE	
						DEBIT	CREDIT
20--							
Apr.	1	Balance	✓				60.00

ACCOUNT _Freight In_ _____ ACCOUNT NO. _514_

DATE		ITEM	POST. REF.	DEBIT	CREDIT	BALANCE	
						DEBIT	CREDIT
20--							
Apr.	1	Balance	✓			712.00	

ACCOUNT _Office Supplies Expense_ _____ ACCOUNT NO. _613_

DATE		ITEM	POST. REF.	DEBIT	CREDIT	BALANCE	
						DEBIT	CREDIT
20--							
Apr.	1	Balance	✓			220.00	

Problem C-1A (continued)

ACCOUNTS RECEIVABLE LEDGER

NAME   *C. N. Hague*

ADDRESS

DATE	ITEM	POST. REF.	DEBIT	CREDIT	BALANCE
20--					

NAME   *Pima and Lane*

ADDRESS

DATE		ITEM	POST. REF.	DEBIT	CREDIT	BALANCE
20--						
Apr.	1	Balance	✓			426.00

NAME   *Schilling and Mark*

ADDRESS

DATE		ITEM	POST. REF.	DEBIT	CREDIT	BALANCE
20--						
Apr.	1	Balance	✓			974.00

NAME   *Slover Company*

ADDRESS

DATE	ITEM	POST. REF.	DEBIT	CREDIT	BALANCE
20--					

Problem C-1A (continued)

ACCOUNTS PAYABLE LEDGER

NAME *Kraig and Company*
ADDRESS _____

DATE		ITEM	POST. REF.	DEBIT	CREDIT	BALANCE
20--						
Apr.	1	Balance	✓			262.00

NAME *M. R. Parker, Inc.*
ADDRESS _____

DATE		ITEM	POST. REF.	DEBIT	CREDIT	BALANCE
20--						
Apr.	1	Balance	✓			116.00

NAME *Pedro Company*
ADDRESS _____

DATE		ITEM	POST. REF.	DEBIT	CREDIT	BALANCE
20--						

NAME *Tillman Stationery Company*
ADDRESS _____

DATE		ITEM	POST. REF.	DEBIT	CREDIT	BALANCE
20--						

Problem C-1A (concluded)

NAME **Varder Company**

ADDRESS _____

DATE	ITEM	POST. REF.	DEBIT	CREDIT	BALANCE	
20--						

Problem C-1B

GENERAL JOURNAL   PAGE _____

	DATE		DESCRIPTION	POST. REF.	DEBIT	CREDIT	
1							1
2							2
3							3
4							4
5							5
6							6
7							7
8							8
9							9
10							10
11							11
12							12
13							13
14							14
15							15
16							16
17							17
18							18
19							19
20							20
21							21
22							22
23							23
24							24
25							25
26							26
27							27
28							28
29							29
30							30
31							31
32							32
33							33
34							34
35							35
36							36
37							37
38							38
39							39
40							40
41							41
42							42
43							43
44							44
45							45

302

Problem C-1B (continued)

GENERAL JOURNAL   PAGE _____

	DATE		DESCRIPTION	POST. REF.	DEBIT	CREDIT	
1							1
2							2
3							3
4							4
5							5
6							6
7							7
8							8
9							9
10							10
11							11
12							12
13							13
14							14
15							15
16							16
17							17
18							18
19							19
20							20
21							21
22							22
23							23
24							24
25							25
26							26
27							27
28							28
29							29
30							30
31							31
32							32
33							33
34							34
35							35
36							36
37							37
38							38
39							39
40							40
41							41
42							42
43							43
44							44
45							45

Problem C-1B (continued)

GENERAL LEDGER

ACCOUNT *Accounts Receivable*   ACCOUNT NO. *113*

DATE		ITEM	POST. REF.	DEBIT	CREDIT	BALANCE	
						DEBIT	CREDIT
20--							
Apr.	1	Balance	✓			1,400.00	

ACCOUNT *Accounts Payable*   ACCOUNT NO. *212*

DATE		ITEM	POST. REF.	DEBIT	CREDIT	BALANCE	
						DEBIT	CREDIT
20--							
Apr.	1	Balance	✓				378.00

ACCOUNT *Sales*   ACCOUNT NO. *411*

DATE		ITEM	POST. REF.	DEBIT	CREDIT	BALANCE	
						DEBIT	CREDIT
20--							
Apr.	1	Balance	✓				11,000.00

ACCOUNT *Sales Returns and Allowances*   ACCOUNT NO. *412*

DATE		ITEM	POST. REF.	DEBIT	CREDIT	BALANCE	
						DEBIT	CREDIT
20--							
Apr.	1	Balance	✓			410.00	

Problem C-1B (continued)

ACCOUNT _Purchases_   ACCOUNT NO. _511_

DATE		ITEM	POST. REF.	DEBIT	CREDIT	BALANCE	
						DEBIT	CREDIT
20--							
Apr.	1	Balance	✓			9,600.00	

ACCOUNT _Purchases Returns and Allowances_   ACCOUNT NO. _512_

DATE		ITEM	POST. REF.	DEBIT	CREDIT	BALANCE	
						DEBIT	CREDIT
20--							
Apr.	1	Balance	✓				60.00

ACCOUNT _Freight In_   ACCOUNT NO. _514_

DATE		ITEM	POST. REF.	DEBIT	CREDIT	BALANCE	
						DEBIT	CREDIT
20--							
Apr.	1	Balance	✓			712.00	

ACCOUNT _Office Supplies Expense_   ACCOUNT NO. _613_

DATE		ITEM	POST. REF.	DEBIT	CREDIT	BALANCE	
						DEBIT	CREDIT
20--							
Apr.	1	Balance	✓			220.00	

Problem C-1B (continued)

ACCOUNTS RECEIVABLE LEDGER

NAME   C. D. Alvarez
ADDRESS

DATE		ITEM	POST. REF.	DEBIT	CREDIT	BALANCE
20--						

NAME   Bocci Stores
ADDRESS

DATE		ITEM	POST. REF.	DEBIT	CREDIT	BALANCE
20--						
Apr.	1	Balance	✓			352.50

NAME   Grady Specialty Company
ADDRESS

DATE		ITEM	POST. REF.	DEBIT	CREDIT	BALANCE
20--						
Apr.	1	Balance	✓			225.50

NAME   Helpful Hardware
ADDRESS

DATE		ITEM	POST. REF.	DEBIT	CREDIT	BALANCE
20--						
Apr.	1	Balance	✓			822.00

Problem C-1B (continued)

ACCOUNTS PAYABLE LEDGER

NAME *Ashley Manufacturing Company*

ADDRESS

DATE	ITEM	POST. REF.	DEBIT	CREDIT	BALANCE
20--					

NAME *Bali Products Company*

ADDRESS

DATE	ITEM	POST. REF.	DEBIT	CREDIT	BALANCE
20--					
Apr. 1	Balance	✓			122.46

NAME *Bjorn, Inc.*

ADDRESS

DATE	ITEM	POST. REF.	DEBIT	CREDIT	BALANCE
20--					
Apr. 1	Balance	✓			255.54

NAME *China anad Duncan*

ADDRESS

DATE	ITEM	POST. REF.	DEBIT	CREDIT	BALANCE
20--					

Problem C-1B (concluded)

NAME   *Rama Manufacturing Company*
ADDRESS

DATE		ITEM	POST. REF.	DEBIT	CREDIT	BALANCE	
20--							

The Cash Receipts Journal and the Cash Payments Journal

PERFORMANCE OBJECTIVES

1. Journalize transactions for a merchandising business in a cash receipts journal.
2. Post from a cash receipts journal to a general ledger and an accounts receivable ledger.
3. Determine cash discounts according to credit terms, and record cash receipts from charge customers who are entitled to deduct the cash discount.
4. Journalize transactions in a cash payments journal for a service enterprise.
5. Post from a cash payments journal to a general ledger and an accounts payable ledger.
6. Journalize transactions involving cash discounts in a cash payments journal for a merchandising enterprise.
7. Journalize transactions in a check register.
8. Journalize transactions involving trade discounts.

KEY TERMS

Bank charge card
Cash discount
Cash payments journal
Cash receipts journal
Check register

Credit period
Notes payable
Promissory note
Trade discounts

STUDY GUIDE QUESTIONS

PART 1   True/False

For each of the following statements, indicate T if the statement is true and F if the statement is false.

T   F   1.   The normal balance of the Sales Discounts account is on the debit side.

T   F   2.   An investment of cash by the owner is always recorded in the general journal.

T   F   3.   In a cash receipts journal, the individual amounts in the Other Accounts credit column are posted at the end of the month.

T   F   4.   Entries in the Accounts Payable Debit column of a cash payments journal are posted daily to the accounts payable ledger.

T   F   5.   The Purchases Discounts account is classified as a revenue account.

T   F   6.   Credit terms of 1/10, n/30 indicate that a discount of 30 percent may be deducted if the bill is paid in thirty days.

T   F   7.   The amount of the discount that the bank deducts for a credit card transaction is usually between 10 and 15 percent.

T   F   8.   The buyer records the purchases discount when payment is made.

T   F   9.   Trade discounts are not recorded on the books of either the buyer or the seller.

T   F   10.   A check register performs the same function as a cash payments journal.

PART 2   Completion—Language of Business

Complete each of the following statements by writing the appropriate word(s) in the spaces provided.

1. Large deductions from the list prices of merchandise are referred to as _____.

2. The time the seller allows the buyer before full payment on a charge sale has to be made is called the _____.

3. The _____ is the amount a customer may deduct for paying a bill within a specified period of time.

PART 3   Matching

For each numbered item, choose the appropriate journal and write the identifying letter.

_____	1. Bought merchandise on account	S	Sales journal
_____	2. Sold merchandise for cash	P	Purchases journal (3 columns)
_____	3. Bought merchandise for cash	CR	Cash receipts journal
_____	4. Collected accounts receivable and allowed a cash discount	CP	Cash payments journal
		J	General journal
_____	5. Bought store equipment on credit		
_____	6. Recorded accrued wages		
_____	7. Received credit memo for merchandise returned		
_____	8. Paid freight bill on merchandise purchased		
_____	9. Sold merchandise on account		
_____	10. Paid state unemployment taxes		

PART 4   Cash Receipts Journal

Label the cash receipts journal columns as Debit or Credit.

OTHER ACCOUNTS	ACCOUNTS RECEIVABLE	SALES	SALES DISCOUNTS	CASH

DEMONSTRATION PROBLEM

Elegant Jewelry, a retail store, sells merchandise (1) for cash, (2) on charge accounts, and (3) on bank credit cards. The store uses a sales journal, a purchases journal, a cash receipts journal, a cash payments journal, and a general journal. The store engaged in the following selected transactions:

June 16   Sold merchandise on account to T. Morgan, invoice no. 1230, $9,757, plus $790.32 sales tax.

17   Sold merchandise paid by bank credit cards, $2,271, plus $183.95 sales tax. The bank charges 4 percent of the total sales plus sales tax.

18   Bought merchandise on account from Gem Central, invoice no. D109, dated June 16; $4,542; terms 1/10, n/30; FOB shipping point, freight prepaid and added to the invoice, $60 (total $4,602).

19   Received credit memorandum no. 926 from Gem Central for merchandise return, $529.

22   Paid Gem Central, their invoice no. D109, Ck. No. 5901, $4,032.87. ($4,542 less $529 return and less 1 percent cash discount. $4,542.00 − $529.00 = $4,013.00; $4,013.00 × .01 = $40.13; $4,013.00 − $40.13 = $3,972.87; $3,972.87 + $60 freight = $4,032.87.)

24   Bought packaging supplies on account from The Box Company, their invoice no. 990, dated June 22; net 30 days; $459.

29   Paid rent for the month, Ck. No. 5902, $1,980.

30   Bought merchandise on account from Todd Company, their invoice no. 1002, dated June 29 list price $2,950 less 40 percent trade discount; terms 2/10, n/30; FOB shipping point.

30   Paid freight bill to Fast Freight, Ck. No. 5903, for merchandise received from Todd Company, $110.

30   Issued Ck. No. 5904 for $258.36 to customer L.O. Sherry, for merchandise returned, $239, plus $19.36 sales tax.

Instructions

1.   Journalize the transactions.
2.   Total and rule the journals.
3.   Prove the equality of the debits and the credits at the bottom of each journal.

SOLUTION

SALES JOURNAL

	DATE	INV. NO.	CUSTOMER'S NAME	POST. REF.	ACCOUNTS RECEIVABLE DEBIT	SALES TAX PAYABLE CREDIT	SALES CREDIT	
1	20--							1
2	June 16	1230	T. Morgan		10,547.32	790.32	9,757.00	2
3	30				10,547.32	790.32	9,757.00	3
4								4

DEBITS	CREDITS
$10,547.32	$ 790.32
	9,757.00
$10,547.32	$10,547.32

PURCHASES JOURNAL

	DATE	SUPPLIER'S NAME	INV. NO.	INV. DATE	TERMS	POST. REF.	ACCOUNTS PAYABLE CREDIT	FREIGHT IN DEBIT	PURCHASES DEBIT	
1	20--									1
2	June 18	Gem Central	D109	6/16	1/10, n/30		4,602.00	60.00	4,542.00	2
3	30	Todd Company	1002	6/29	2/10, n/30		1,770.00		1,770.00	3
4	30						6,372.00	60.00	6,312.00	4
5										5

DEBITS	CREDITS
$ 60.00	$6,372.00
6,312.00	
$6,372.00	$6,372.00

SOLUTION *(concluded)*

CASH RECEIPTS JOURNAL

	DATE	ACCOUNT CREDITED	POST. REF.	OTHER ACCOUNTS CREDIT	ACCOUNTS RECEIVABLE CREDIT	SALES CREDIT	SALES TAX PAYABLE CREDIT	CREDIT CARD EXPENSE DEBIT	CASH DEBIT	
1	20--									1
2	June 17					2,271.00	183.95	98.20	2,356.75	2
3	30					2,271.00	183.95	98.20	2,356.75	3
4										4

DEBITS	CREDITS
$ 98.20	$2,271.00
2,356.75	183.95
$2,454.95	$2,454.95

CASH PAYMENTS JOURNAL

	DATE	CK. NO.	ACCOUNT DEBITED	POST. REF.	OTHER ACCOUNTS DEBIT	ACCOUNTS PAYABLE DEBIT	PURCHASES DISCOUNTS CREDIT	CASH CREDIT	
1	20--								1
2	June 22	5901	Gem Central			4,073.00	40.13	4,032.87	2
3	29	5902	Rent Expense		1,980.00			1,980.00	3
4	30	5903	Freight In		110.00			110.00	4
5	30	5904	Sales Returns and Allowances		258.36			258.36	5
6	30				2,348.36	4,073.00	40.13	6,381.23	6
7									7
8									8

DEBITS	CREDITS
$2,348.36	$ 40.13
4,073.00	6,381.23
$6,421.36	$6,421.36

GENERAL JOURNAL

	DATE		DESCRIPTION	POST. REF.	DEBIT	CREDIT	
1	20--						1
2	June	19	Accounts Payable, Gem Central		529.00		2
3			Purchases Returns and Allowances			529.00	3
4			Credit memo no. 926.				4
5							5
6		24	Supplies Expense		459.00		6
7			Accounts Payable, The Box Company			459.00	7
8			Packing supplies, invoice no. 990,				8
9			dated June 22, net 30 days.				9
10							10

EXERCISES

Exercise 11-1

_____
_____
_____
_____
_____
_____
_____

Exercise 11-2

CASH RECEIPTS JOURNAL   PAGE _____

	DATE	ACCOUNT CREDITED	POST. REF.	OTHER ACCOUNTS	ACCOUNTS RECEIVABLE	SALES	SALES DISCOUNTS	CASH	
1									1
2									2
3									3

Exercise 11-3

a. _____
_____
b. _____
_____
c. _____
_____

Exercise 11-4

a. _____
b. _____
c. _____
d. _____
e. _____

Exercise 11-5

TRANSACTION	JOURNAL				
	S	P (3-col.)	CR	CP	J
a. Paid a creditor on account.					
b. Bought merchandise on account.					
c. Sold merchandise for cash					
d. Adjusted for insurance expired.					
e. Received payment on account from a charge customer.					
f. Received a credit memo for merchandise returned.					
g. Bought equipment on credit.					
h. Sold merchandise on account.					
i. Recorded a customer's NSF check.					
j. Invested personal noncash assets in the business.					
k. Withdrew cash for personal use.					

Exercise 11-6

GENERAL JOURNAL

PAGE _____

	DATE	DESCRIPTION	POST. REF.	DEBIT	CREDIT	
1						1
2						2
3						3
4						4
5						5
6						6
7						7
8						8
9						9
10						10
11						11
12						12
13						13
14						14
15						15
16						16
17						17
18						18
19						19
20						20
21						21
22						22
23						23
24						24
25						25
26						26
27						27
28						28
29						29
30						30
31						31
32						32
33						33
34						34
35						35
36						36
37						37

Exercise 11-7

Seller's Books (Fry Company)

GENERAL JOURNAL   PAGE _____

	DATE		DESCRIPTION	POST. REF.	DEBIT	CREDIT	
1							1
2							2
3							3
4							4
5							5
6							6
7							7
8							8
9							9
10							10
11							11
12							12
13							13
14							14

Buyer's Books (Lee Company)

GENERAL JOURNAL   PAGE _____

	DATE		DESCRIPTION	POST. REF.	DEBIT	CREDIT	
1							1
2							2
3							3
4							4
5							5
6							6
7							7
8							8
9							9
10							10
11							11
12							12
13							13
14							14

Exercise 11-8

GENERAL JOURNAL   PAGE _____

	DATE	DESCRIPTION	POST. REF.	DEBIT	CREDIT	
1						1
2						2
3						3
4						4
5						5
6						6
7						7
8						8
9						9
10						10
11						11
12						12
13						13
14						14
15						15
16						16
17						17
18						18
19						19
20						20
21						21
22						22
23						23
24						24
25						25
26						26
27						27
28						28
29						29
30						30
31						31
32						32
33						33
34						34
35						35
36						36
37						37
38						38
39						39
40						40

NAME _____

DATE _____

Problem 11-1A or 11-1B

CASH RECEIPTS JOURNAL

PAGE _____

	DATE	ACCOUNT CREDITED	POST. REF.	OTHER ACCOUNTS CREDIT	ACCOUNTS RECEIVABLE CREDIT	SALES CREDIT	SALES TAX PAYABLE CREDIT	CREDIT CARD EXPENSE DEBIT	CASH DEBIT	
1										1
2										2
3										3
4										4
5										5
6										6
7										7
8										8
9										9
10										10
11										11
12										12
13										13
14										14
15										15
16										16
17										17
18										18
19										19
20										20
21										21

EQUALITY OF DEBITS AND CREDITS

DEBITS _____

CREDITS _____

Problem 11-1A or 11-1B (continued)

GENERAL LEDGER

ACCOUNT *Accounts Receivable*   ACCOUNT NO. *113*

DATE		ITEM	POST. REF.	DEBIT	CREDIT	BALANCE	
						DEBIT	CREDIT

ACCOUNTS RECEIVABLE LEDGER

NAME _____

ADDRESS _____

DATE		ITEM	POST. REF.	DEBIT	CREDIT	BALANCE

NAME _____

ADDRESS _____

DATE		ITEM	POST. REF.	DEBIT	CREDIT	BALANCE

NAME _____

ADDRESS _____

DATE		ITEM	POST. REF.	DEBIT	CREDIT	BALANCE

Problem 11-1A or 11-1B (concluded)

NAME _____

ADDRESS _____

DATE		ITEM	POST. REF.	DEBIT	CREDIT	BALANCE	

NAME _____

ADDRESS _____

DATE		ITEM	POST. REF.	DEBIT	CREDIT	BALANCE	

NAME _____

ADDRESS _____

DATE		ITEM	POST. REF.	DEBIT	CREDIT	BALANCE	

Problem 11-2A or 11-2B

CASH RECEIPTS JOURNAL

PAGE ___71___

	DATE	ACCOUNT CREDITED	POST. REF.	OTHER ACCOUNTS CREDIT	ACCOUNTS RECEIVABLE CREDIT	SALES CREDIT	SALES DISCOUNTS DEBIT	CASH DEBIT	
1									1
2									2
3									3
4									4
5									5
6									6
7									7
8									8
9									9
10									10
11									11
12									12

SALES JOURNAL

PAGE ___43___

	DATE	CUSTOMER'S NAME	INV. NO.	POST. REF.	ACCOUNTS RECEIVABLE DR., SALES CR.	
1						1
2						2
3						3
4						4
5						5
6						6

EQUALITY OF DEBITS AND CREDITS

DEBITS _____   CREDITS _____

NAME _____ DATE _____ CLASS _____

Problem 11-3A or 11-3B

CHECK REGISTER

PAGE _____ 16 _____

DATE	CK. NO.	PAYEE	ACCOUNT DEBITED	POST. REF.	OTHER ACCOUNTS DEBIT	ACCOUNTS PAYABLE DEBIT	PURCHASES DISCOUNTS CREDIT	FIRST NAT'L BANK CREDIT	
									1
									2
									3
									4
									5
									6
									7
									8
									9
									10
									11
									12
									13
									14
									15
									16
									17
									18

EQUALITY OF DEBITS AND CREDITS

DEBITS _____   CREDITS _____

Problem 11-4A or 11-4B

SALES JOURNAL   PAGE _____

	DATE	INV. NO.	CUSTOMER'S NAME	POST. REF.	ACCOUNTS RECEIVABLE DR. SALES CR.	
1						1
2						2
3						3
4						4
5						5
6						6
7						7
8						8
9						9
10						10
11						11

PURCHASES JOURNAL   PAGE _____

	DATE	SUPPLIER'S NAME	INV. NO.	INV. DATE	TERMS	POST. REF.	ACCOUNTS PAYABLE CREDIT	FREIGHT IN DEBIT	PURCHASES DEBIT	
1										1
2										2
3										3
4										4
5										5
6										6
7										7
8										8
9										9

EQUALITY OF DEBITS AND CREDITS

DEBITS   CREDITS

NAME _____ DATE _____ CLASS _____

Problem 11-4A or 11-4B (continued)

CASH RECEIPTS JOURNAL

PAGE _____

	DATE	ACCOUNT CREDITED	POST. REF.	OTHER ACCOUNTS CREDIT	ACCOUNTS RECEIVABLE CREDIT	SALES CREDIT	SALES DISCOUNTS DEBIT	CASH DEBIT	
1									1
2									2
3									3
4									4
5									5
6									6
7									7
8									8
9									9
10									10
11									11
12									12

EQUALITY OF DEBITS AND CREDITS

DEBITS _____   CREDITS _____

Problem 11-4A or 11-4B (continued)

CASH PAYMENTS JOURNAL   PAGE _____

	DATE	CK. NO.	ACCOUNT DEBITED	POST. REF.	OTHER ACCOUNTS DEBIT	ACCOUNTS PAYABLE DEBIT	PURCHASES DISCOUNTS CREDIT	CASH CREDIT	
1									1
2									2
3									3
4									4
5									5
6									6
7									7
8									8
9									9
10									10
11									11
12									12

EQUALITY OF DEBITS AND CREDITS

DEBITS   CREDITS

NAME _____ DATE _____ CLASS _____

Problem 11-4A or 11-4B (continued)

GENERAL JOURNAL   PAGE _____

	DATE		DESCRIPTION	POST. REF.	DEBIT	CREDIT	
1							1
2							2
3							3
4							4
5							5
6							6
7							7
8							8
9							9
10							10
11							11
12							12
13							13
14							14
15							15
16							16
17							17
18							18
19							19
20							20
21							21
22							22
23							23
24							24
25							25
26							26
27							27
28							28
29							29
30							30
31							31
32							32
33							33
34							34
35							35
36							36
37							37
38							38
39							39
40							40
41							41
42							42

Problem 11-4A or 11-4B (continued)

GENERAL LEDGER

ACCOUNT   *Cash*   ACCOUNT NO.   *111*

DATE		ITEM	POST. REF.	DEBIT	CREDIT	BALANCE	
						DEBIT	CREDIT
20--							
Jan.	1	Balance	✓			8,740.00	

ACCOUNT   *Accounts Receivable*   ACCOUNT NO.   *113*

DATE		ITEM	POST. REF.	DEBIT	CREDIT	BALANCE	
						DEBIT	CREDIT
20--							
Jan.	1	Balance	✓			1,650.00	

ACCOUNT   *Merchandise Inventory*   ACCOUNT NO.   *114*

DATE		ITEM	POST. REF.	DEBIT	CREDIT	BALANCE	
						DEBIT	CREDIT
20--							
Jan.	1	Balance	✓			20,584.00	

Problem 11-4A or 11-4B (continued)

ACCOUNT   *Prepaid Insurance* _____   ACCOUNT NO. ___116___

DATE		ITEM	POST. REF.	DEBIT	CREDIT	BALANCE DEBIT	CREDIT
20--							
Jan.	1	Balance	✓			390.00	

ACCOUNT   *Equipment* _____   ACCOUNT NO. ___121___

DATE		ITEM	POST. REF.	DEBIT	CREDIT	BALANCE DEBIT	CREDIT
20--							
Jan.	1	Balance	✓			3,644.00	

ACCOUNT   *Accounts Payable* _____   ACCOUNT NO. ___212___

DATE		ITEM	POST. REF.	DEBIT	CREDIT	BALANCE DEBIT	CREDIT
20--							
Jan.	1		✓				600.00

ACCOUNT   *Salaries Payable* _____   ACCOUNT NO. ___215___

DATE		ITEM	POST. REF.	DEBIT	CREDIT	BALANCE DEBIT	CREDIT

Problem 11-4A or 11-4B (continued)

ACCOUNT   *Employees' Federal Income Tax Payable*   ACCOUNT NO.   *216*

DATE		ITEM	POST. REF.	DEBIT	CREDIT	BALANCE	
						DEBIT	CREDIT

ACCOUNT   *FICA Tax Payable*   ACCOUNT NO.   *217*

DATE		ITEM	POST. REF.	DEBIT	CREDIT	BALANCE	
						DEBIT	CREDIT

ACCOUNT   *State Unemployment Tax Payable*   ACCOUNT NO.   *218*

DATE		ITEM	POST. REF.	DEBIT	CREDIT	BALANCE	
						DEBIT	CREDIT

ACCOUNT   *Federal Unemployment Tax Payable*   ACCOUNT NO.   *219*

DATE		ITEM	POST. REF.	DEBIT	CREDIT	BALANCE	
						DEBIT	CREDIT

ACCOUNT   *, Capital*   ACCOUNT NO.   *311*

DATE		ITEM	POST. REF.	DEBIT	CREDIT	BALANCE	
						DEBIT	CREDIT
20--							
Jan.	*1*	*Balance*	✓				*35,000.00*

330

Problem 11-4A or 11-4B (continued)

ACCOUNT _____ **, Drawing** _____ ACCOUNT NO. _____ *312*

DATE		ITEM	POST. REF.	DEBIT	CREDIT	BALANCE	
						DEBIT	CREDIT

ACCOUNT _____ *Sales* _____ ACCOUNT NO. _____ *411*

DATE		ITEM	POST. REF.	DEBIT	CREDIT	BALANCE	
						DEBIT	CREDIT

ACCOUNT _____ *Sales Returns and Allowances* _____ ACCOUNT NO. _____ *412*

DATE		ITEM	POST. REF.	DEBIT	CREDIT	BALANCE	
						DEBIT	CREDIT

ACCOUNT _____ *Sales Discounts* _____ ACCOUNT NO. _____ *413*

DATE		ITEM	POST. REF.	DEBIT	CREDIT	BALANCE	
						DEBIT	CREDIT

ACCOUNT _____ *Purchases* _____ ACCOUNT NO. _____ *511*

DATE		ITEM	POST. REF.	DEBIT	CREDIT	BALANCE	
						DEBIT	CREDIT

Problem 11-4A or 11-4B (continued)

ACCOUNT   *Purchases Returns and Allowances*   ACCOUNT NO.   *512*

DATE		ITEM	POST. REF.	DEBIT	CREDIT	BALANCE	
						DEBIT	CREDIT

ACCOUNT   *Purchases Discounts*   ACCOUNT NO.   *513*

DATE		ITEM	POST. REF.	DEBIT	CREDIT	BALANCE	
						DEBIT	CREDIT

ACCOUNT   *Freight In*   ACCOUNT NO.   *514*

DATE		ITEM	POST. REF.	DEBIT	CREDIT	BALANCE	
						DEBIT	CREDIT

ACCOUNT   *Salary Expense*   ACCOUNT NO.   *621*

DATE		ITEM	POST. REF.	DEBIT	CREDIT	BALANCE	
						DEBIT	CREDIT

ACCOUNT   *Payroll Tax Expense*   ACCOUNT NO.   *622*

DATE		ITEM	POST. REF.	DEBIT	CREDIT	BALANCE	
						DEBIT	CREDIT

Problem 11-4A or 11-4B (continued)

ACCOUNT *Supplies Expense* _____ ACCOUNT NO. _____ 625 _____

DATE		ITEM	POST. REF.	DEBIT	CREDIT	BALANCE	
						DEBIT	CREDIT
20--							
Jan.	1	Balance	✓			592.00	

ACCOUNT *Rent Expense* _____ ACCOUNT NO. _____ 627 _____

DATE		ITEM	POST. REF.	DEBIT	CREDIT	BALANCE	
						DEBIT	CREDIT

ACCOUNT *Miscellaneous Expense* _____ ACCOUNT NO. _____ 631 _____

DATE		ITEM	POST. REF.	DEBIT	CREDIT	BALANCE	
						DEBIT	CREDIT

ACCOUNTS RECEIVABLE LEDGER

NAME *Bryan Supply* _____
ADDRESS _____

DATE		ITEM	POST. REF.	DEBIT	CREDIT	BALANCE

NAME *English and Cole* _____
ADDRESS _____

DATE		ITEM	POST. REF.	DEBIT	CREDIT	BALANCE

Problem 11-4A or 11-4B (continued)

NAME   *L. Parker*

ADDRESS

DATE		ITEM	POST. REF.	DEBIT	CREDIT	BALANCE	

NAME   *Peterson, Inc.*

ADDRESS

DATE		ITEM	POST. REF.	DEBIT	CREDIT	BALANCE	
20--							
Jan.	1	Balance	✓			650.00	

NAME   *Vessey Appliance*

ADDRESS

DATE		ITEM	POST. REF.	DEBIT	CREDIT	BALANCE	
20--							
Jan.	1	Balance	✓			1,000.00	

Problem 11-4A or 11-4B (continued)

ACCOUNTS PAYABLE LEDGER

NAME   *Crosby Products*

ADDRESS

DATE		ITEM	POST. REF.	DEBIT	CREDIT	BALANCE

NAME   *Duncan Office Supply*

ADDRESS

DATE		ITEM	POST. REF.	DEBIT	CREDIT	BALANCE

NAME   *Franklin and Son*

ADDRESS

DATE		ITEM	POST. REF.	DEBIT	CREDIT	BALANCE
20--						
Jan.	1	Balance	✓			600.00

NAME   *Vaughn and Company*

ADDRESS

DATE		ITEM	POST. REF.	DEBIT	CREDIT	BALANCE

Problem 11-4A or 11-4B (continued)

ACCOUNT NAME	DEBIT	CREDIT	

Problem 11-4A or 11-4B (concluded)

NAME_____   DATE_____   CLASS_____

BEFORE A TEST CHECK SOLUTIONS: CHAPTERS 10–11

Part I: 1._____   2._____   3._____

4._____   5._____   6._____   7._____

8._____   9._____

10._____

Part II: 1.____   2.____   3.____   4.____   5.____   6.____   7.____   8.____   9.____   10.____

Part III: 1.____   2.____   3.____   4.____   5.____

Problem D-1A or D-1B

GENERAL JOURNAL   PAGE ___1___

	DATE		DESCRIPTION	POST. REF.	DEBIT	CREDIT	
1							1
2							2
3							3
4							4
5							5
6							6
7							7
8							8
9							9
10							10
11							11
12							12
13							13
14							14
15							15
16							16
17							17
18							18
19							19
20							20
21							21
22							22
23							23
24							24
25							25
26							26
27							27
28							28
29							29
30							30
31							31
32							32
33							33
34							34
35							35
36							36
37							37
38							38
39							39
40							40
41							41
42							42
43							43
44							44
45							45

Problem D-1A or D-1B (continued)

GENERAL JOURNAL　　　　　　　PAGE ___2___

	DATE		DESCRIPTION	POST. REF.	DEBIT	CREDIT	
1							1
2							2
3							3
4							4
5							5
6							6
7							7
8							8
9							9
10							10
11							11
12							12
13							13
14							14
15							15
16							16
17							17
18							18
19							19
20							20
21							21
22							22
23							23
24							24
25							25
26							26
27							27
28							28
29							29
30							30
31							31
32							32
33							33
34							34
35							35
36							36
37							37
38							38
39							39
40							40
41							41
42							42
43							43
44							44
45							45

Problem D-1A or D-1B (continued)

GENERAL JOURNAL   PAGE ___3___

	DATE	DESCRIPTION	POST. REF.	DEBIT	CREDIT	
1						1
2						2
3						3
4						4
5						5
6						6
7						7
8						8
9						9
10						10
11						11
12						12
13						13
14						14
15						15
16						16
17						17
18						18
19						19
20						20
21						21
22						22
23						23
24						24
25						25
26						26
27						27
28						28
29						29
30						30
31						31
32						32
33						33
34						34
35						35
36						36
37						37
38						38
39						39
40						40
41						41
42						42
43						43
44						44
45						45

Problem D-1A or D-1B (continued)

GENERAL LEDGER

ACCOUNT   *Cash*   ACCOUNT NO.   *111*

DATE		ITEM	POST. REF.	DEBIT	CREDIT	BALANCE	
						DEBIT	CREDIT
20--							
Jan.	1	Balance	✓			8,740.00	

ACCOUNT   *Accounts Receivable*   ACCOUNT NO.   *113*

DATE		ITEM	POST. REF.	DEBIT	CREDIT	BALANCE	
						DEBIT	CREDIT
20--							
Jan.	1	Balance	✓			1,650.00	

ACCOUNT   *Merchandise Inventory*   ACCOUNT NO.   *114*

DATE		ITEM	POST. REF.	DEBIT	CREDIT	BALANCE	
						DEBIT	CREDIT
20--							
Jan.	1	Balance	✓			20,584.00	

Problem D-1A or D-1B (continued)

ACCOUNT *Prepaid Insurance*   ACCOUNT NO. _____116_____

DATE		ITEM	POST. REF.	DEBIT	CREDIT	BALANCE	
						DEBIT	CREDIT
20--							
Jan.	1	Balance	✓			390.00	

ACCOUNT *Equipment*   ACCOUNT NO. _____121_____

DATE		ITEM	POST. REF.	DEBIT	CREDIT	BALANCE	
						DEBIT	CREDIT
20--							
Jan.	1	Balance	✓			3,644.00	

ACCOUNT *Accounts Payable*   ACCOUNT NO. _____212_____

DATE		ITEM	POST. REF.	DEBIT	CREDIT	BALANCE	
						DEBIT	CREDIT
20--							
Jan.	1	Balance	✓				600.00

ACCOUNT *Salaries Payable*   ACCOUNT NO. _____215_____

DATE		ITEM	POST. REF.	DEBIT	CREDIT	BALANCE	
						DEBIT	CREDIT
20--							

ACCOUNT *Employees' Federal Income Tax Payable*   ACCOUNT NO. _____216_____

DATE		ITEM	POST. REF.	DEBIT	CREDIT	BALANCE	
						DEBIT	CREDIT
20--							

Problem D-1A or D-1B (continued)

ACCOUNT *FICA Tax Payable*   ACCOUNT NO. *217*

DATE	ITEM	POST. REF.	DEBIT	CREDIT	BALANCE	
					DEBIT	CREDIT
20--						

ACCOUNT *State Unemployment Tax Payable*   ACCOUNT NO. *218*

DATE	ITEM	POST. REF.	DEBIT	CREDIT	BALANCE	
					DEBIT	CREDIT
20--						

ACCOUNT *Federal Unemployment Tax Payable*   ACCOUNT NO. *219*

DATE	ITEM	POST. REF.	DEBIT	CREDIT	BALANCE	
					DEBIT	CREDIT
20--						

ACCOUNT *, Capital*   ACCOUNT NO. *311*

DATE	ITEM	POST. REF.	DEBIT	CREDIT	BALANCE	
					DEBIT	CREDIT
20--						
Jan. 1		✓				35,000.00

ACCOUNT *, Drawing*   ACCOUNT NO. *312*

DATE	ITEM	POST. REF.	DEBIT	CREDIT	BALANCE	
					DEBIT	CREDIT
20--						

NAME _____ DATE _____ CLASS _____

Problem D-1A or D-1B (continued)

ACCOUNT _Sales_   ACCOUNT NO. _411_

DATE	ITEM		POST. REF.	DEBIT	CREDIT	BALANCE DEBIT	CREDIT
20--							

ACCOUNT _Sales Returns and Allowances_   ACCOUNT NO. _412_

DATE	ITEM		POST. REF.	DEBIT	CREDIT	BALANCE DEBIT	CREDIT
20--							

ACCOUNT _Sales Discounts_   ACCOUNT NO. _413_

DATE	ITEM		POST. REF.	DEBIT	CREDIT	BALANCE DEBIT	CREDIT
20--							

ACCOUNT _Purchases_   ACCOUNT NO. _511_

DATE	ITEM		POST. REF.	DEBIT	CREDIT	BALANCE DEBIT	CREDIT
20--							

Problem D-1A or D-1B (continued)

ACCOUNT **Purchases Returns and Allowances**   ACCOUNT NO. *512*

DATE	ITEM	POST. REF.	DEBIT	CREDIT	BALANCE DEBIT	BALANCE CREDIT
20--						

ACCOUNT **Purchases Discounts**   ACCOUNT NO. *513*

DATE	ITEM	POST. REF.	DEBIT	CREDIT	BALANCE DEBIT	BALANCE CREDIT
20--						

ACCOUNT **Freight In**   ACCOUNT NO. *514*

DATE	ITEM	POST. REF.	DEBIT	CREDIT	BALANCE DEBIT	BALANCE CREDIT
20--						

ACCOUNT **Salary Expense**   ACCOUNT NO. *621*

DATE	ITEM	POST. REF.	DEBIT	CREDIT	BALANCE DEBIT	BALANCE CREDIT
20--						

ACCOUNT **Payroll Tax Expense**   ACCOUNT NO. *622*

DATE	ITEM	POST. REF.	DEBIT	CREDIT	BALANCE DEBIT	BALANCE CREDIT
20--						

Problem D-1A or D-1B (continued)

ACCOUNT *Supplies Expense*　　　　　　　　　　　　　　ACCOUNT NO. *625*

DATE		ITEM	POST. REF.	DEBIT	CREDIT	BALANCE	
						DEBIT	CREDIT
20--							
Jan.	1	Balance	✓			592.00	

ACCOUNT *Rent Expense*　　　　　　　　　　　　　　ACCOUNT NO. *627*

DATE	ITEM	POST. REF.	DEBIT	CREDIT	BALANCE	
					DEBIT	CREDIT
20--						

ACCOUNT *Miscellaneous Expense*　　　　　　　　　　　ACCOUNT NO. *631*

DATE	ITEM	POST. REF.	DEBIT	CREDIT	BALANCE	
					DEBIT	CREDIT
20--						

Problem D-1A or D-1B (continued)

ACCOUNTS RECEIVABLE LEDGER

NAME   *Bryan Supply*

ADDRESS

DATE	ITEM	POST. REF.	DEBIT	CREDIT	BALANCE
20--					

NAME   *English and Cole*

ADDRESS

DATE	ITEM	POST. REF.	DEBIT	CREDIT	BALANCE
20--					

NAME   *L. Parker*

ADDRESS

DATE	ITEM	POST. REF.	DEBIT	CREDIT	BALANCE
20--					

NAME   *Peterson, Inc.*

ADDRESS

DATE		ITEM	POST. REF.	DEBIT	CREDIT	BALANCE
20--						
Jan.	1	Balance	✓			650.00

NAME   *Vessey Appliance*

ADDRESS

DATE		ITEM	POST. REF.	DEBIT	CREDIT	BALANCE
20--						
Jan.	1	Balance	✓			1,000.00

NAME _____ DATE _____ CLASS _____

Problem D-1A or D-1B (continued)

ACCOUNTS PAYABLE LEDGER

NAME **Crosby Products**

ADDRESS

DATE	ITEM	POST. REF.	DEBIT	CREDIT	BALANCE
20--					

NAME **Duncan Office Supply**

ADDRESS

DATE	ITEM	POST. REF.	DEBIT	CREDIT	BALANCE
20--					

NAME **Franklin and Son**

ADDRESS

DATE		ITEM	POST. REF.	DEBIT	CREDIT	BALANCE
20--						
Jan.	1	Balance	✓			600.00

NAME **Vaughn and Company**

ADDRESS

DATE	ITEM	POST. REF.	DEBIT	CREDIT	BALANCE
20--					

Problem D-1A or D-1B (continued)

ACCOUNT NAME	DEBIT	CREDIT

Problem D-1A or D-1B (concluded)

NAME _____   DATE _____   CLASS _____

Extra Form

GENERAL JOURNAL   PAGE _____

	DATE		DESCRIPTION	POST. REF.	DEBIT	CREDIT	
1							1
2							2
3							3
4							4
5							5
6							6
7							7
8							8
9							9
10							10
11							11
12							12
13							13
14							14
15							15
16							16
17							17
18							18
19							19
20							20
21							21
22							22
23							23
24							24
25							25
26							26
27							27
28							28
29							29
30							30
31							31
32							32
33							33
34							34
35							35
36							36
37							37
38							38
39							39
40							40
41							41
42							42
43							43
44							44
45							45

352

PERFORMANCE OBJECTIVES

1. Prepare an adjustment for supplies.
2. Prepare an adjustment for merchandise inventory under the periodic inventory system.
3. Prepare an adjustment for unearned revenue.
4. Record the adjustment data in a work sheet (including merchandise inventory, unearned revenue, supplies remaining, expired insurance, depreciation, and accrued wages or salaries).
5. Complete the work sheet.
6. Journalize the adjusting entries for a merchandising business under the periodic inventory system.
7. Journalize the adjusting entry for merchandise inventory under the perpetual inventory system.

KEY TERMS

Periodic inventory system
Perpetual inventory system
Physical inventory
Unearned revenue

STUDY GUIDE QUESTIONS

PART 1   True/False

For each of the following statements, indicate T if the statement is true and F if the statement is false.

T   F   1. An actual count of a stock of goods on hand is called a physical inventory.

T   F   2. The first adjustment for Merchandise Inventory is to debit Merchandise Inventory for the amount of the beginning inventory.

T   F   3. The value of the ending Merchandise Inventory appears in the Balance Sheet Credit column of the work sheet.

T   F   4. The balance of the Sales Discounts account appears in the Income Statement Credit column.

T   F   5. Under the periodic inventory system, entries are recorded in the Merchandise Inventory account at the end of the fiscal period only.

T   F   6. When a business receives cash for a product or service that is to be delivered in the future, the Unearned Revenue account is credited.

T   F   7. The balance of the Unearned Revenue account appears in the Balance Sheet Credit column.

| T | F | 8. | In the Balance Sheet columns of the work sheet, Income Summary is shown in two figures. |

| T | F | 9. | The balance of the Purchases Discounts account appears in the Income Statement Credit column. |

| T | F | 10. | If Income Summary has a debit of $80,000 and a credit of $70,000 in the Adjustments columns of the work sheet, these will be combined into a debit of $10,000 in the Income Statement Debit column. |

PART 2   Identifying Work Sheet Columns

Below is a list of selected accounts. Using a check mark, identify the columns in which the balance of each of the accounts would appear.

ACCOUNT NAME	INCOME STATEMENT		BALANCE SHEET	
	DEBIT	CREDIT	DEBIT	CREDIT
0. *Rent Income*		✓		
1. Sales Discounts				
2. C. Carr, Drawing				
3. Supplies Expense				
4. Sales				
5. Merchandise Inventory				
6. Purchases Returns and Allowances				
7. Income Summary				
8. C. Carr, Capital				
9. Accumulated Depreciation, Equipment				
10. Purchases				
11. Sales Returns and Allowances				
12. Purchases Discounts				
13. Unearned Rent				
14. Salaries Payable				

DEMONSTRATION PROBLEM

Office Specialists sells and services copiers and fax machines. The trial balance as of December 31, the end of its fiscal year, is as follows:

Office Specialists
Trial Balance
December 31, 20--

ACCOUNT NAME	DEBIT	CREDIT
Cash	4,000.00	
Merchandise Inventory	151,000.00	
Prepaid Insurance	1,000.00	
Store Equipment	26,000.00	
Accumulated Depreciation, Store Equipment		12,500.00
Accounts Payable		50,000.00
Employees' Income Tax Payable		3,000.00
Payroll Taxes and Employees' Withholding Payable		1,500.00
Unearned Service Contracts		15,000.00
L. Griswald, Capital		44,100.00
L. Griswald, Drawing	60,000.00	
Sales		453,000.00
Service Contract Income		56,000.00
Purchases	280,000.00	
Purchases Discounts		3,800.00
Freight In	3,900.00	
Salary Expense	80,000.00	
Payroll Tax Expense	8,000.00	
Rent Expense	20,000.00	
Supplies Expense	2,000.00	
Miscellaneous Expense	3,000.00	
	638,900.00	638,900.00

The earnings from short-term contracts completed during the year have been recorded in Service Contract Income. Amounts received in advance for longer-term service contracts have been recorded in Unearned Service Contracts. To save space by reducing the number of accounts, we use the account called Payroll Taxes and Employees' Withholding Payable for the FICA and unemployment tax liabilities. Data for the adjustments are as follows:

a–b. Merchandise inventory at December 31, $139,500.
c. Supplies inventory, $1,700.
d. Insurance expired, $600.
e. Salaries accrued, $2,000.
f. Depreciation of store equipment, $5,200.
g. Unearned service contract income now earned, $4,800.

Instructions

Complete the work sheet.

SOLUTION

Office Specialists

Work Sheet

For Year Ended December 31, 20--

	ACCOUNT NAME	TRIAL BALANCE	
		DEBIT	CREDIT
1	Cash	4,000.00	
2	Merchandise Inventory	151,000.00	
3	Prepaid Insurance	1,000.00	
4	Store Equipment	26,000.00	
5	Accumulated Depreciation, Store Equipment		12,500.00
6	Accounts Payable		50,000.00
7	Employees' Income Tax Payable		3,000.00
8	Payroll Taxes and Employees' Withholding Payable		1,500.00
9	Unearned Service Contracts		15,000.00
10	L. Griswald, Capital		44,100.00
11	L. Griswald, Drawing	60,000.00	
12	Sales		453,000.00
13	Service Contract Income		56,000.00
14	Purchases	280,000.00	
15	Purchases Discounts		3,800.00
16	Freight In	3,900.00	
17	Salary Expense	80,000.00	
18	Payroll Tax Expense	8,000.00	
19	Rent Expense	20,000.00	
20	Supplies Expense	2,000.00	
21	Miscellaneous Expense	3,000.00	
22		638,900.00	638,900.00
23	Income Summary		
24	Supplies		
25	Insurance Expense		
26	Salaries Payable		
27	Depreciation Expense, Store Equipment		
28			
29	Net Income		
30			
31			
32			
33			
34			
35			

SOLUTION *(concluded)*

ADJUSTMENTS				INCOME STATEMENT		BALANCE SHEET		
DEBIT		CREDIT		DEBIT	CREDIT	DEBIT	CREDIT	
						4,000.00		1
(b)	139,500.00	(a)	151,000.00			139,500.00		2
		(d)	600.00			400.00		3
						26,000.00		4
		(f)	5,200.00				17,700.00	5
							50,000.00	6
							3,000.00	7
							1,500.00	8
(g)	4,800.00						10,200.00	9
							44,100.00	10
						60,000.00		11
					453,000.00			12
		(g)	4,800.00		60,800.00			13
				280,000.00				14
					3,800.00			15
				3,900.00				16
(e)	2,000.00			82,000.00				17
				8,000.00				18
		(c)	1,700.00	300.00				19
				20,000.00				20
				3,000.00				21
								22
(a)	151,000.00	(b)	139,500.00	151,000.00	139,500.00			23
(c)	1,700.00					1,700.00		24
(d)	600.00			600.00				25
		(e)	2,000.00				2,000.00	26
(f)	5,200.00			5,200.00				27
	304,800.00		304,800.00	554,000.00	657,100.00	231,600.00	128,500.00	28
				103,100.00			103,100.00	29
				657,100.00	657,100.00	231,600.00	231,600.00	30
								31
								32
								33
								34
								35

EXERCISES

Exercise 12-1

GENERAL JOURNAL   PAGE _____ *112* _____

	DATE	DESCRIPTION	POST. REF.	DEBIT	CREDIT	
1						1
2						2
3						3
4						4
5						5
6						6
7						7

Exercise 12-2

a.

GENERAL JOURNAL   PAGE _____

	DATE	DESCRIPTION	POST. REF.	DEBIT	CREDIT	
1						1
2						2
3						3
4						4
5						5
6						6

b. _____

_____

c. _____

_____

Exercise 12-3

Exercise 12-4

Exercise 12-5

a. _____

b. _____

c. _____

d. _____

e. _____

f. _____

g. _____

h. _____

i. _____

j. _____

Exercise 12-6

GENERAL JOURNAL   PAGE ___42___

	DATE	DESCRIPTION	POST. REF.	DEBIT	CREDIT	
1						1
2						2
3						3
4						4
5						5
6						6
7						7
8						8
9						9
10						10
11						11
12						12
13						13
14						14
15						15
16						16
17						17
18						18
19						19
20						20
21						21
22						22
23						23
24						24
25						25
26						26

Exercise 12-7

GENERAL JOURNAL PAGE _____

	DATE		DESCRIPTION	POST. REF.	DEBIT	CREDIT	
1							1
2							2
3							3
4							4
5							5
6							6
7							7
8							8
9							9
10							10
11							11
12							12
13							13
14							14
15							15
16							16
17							17
18							18

Exercise 12-8

GENERAL JOURNAL PAGE _____

	DATE		DESCRIPTION	POST. REF.	DEBIT	CREDIT	
1							1
2							2
3							3
4							4

Problem 12-1A or 12-1B

	ACCOUNT NAME	TRIAL BALANCE	
		DEBIT	CREDIT
1			
2			
3			
4			
5			
6			
7			
8			
9			
10			
11			
12			
13			
14			
15			
16			
17			
18			
19			
20			
21			
22			
23			
24			
25			
26			
27			
28			
29			
30			
31			
32			
33			
34			
35			

Problem 12-1A or 12-1B (concluded)

ADJUSTMENTS		INCOME STATEMENT		BALANCE SHEET		
DEBIT	CREDIT	DEBIT	CREDIT	DEBIT	CREDIT	
						1
						2
						3
						4
						5
						6
						7
						8
						9
						10
						11
						12
						13
						14
						15
						16
						17
						18
						19
						20
						21
						22
						23
						24
						25
						26
						27
						28
						29
						30
						31
						32
						33
						34
						35

Problem 12-2A or 12-2B

	ACCOUNT NAME	TRIAL BALANCE	
		DEBIT	CREDIT
1			
2			
3			
4			
5			
6			
7			
8			
9			
10			
11			
12			
13			
14			
15			
16			
17			
18			
19			
20			
21			
22			
23			
24			
25			
26			
27			
28			
29			
30			
31			
32			
33			
34			
35			

Problem 12-2A or 12-2B (continued)

ADJUSTMENTS		INCOME STATEMENT		BALANCE SHEET		
DEBIT	CREDIT	DEBIT	CREDIT	DEBIT	CREDIT	
						1
						2
						3
						4
						5
						6
						7
						8
						9
						10
						11
						12
						13
						14
						15
						16
						17
						18
						19
						20
						21
						22
						23
						24
						25
						26
						27
						28
						29
						30
						31
						32
						33
						34
						35

Problem 12-2A or 12-2B (concluded)

GENERAL JOURNAL   PAGE _____16_____

	DATE		DESCRIPTION	POST. REF.	DEBIT	CREDIT	
1							1
2							2
3							3
4							4
5							5
6							6
7							7
8							8
9							9
10							10
11							11
12							12
13							13
14							14
15							15
16							16
17							17
18							18
19							19
20							20
21							21
22							22
23							23
24							24
25							25
26							26
27							27
28							28
29							29
30							30
31							31
32							32
33							33
34							34
35							35
36							36
37							37

NOTES AND CALCULATIONS

Problem 12-3A or 12-3B

	ACCOUNT NAME	TRIAL BALANCE	
		DEBIT	CREDIT
1			
2			
3			
4			
5			
6			
7			
8			
9			
10			
11			
12			
13			
14			
15			
16			
17			
18			
19			
20			
21			
22			
23			
24			
25			
26			
27			
28			
29			
30			
31			
32			
33			
34			
35			
36			
37			
38			
39			

Problem 12-3A or 12-3B (continued)

ADJUSTMENTS		INCOME STATEMENT		BALANCE SHEET		
DEBIT	CREDIT	DEBIT	CREDIT	DEBIT	CREDIT	
						1
						2
						3
						4
						5
						6
						7
						8
						9
						10
						11
						12
						13
						14
						15
						16
						17
						18
						19
						20
						21
						22
						23
						24
						25
						26
						27
						28
						29
						30
						31
						32
						33
						34
						35
						36
						37
						38
						39

Problem 12-3A or 12-3B (concluded)

GENERAL JOURNAL   PAGE ____63____

	DATE		DESCRIPTION	POST. REF.	DEBIT	CREDIT	
1							1
2							2
3							3
4							4
5							5
6							6
7							7
8							8
9							9
10							10
11							11
12							12
13							13
14							14
15							15
16							16
17							17
18							18
19							19
20							20
21							21
22							22
23							23
24							24
25							25
26							26
27							27
28							28
29							29
30							30
31							31
32							32
33							33
34							34
35							35
36							36
37							37

Problem 12-4A or 12-4B

1.

GENERAL JOURNAL   41

	DATE		DESCRIPTION	POST. REF.	DEBIT	CREDIT	
1							1
2							2
3							3
4							4
5							5
6							6
7							7
8							8
9							9
10							10
11							11
12							12
13							13
14							14
15							15
13							13
14							14
15							15
16							16
17							17
18							18
19							19
20							20
21							21
22							22
23							23
24							24

2. _____

   _____ $_____

   _____

   _____ $_____

3. _____

   _____ $_____

   _____ $_____

   _____

   _____ $_____

13   Financial Statements, Closing Entries, and Reversing Entries

PERFORMANCE OBJECTIVES

1. Prepare a classified income statement for a merchandising firm.
2. Prepare a classified balance sheet for any type of business.
3. Compute working capital and current ratio.
4. Journalize the closing entries for a merchandising firm.
5. Determine which adjusting entries can be reversed, and journalize the reversing entries.

KEY TERMS

Cost of Goods Sold	Net Income or Net Profit
Current Assets	Net Purchases
Current Liabilities	Net Sales
Current ratio	Notes Receivable (current)
Delivered Cost of Purchases	Property and Equipment
General Expenses	Reversing entries
Gross Profit	Selling Expenses
Liquidity	Temporary-equity accounts
Long-Term Liabilities	Working capital

STUDY GUIDE QUESTIONS

PART 1   True/False

For each of the following statements, indicate T if the statement is true and F if the statement is false.

T   F   1. The cost of goods sold is obtained by subtracting the goods available for sale from the gross sales.

T   F   2. An increase in Sales Returns and Allowances represents a decrease in gross profit.

T   F   3. Gross profit is equal to net sales minus goods available for sale.

T   F   4. Insurance Expense is classified in the Other Expenses section of an income statement.

T   F   5. Freight In is classified in the Operating Expenses section of an income statement.

T   F   6. In the Current Liabilities section of a balance sheet, Accounts Payable precedes Notes Payable.

T   F   7. An unearned revenue account is classified as a current liability.

T   F   8. Reversing entries are required for all adjusting entries.

T   F   9. On a balance sheet, Prepaid Insurance is classified in the Property and Equipment section.

T   F   10. An increase in Rent Expense results in a decrease in gross profit.

PART 2   Completion—Language of Business

Complete each of the following statements by writing the appropriate word(s) in the spaces provided.

1. Current Assets minus Current Liabilities equals _____.

2. Net Sales minus Cost of Goods Sold is _____.

3. Cost of Goods Available for Sale minus ending Merchandise Inventory is called

   _____.

4. Gross Profit minus Operating Expenses is called _____.

5. Gross Purchases minus Purchase Returns and Allowances minus Purchases Discounts

   plus _____ equals Delivered Cost of Purchases.

PART 3   Financial Statement Classifications

Classify the following accounts according to the title of the financial statement and the statement classification. The first two accounts are provided as examples.

ACCOUNT NAME	FINANCIAL STATEMENT	CLASSIFICATION
0. *Example:* Wages Expense	Income Statement	Operating Expenses
0. *Example:* Accounts Payable	Balance Sheet	Current Liabilities
1. Purchases		
2. Accounts Receivable		
3. Building		
4. Freight In		
5. Interest Expense		
6. Supplies Expense		
7. Sales Discounts		
8. Unearned Subscriptions		
9. Accumulated Depreciation, Equipment		
10. Purchases Returns and Allowances		

CHAPTER 13

DEMONSTRATION PROBLEM

Christy's Apparel has a fiscal year extending from January 1 through December 31. Its account balances after adjustments are presented below in random order. The beginning merchandise inventory amounts to $35,870.

Notes Receivable	$ 7,000	Freight In	$ 7,040
Interest Income	5,362	Office Salary Expense	11,119
Building	45,400	Accounts Receivable	46,627
Accounts Payable	25,245	Store Supplies	1,094
Prepaid Insurance	1,090	Interest Expense	2,100
Insurance Expense	2,505	Cash	3,305
Accumulated Depreciation,		Depreciation Expense, Building	1,297
Building	15,133	Purchases Discounts	1,335
Notes Payable	10,250	Accumulated Depreciation,	
Sales	267,111	Store Equipment	10,750
Sales Salary Expense	60,377	Salaries Payable	3,420
Rent Income	2,400	C.P. Bennett, Drawing	60,000
Store Equipment	21,500	Office Equipment	8,875
Mortgage Payable (current		Taxes Expense	4,006
portion is $2,000)	31,000	Accumulated Depreciation,	
Land	10,000	Office Equipment	4,438
Sales Commission Expense	6,400	Miscellaneous General Expense	1,750
Sales Discounts	2,671	Store Supplies Expense	1,918
Merchandise Inventory,		C.P. Bennett, Capital,	
Dec. 31, 20—	41,998	Jan. 1, 20—	110,980
Purchases	133,556	Depreciation Expense, Office	
Advertising Expense	5,342	Equipment	1,775
Sales Returns and Allowances	3,149	Depreciation Expense,	
Purchases Returns and Allowanc	2,642	Store Equipment	4,300

Instructions

1. Prepare a classified income statement and subdivide operating expenses.
2. Prepare a statement of owner's equity.
3. Prepare balance sheet.
4. Determine the amount of working capital and the current ratio.

SOLUTION

1.

Christy's Apparel				
Income Statement				
For Year Ended December 31, 20--				
Revenue from Sales:				
Sales		$267,111.00		
Less: Sales Returns and Allowances	$ 3,149.00			
Sales Discounts	2,671.00	5,820.00		
Net Sales			$261,291.00	
Cost of Goods Sold:				
Merchandise Inventory, January 1, 20--		$ 35,870.00		
Purchases	$133,556.00			
Less: Purchases Returns and				
Allowances	$2,642.00			
Purchases Discounts	1,335.00	3,977.00		
Net Purchases		$129,579.00		
Add Freight In		7,040.00		
Delivered Cost of Purchases			136,619.00	
Cost of Goods Available for Sale			$172,489.00	
Less Merchandise Inventory,				
December 31, 20--			41,998.00	
Cost of Goods Sold				130,491.00
Gross Profit				$130,800.00
Operating Expenses:				
Selling Expenses:				
Sales Salary Expense		$ 60,377.00		
Sales Commission Expense		6,400.00		
Advertising Expense		5,342.00		
Store Supplies Expense		1,918.00		
Depreciation Expense, Store Equipment		4,300.00		
Total Selling Expenses			$ 78,337.00	
General Expenses:				
Insurance Expense		$ 2,505.00		
Office Salary Expense		11,119.00		
Depreciation Expense, Building		1,297.00		
Depreciation Expense, Office Equipment		1,775.00		
Taxes Expense		4,006.00		
Miscellaneous General Expense		1,750.00		
Total General Expenses			22,452.00	
Total Operating Expenses				100,789.00
Income from Operations				$ 30,011.00
Other Income:				
Interest Income			$ 5,362.00	
Rent Income			2,400.00	
Total Other Income			$ 7,762.00	
Other Expenses:				
Interest Expense			2,100.00	5,662.00
Net Income				$ 35,673.00

SOLUTION (continued)

2.

Christy's Apparel
Statement of Owner's Equity
For Year Ended December 31, 20--

C. P. Bennett, Capital, January 1, 20--			$110,980.00
Net Income for the Year		$ 35,673.00	
Less Withdrawals for the Year		60,000.00	
Decrease in Capital			24,327.00
C. P. Bennett, Capital, December 31, 20--			$ 86,653.00

3.

Christy's Apparel
Balance Sheet
December 31, 20--

Assets			
Current Assets:			
Cash		$ 3,305.00	
Notes Receivable		7,000.00	
Accounts Receivable		46,627.00	
Merchandise Inventory		41,998.00	
Store Supplies		1,094.00	
Prepaid Insurance		1,090.00	
Total Current Assets			$101,114.00
Property and Equipment:			
Land		$10,000.00	
Building	$45,400.00		
Less Accumulated Depreciation	15,133.00	30,267.00	
Office Equipment	$ 8,875.00		
Less Accumulated Depreciation	4,438.00	4,437.00	
Store Equipment	$21,500.00		
Less Accumulated Depreciation	10,750.00	10,750.00	
Total Property and Equipment			55,454.00
Total Assets			$156,568.00
Liabilities			
Current Liabilities:			
Notes Payable		$10,250.00	
Mortgage Payable (current portion)		2,000.00	
Accounts Payable		25,245.00	
Salaries Payable		3,420.00	
Total Current Liabilities			$ 40,915.00
Long-Term Liabilities:			
Mortgage Payable			29,000.00
Total Liabilities			$ 69,915.00
Owner's Equity			
C. P. Bennett, Capital			86,653.00
Total Liabilities and Owner's Equity			$156,568.00

SOLUTION *(concluded)*

4.   Working capital   =   Current assets   −   Current liabilities

= $101,114   − $40,915   = $60,199

$$\text{Current ratio} \quad = \quad \frac{\text{Current assets}}{\text{Current liabilities}} \quad = \quad \frac{\$101,114}{\$40,915} \quad = \quad \underline{\underline{2.47}}$$

EXERCISES

Exercise 13-1

a. _____
_____
_____
_____

b. _____
_____
_____
_____

c. _____
_____
_____
_____

Exercise 13-2

Exercise 13-3

a. _____   f. _____
b. _____   g. _____
c. _____   h. _____
d. _____   i. _____
e. _____   j. _____

Exercise 13-4

Exercise 13-5

a. _____ f. _____

b. _____ g. _____

c. _____ h. _____

d. _____ i. _____

e. _____

Exercise 13-6

Current Assets:

_____ $ _____

_____

_____

_____ _____

· Total $ _____

Current Liabilities:

_____ $ _____

_____

_____

_____

Total $ _____

Working capital = _____ − _____ = _____

Current ratio = ———— = _____

Exercise 13-7

GENERAL JOURNAL   PAGE _____

	DATE	DESCRIPTION	POST. REF.	DEBIT	CREDIT	
1						1
2						2
3						3
4						4
5						5
6						6
7						7
8						8
9						9
10						10
11						11
12						12
13						13
14						14
15						15
16						16
17						17
18						18
19						19
20						20
21						21
22						22

Exercise 13-8

GENERAL JOURNAL   PAGE _____

	DATE		DESCRIPTION	POST. REF.	DEBIT	CREDIT	
1							1
2							2
3							3
4							4
5							5
6							6
7							7

Problem 13-1A or 13-1B

Problem 13-1A or 13-1B (concluded)

GENERAL JOURNAL   PAGE ____ _69_

	DATE		DESCRIPTION	POST. REF.	DEBIT	CREDIT	
1							1
2							2
3							3
4							4
5							5
6							6
7							7
8							8
9							9
10							10
11							11
12							12
13							13
14							14
15							15
16							16
17							17
18							18
19							19
20							20
21							21
22							22
23							23
24							24
25							25
26							26
27							27
28							28
29							29
30							30
31							31
32							32
33							33
34							34
35							35
36							36
37							37
38							38
39							39
40							40

Problem 13-2A or 13-2B

Problem 13-2A or 13-2B (concluded)

Working Capital = _____ – _____

_____ – _____ = _____

Current Ratio = ——————————— = ——————————— = ————

Problem 13-3A or 13-3B

GENERAL JOURNAL   PAGE ____ *81* ____

	DATE		DESCRIPTION	POST. REF.	DEBIT	CREDIT	
1							1
2							2
3							3
4							4
5							5
6							6
7							7
8							8
9							9
10							10
11							11
12							12
13							13
14							14
15							15
16							16
17							17
18							18
19							19
20							20
21							21
22							22
23							23
24							24
25							25
26							26
27							27
28							28
29							29
30							30
31							31
32							32
33							33
34							34
35							35
36							36
37							37
38							38
39							39
40							40

Problem 13-3A or 13-3B (concluded)

GENERAL JOURNAL   PAGE _____ *82* _____

	DATE		DESCRIPTION	POST. REF.	DEBIT	CREDIT	
1							1
2							2
3							3
4							4
5							5
6							6
7							7
8							8
9							9
10							10
11							11
12							12
13							13
14							14
15							15
16							16
17							17
18							18
19							19
20							20
21							21
22							22
23							23
24							24
25							25
26							26
27							27
28							28
29							29
30							30
31							31
32							32
33							33
34							34

NAME _____ DATE _____ CLASS _____

Problem 13-4A or 13-4B

	ACCOUNT NAME	TRIAL BALANCE	
		DEBIT	CREDIT
1			
2			
3			
4			
5			
6			
7			
8			
9			
10			
11			
12			
13			
14			
15			
16			
17			
18			
19			
20			
21			
22			
23			
24			
25			
26			
27			
28			
29			
30			
31			
32			
33			
34			
35			
36			
37			
38			

Problem 13-4A or 13-4B (continued)

ADJUSTMENTS		INCOME STATEMENT		BALANCE SHEET		
DEBIT	CREDIT	DEBIT	CREDIT	DEBIT	CREDIT	
						1
						2
						3
						4
						5
						6
						7
						8
						9
						10
						11
						12
						13
						14
						15
						16
						17
						18
						19
						20
						21
						22
						23
						24
						25
						26
						27
						28
						29
						30
						31
						32
						33
						34
						35
						36
						37
						38

Problem 13-4A or 13-4B (continued)

Problem 13-4A or 13-4B (continued)

Problem 13-4A or 13-4B (continued)

GENERAL JOURNAL   PAGE ___76___

	DATE		DESCRIPTION	POST. REF.	DEBIT	CREDIT	
1							1
2							2
3							3
4							4
5							5
6							6
7							7
8							8
9							9
10							10
11							11
12							12
13							13
14							14
15							15
16							16
17							17
18							18
19							19
20							20
21							21
22							22
23							23
24							24
25							25
26							26
27							27
28							28
29							29
30							30
31							31
32							32
33							33
34							34
35							35
36							36
37							37
38							38
39							39
40							40

Problem 13-4A or 13-4B (concluded)

GENERAL JOURNAL   PAGE   77

	DATE		DESCRIPTION	POST. REF.	DEBIT	CREDIT	
1							1
2							2
3							3
4							4
5							5
6							6
7							7
8							8
9							9
10							10
11							11
12							12
13							13
14							14
15							15
16							16
17							17
18							18
19							19
20							20
21							21
22							22
23							23
24							24
25							25
26							26
27							27
28							28
29							29
30							30
31							31
32							32
33							33
34							34
35							35
36							36
37							37
38							38
39							39
40							40

BEFORE A TEST CHECK SOLUTIONS: CHAPTERS 12–13

Part I:

1. _____ 2. _____ 3. _____
4. _____ 5. _____
6. _____ 7. _____ 8. _____
9. _____ 10. _____

Part II: 1. ___ 2. ___ 3. ___ 4. ___ 5. ___ 6. ___ 7. ___ 8. ___ 9. ___ 10. ___

Part III: 1.   GENERAL JOURNAL   PAGE _____

	DATE	DESCRIPTION	POST. REF.	DEBIT	CREDIT	
1						1
2						2
3						3
4						4
5						5
6						6
7						7

2.   GENERAL JOURNAL   PAGE _____

	DATE	DESCRIPTION	POST. REF.	DEBIT	CREDIT	
1						1
2						2
3						3
4						4
5						5

BEFORE A TEST CHECK SOLUTIONS (concluded)

3.

GENERAL JOURNAL   PAGE _____

	DATE	DESCRIPTION	POST. REF.	DEBIT	CREDIT	
1						1
2						2
3						3
4						4
5						5
6						6
7						7
8						8
9						9
10						10
11						11
12						12

4.   a. _____

        _____

        _____

    b. _____ =

Extra Form

GENERAL JOURNAL   PAGE _____

	DATE		DESCRIPTION	POST. REF.	DEBIT	CREDIT	
1							1
2							2
3							3
4							4
5							5
6							6
7							7
8							8
9							9
10							10
11							11
12							12
13							13
14							14
15							15
16							16
17							17
18							18
19							19
20							20
21							21
22							22
23							23
24							24
25							25
26							26
27							27
28							28
29							29
30							30
31							31
32							32
33							33
34							34
35							35
36							36
37							37
38							38
39							39
40							40

COMPREHENSIVE REVIEW PROBLEM

SALES JOURNAL   PAGE ___56___

	DATE	INV. NO.	CUSTOMER'S NAME	POST. REF.	ACCOUNTS RECEIVABLE DEBIT SALES CREDIT	
1						1
2						2
3						3
4						4
5						5
6						6
7						7
8						8

PURCHASES JOURNAL   PAGE ___62___

	DATE	SUPPLIER'S NAME	INV. NO.	INV. DATE	TERMS	POST. REF.	ACCOUNTS PAYABLE CREDIT	FREIGHT IN DEBIT	PURCHASES DEBIT	
1										1
2										2
3										3
4										4
5										5
6										6
7										7
8										8

COMPREHENSIVE REVIEW PROBLEM (continued)

CASH RECEIPTS JOURNAL   PAGE   *69*

	DATE		ACCOUNT CREDITED	POST. REF.	OTHER ACCOUNTS CREDIT	ACCOUNTS RECEIVABLE CREDIT	SALES CREDIT	CASH DEBIT	
1									1
2									2
3									3
4									4
5									5
6									6
7									7
8									8
9									9
10									10
11									11
12									12
13									13
14									14

COMPREHENSIVE REVIEW PROBLEM (continued)

CASH PAYMENTS JOURNAL   PAGE ___75___

	DATE	CK. NO.	ACCOUNT NAME	POST. REF.	OTHER ACCOUNTS DEBIT	ACCOUNTS PAYABLE DEBIT	PURCHASES DISCOUNTS CREDIT	CASH CREDIT	
1									1
2									2
3									3
4									4
5									5
6									6
7									7
8									8
9									9
10									10
11									11
12									12
13									13
14									14
15									15
16									16
17									17
18									18
19									19
20									20
21									21
22									22
23									23
24									24

COMPREHENSIVE REVIEW PROBLEM (continued)

GENERAL JOURNAL   PAGE _____89_____

	DATE	DESCRIPTION	POST. REF.	DEBIT	CREDIT	
1						1
2						2
3						3
4						4
5						5
6						6
7						7
8						8
9						9
10						10
11						11
12						12
13						13
14						14
15						15
16						16
17						17
18						18
19						19
20						20
21						21
22						22
23						23
24						24
25						25
26						26
27						27
28						28
29						29
30						30
31						31
32						32
33						33
34						34
35						35
36						36
37						37
38						38
39						39
40						40

COMPREHENSIVE REVIEW PROBLEM (continued)

GENERAL JOURNAL   PAGE ___90___

	DATE		DESCRIPTION	POST. REF.	DEBIT	CREDIT	
1							1
2							2
3							3
4							4
5							5
6							6
7							7
8							8
9							9
10							10
11							11
12							12
13							13
14							14
15							15
16							16

GENERAL JOURNAL   PAGE ___91___

	DATE		DESCRIPTION	POST. REF.	DEBIT	CREDIT	
1							1
2							2
3							3
4							4
5							5
6							6
7							7
8							8
9							9
10							10
11							11
12							12
13							13
14							14
15							15
16							16
17							17
18							18
19							19
20							20

COMPREHENSIVE REVIEW PROBLEM (continued)

GENERAL JOURNAL   PAGE ___92___

	DATE		DESCRIPTION	POST. REF.	DEBIT	CREDIT	
1							1
2							2
3							3
4							4
5							5
6							6
7							7
8							8
9							9
10							10
11							11
12							12
13							13
14							14
15							15
16							16
17							17
18							18
19							19
20							20
21							21
22							22
23							23
24							24
25							25
26							26
27							27
28							28
29							29
30							30
31							31
32							32
33							33
34							34
35							35
36							36
37							37
38							38
39							39
40							40

COMPREHENSIVE REVIEW PROBLEM (continued)
ACCOUNTS RECEIVABLE LEDGER

ACCOUNT *Hotel Bentnor*

ADDRESS *4600 Beaumont Drive*

Dallas, TX 75294

DATE		ITEM	POST. REF.	DEBIT	CREDIT	BALANCE

ACCOUNT *Jerome and Woods*

ADDRESS *1420 Favela Road*

Dallas, TX 75294

DATE		ITEM	POST. REF.	DEBIT	CREDIT	BALANCE
20--						
Feb.	1	Balance	✓			11,619.50

ACCOUNT *Wilkes Decorators*

ADDRESS *642 Guthrie St.*

Dallas, TX 75294

DATE		ITEM	POST. REF.	DEBIT	CREDIT	BALANCE
20--						
Feb.	1	Balance	✓			4,920.14

COMPREHENSIVE REVIEW PROBLEM (continued)

ACCOUNTS PAYABLE LEDGER

ACCOUNT *Byran, Inc.*
ADDRESS *400 W. Tatum St.*
Amarillo, TX 79177

DATE		ITEM	POST. REF.	DEBIT	CREDIT	BALANCE

ACCOUNT. *Keller Textiles*
ADDRESS *1464 Harding Drive*
Dallas, TX 75294

DATE		ITEM	POST. REF.	DEBIT	CREDIT	BALANCE
20--						
Feb.	1	Balance	✓			17,624.10

ACCOUNT *Meldon Fabrics*
ADDRESS *620 W. Huber St.*
Corpus Christi, TX 78487

DATE		ITEM	POST. REF.	DEBIT	CREDIT	BALANCE
20--						
Feb.	1	Balance	✓			9,616.00

ACCOUNT *Taylor Manufacturing Company*
ADDRESS *842 N. Howard Ave.*
Fort Worth, TX 76196

DATE		ITEM	POST. REF.	DEBIT	CREDIT	BALANCE
20--						
Feb.	1	Balance	✓			12,710.00

NAME _____   DATE _____   CLASS _____

COMPREHENSIVE REVIEW PROBLEM (continued)

GENERAL LEDGER

ACCOUNT __Cash__   ACCOUNT NO. __111__

DATE		ITEM	POST. REF.	DEBIT	CREDIT	BALANCE DEBIT	BALANCE CREDIT
20--							
Feb.	1	Balance	✓			36,510.50	

ACCOUNT __Petty Cash Fund__   ACCOUNT NO. __112__

DATE		ITEM	POST. REF.	DEBIT	CREDIT	BALANCE DEBIT	BALANCE CREDIT
20--							
Feb.	1	Balance	✓			70.00	

ACCOUNT __Accounts Receivable__   ACCOUNT NO. __113__

DATE		ITEM	POST. REF.	DEBIT	CREDIT	BALANCE DEBIT	BALANCE CREDIT
20--							
Feb.	1	Balance	✓			16,539.64	

ACCOUNT __Merchandise Inventory__   ACCOUNT NO. __114__

DATE		ITEM	POST. REF.	DEBIT	CREDIT	BALANCE DEBIT	BALANCE CREDIT
20--							
Feb.	1	Balance	✓			52,640.00	

ACCOUNT __Prepaid Insurance__   ACCOUNT NO. __118__

DATE		ITEM	POST. REF.	DEBIT	CREDIT	BALANCE DEBIT	BALANCE CREDIT
20--							
Feb.	1	Balance	✓			480.00	

COMPREHENSIVE REVIEW PROBLEM (continued)

ACCOUNT _Equipment_ ACCOUNT NO. _122_

DATE		ITEM	POST. REF.	DEBIT	CREDIT	BALANCE	
						DEBIT	CREDIT
20--							
Feb.	1	Balance	✓			9,324.00	

ACCOUNT **Accumulated Depreciation, Equipment** ACCOUNT NO. _123_

DATE		ITEM	POST. REF.	DEBIT	CREDIT	BALANCE	
						DEBIT	CREDIT
20--							
Feb.	1	Balance	✓				5,328.00

ACCOUNT **Accounts Payable** ACCOUNT NO. _221_

DATE		ITEM	POST. REF.	DEBIT	CREDIT	BALANCE	
						DEBIT	CREDIT
20--							
Feb.	1	Balance	✓				39,950.10

ACCOUNT **Employees' Income Tax Payable** ACCOUNT NO. _226_

DATE		ITEM	POST. REF.	DEBIT	CREDIT	BALANCE	
						DEBIT	CREDIT
20--							
Feb.	1	Balance	✓				1,391.60

ACCOUNT **FICA Tax Payable** ACCOUNT NO. _227_

DATE		ITEM	POST. REF.	DEBIT	CREDIT	BALANCE	
						DEBIT	CREDIT
20--							
Feb.	1	Balance	✓				1,520.84

COMPREHENSIVE REVIEW PROBLEM (continued)

ACCOUNT *State Unemployment Tax Payable* ACCOUNT NO. 228

DATE		ITEM	POST. REF.	DEBIT	CREDIT	BALANCE DEBIT	BALANCE CREDIT
20--							
Feb.	1	Balance	✓				536.76

ACCOUNT *Federal Unemployment Tax Payable* ACCOUNT NO. 229

DATE		ITEM	POST. REF.	DEBIT	CREDIT	BALANCE DEBIT	BALANCE CREDIT
20--							
Feb.	1	Balance	✓				79.52

ACCOUNT *Salaries Payable* ACCOUNT NO. 230

DATE		ITEM	POST. REF.	DEBIT	CREDIT	BALANCE DEBIT	BALANCE CREDIT
20--							
Feb.	1	Balance	✓				710.00

ACCOUNT *J. L. Fisher, Capital* ACCOUNT NO. 311

DATE		ITEM	POST. REF.	DEBIT	CREDIT	BALANCE DEBIT	BALANCE CREDIT
20--							
Feb.	1	Balance	✓				66,047.32

COMPREHENSIVE REVIEW PROBLEM (continued)

ACCOUNT *J. L. Fisher, Drawing*   ACCOUNT NO. *312*

DATE		ITEM	POST. REF.	DEBIT	CREDIT	BALANCE	
						DEBIT	CREDIT

ACCOUNT *Income Summary*   ACCOUNT NO. *313*

DATE		ITEM	POST. REF.	DEBIT	CREDIT	BALANCE	
						DEBIT	CREDIT

ACCOUNT *Sales*   ACCOUNT NO. *411*

DATE		ITEM	POST. REF.	DEBIT	CREDIT	BALANCE	
						DEBIT	CREDIT

ACCOUNT *Sales Returns and Allowances*   ACCOUNT NO. *412*

DATE		ITEM	POST. REF.	DEBIT	CREDIT	BALANCE	
						DEBIT	CREDIT

ACCOUNT *Purchases*   ACCOUNT NO. *511*

DATE		ITEM	POST. REF.	DEBIT	CREDIT	BALANCE	
						DEBIT	CREDIT

COMPREHENSIVE REVIEW PROBLEM (continued)

ACCOUNT _Purchases Returns and Allowances_ ACCOUNT NO. _512_

DATE	ITEM	POST. REF.	DEBIT	CREDIT	BALANCE	
					DEBIT	CREDIT

ACCOUNT _Purchases Discounts_ ACCOUNT NO. _513_

DATE	ITEM	POST. REF.	DEBIT	CREDIT	BALANCE	
					DEBIT	CREDIT

ACCOUNT _Freight In_ ACCOUNT NO. _514_

DATE	ITEM	POST. REF.	DEBIT	CREDIT	BALANCE	
					DEBIT	CREDIT

ACCOUNT _Salary Expense_ ACCOUNT NO. _611_

DATE	ITEM	POST. REF.	DEBIT	CREDIT	BALANCE	
					DEBIT	CREDIT

ACCOUNT _Payroll Tax Expense_ ACCOUNT NO. _612_

DATE	ITEM	POST. REF.	DEBIT	CREDIT	BALANCE	
					DEBIT	CREDIT

COMPREHENSIVE REVIEW PROBLEM (continued)

ACCOUNT *Rent Expense*   ACCOUNT NO. *613*

DATE	ITEM	POST. REF.	DEBIT	CREDIT	BALANCE	
					DEBIT	CREDIT

ACCOUNT *Utilities Expense*   ACCOUNT NO. *614*

DATE	ITEM	POST. REF.	DEBIT	CREDIT	BALANCE	
					DEBIT	CREDIT

ACCOUNT *Supplies Expense*   ACCOUNT NO. *616*

DATE	ITEM	POST. REF.	DEBIT	CREDIT	BALANCE	
					DEBIT	CREDIT

ACCOUNT *Insurance Expense*   ACCOUNT NO. *617*

DATE	ITEM	POST. REF.	DEBIT	CREDIT	BALANCE	
					DEBIT	CREDIT

ACCOUNT *Depreciation Expense, Equipment*   ACCOUNT NO. *618*

DATE	ITEM	POST. REF.	DEBIT	CREDIT	BALANCE	
					DEBIT	CREDIT

COMPREHENSIVE REVIEW PROBLEM (continued)

ACCOUNT *Miscellaneous Expense*   ACCOUNT NO. *619*

DATE		ITEM	POST. REF.	DEBIT	CREDIT	BALANCE	
						DEBIT	CREDIT

COMPREHENSIVE REVIEW PROBLEM (continued)

Fine Fabrics

Schedule of Accounts Receivable

February 28, 20--

COMPREHENSIVE REVIEW PROBLEM (continued)

Fine Fabrics

Schedule of Accounts Payable

February 28, 20--

COMPREHENSIVE REVIEW PROBLEM (continued)

Fine Fabrics

Work Sheet

For Month Ended February 28, 20--

	ACCOUNT NAME	TRIAL BALANCE	
		DEBIT	CREDIT
1	Cash		
2	Petty Cash Fund		
3	Accounts Receivable		
4	Merchandise Inventory		
5	Prepaid Insurance		
6	Equipment		
7	Accumulated Depreciation, Equipment		
8	Accounts Payable		
9	Employees' Income Tax Payable		
10	FICA Tax Payable		
11	State Unemployment Tax Payable		
12	Federal Unemployment Tax Payable		
13	J. L. Fisher, Capital		
14	J. L. Fisher, Drawing		
15	Sales		
16	Sales Returns and Allowances		
17	Purchases		
18	Purchases Returns and Allowances		
19	Purchases Discounts		
20	Freight In		
21	Salary Expense		
22	Payroll Tax Expense		
23	Rent Expense		
24	Utilities Expense		
25	Supplies Expense		
26	Miscellaneous Expense		
27			
28			
29			
30			
31			
32			
33			
34			
35			
36			
37			
38			

COMPREHENSIVE REVIEW PROBLEM (continued)

ADJUSTMENTS		INCOME STATEMENT		BALANCE SHEET		
DEBIT	CREDIT	DEBIT	CREDIT	DEBIT	CREDIT	
						1
						2
						3
						4
						5
						6
						7
						8
						9
						10
						11
						12
						13
						14
						15
						16
						17
						18
						19
						20
						21
						22
						23
						24
						25
						26
						27
						28
						29
						30
						31
						32
						33
						34
						35
						36
						37
						38

COMPREHENSIVE REVIEW PROBLEM (continued)

Fine Fabrics
Income Statement
For Month Ended February 28, 20--

COMPREHENSIVE REVIEW PROBLEM (continued)

Fine Fabrics
Statement of Owner's Equity
For Month Ended February 28, 20--

COMPREHENSIVE REVIEW PROBLEM (continued)

Fine Fabrics

Balance Sheet

February 28, 20--

COMPREHENSIVE REVIEW PROBLEM (continued)

Fine Fabrics

Post-Closing Trial Balance

February 28, 20--

ACCOUNT NAME	DEBIT	CREDIT

COMPREHENSIVE REVIEW PROBLEM (continued)

PAYROLL REGISTER FOR SEMIMONTHLY ENDED _____

	NAME	TOTAL HOURS	BEGINNING CUMULATIVE EARNINGS	TOTAL EARNINGS	ENDING CUMULATIVE EARNINGS	TAXABLE EARNINGS		
						UNEMPLOY-MENT	SOCIAL SECURITY	MEDICARE
1		40	5,460.00					
2		40	4,480.00					
3			9,940.00					
4								
5								

PAYROLL REGISTER FOR SEMIMONTHLY ENDED _____

	NAME	TOTAL HOURS	BEGINNING CUMULATIVE EARNINGS	TOTAL EARNINGS	ENDING CUMULATIVE EARNINGS	TAXABLE EARNINGS		
						UNEMPLOY-MENT	SOCIAL SECURITY	MEDICARE
1		40						
2		40						
3								
4								
5								

COMPREHENSIVE REVIEW PROBLEM (concluded)

(continuation of PAYROLL REGISTER)   PAGE _____12_____

| DEDUCTIONS | | | | PAYMENTS | | SALARY EXPENSE DEBIT | |
INCOME TAX	SOCIAL SECURITY TAX	MEDICARE TAX	TOTAL	NET AMOUNT	CK. NO.		
							1
							2
							3
							4
							5

(continuation of PAYROLL REGISTER)   PAGE _____13_____

| DEDUCTIONS | | | | PAYMENTS | | SALARY EXPENSE DEBIT | |
INCOME TAX	SOCIAL SECURITY TAX	MEDICARE TAX	TOTAL	NET AMOUNT	CK. NO.		
							1
							2
							3
							4
							5

APPENDIX E

Problem E-1

_____   cu. yds. @ _____ per cu. yd. =
_____   cu. yds. @ _____ per cu. yd. =
_____   cu. yds. @ _____ per cu. yd. =
_____   cu. yds. @ _____ per cu. yd. = _____
_____   =========

                                          average cost per cu. yd. (rounded)
                         _____ cu. yds.   ) _____

                         _____ cu. yds.   x   _____   = _____

Problem E-2

           cu. yds. @ _____ per cu. yd. =
_____ cu. yds. @ _____ per cu. yd. = _____
_____ cu. yds.
=======   =========

Problem E-3

_____ cu. yds. @ _____ per cu. yd. = =========

APPENDIX F

Problem F-1

1. *Gross Profit % (2008)* = —————— = —————— = ——————

    Gross Profit % (2007) = —————— = —————— = ——————

2. *Net Income % (2008)* = —————— = —————— = ——————

    Net Income % (2007) = —————— = —————— = ——————

Problem F-2

Average Merchandise Inventory (2008) = ——————— + ——————— = ——————

Merchandise Inventory Turnover (2008) = —————— = **times per year**

Average Merchandise Inventory (2007) = ——————— + ——————— = ——————

Merchandise Inventory Turnover (2007) = —————— = **times per year**

Problem F-3

Average Capital (2008) = ——————— + ——————— = ——————

Return on Investment (2008) = —————— = —————— = ——————

Average Capital (2007) = ——————— + ——————— = ——————

Return on Investment (2007) = —————— = —————— = ——————

APPENDIX G

Problem G-1

APPENDIX G (continued)

Problem G-2

APPENDIX G (concluded)

Problem G-3

Answers to Study Guide Questions

CHAPTER 1

PART 1   True/False

1. T
2. F
3. F
4. T
5. T

6. T
7. T
8. T
9. T
10. T

PART 2   Completion—Language of Business

1. sole proprietorship
2. liabilities
3. creditor
4. accounts
5. transaction
6. capital
7. fundamental accounting equation
8. chart of accounts
9. equity
10. Revenue
11. withdrawal
12. Accounts Receivable
13. Expenses

PART 3   Classifying Accounts

Assets
Office Equipment
Building
Cash
Land
Prepaid Insurance
Neon Sign

Liabilities
Accounts Payable
Mortgage Payable

Owner's Equity
S. Acevedo, Capital
S. Acevedo, Drawing

Revenue
Income from Services

Expenses
Supplies Expense
Rent Expense
Wages Expense

PART 4   Analyzing Transactions

0. *Example:* Owner invested cash
1. Payment of rent
2. Sales of services for cash
3. Investment of equipment by owner
4. Payment of insurance premium for two years
5. Payment of wages
6. Sales of services on account
7. Withdrawal of cash by owner
8. Purchase of supplies on account
9. Collection from charge customer previously billed
10. Payment made to creditor on account

A	L	OE	R	E
+		+		
−				+
+			+	
+		+		
+ −				
−				+
+			+	
−		−		
	+			+
+ −				
−	−			

CHAPTER 2

PART 1   True/False

1. F	6. F
2. T	7. F
3. T	8. T
4. F	9. T
5. T	10. F

PART 2   Completion—Language of Business

1. debit
2. footings
3. transposition
4. trial balance
5. compound entry
6. credit

PART 3   Accounting Entries

Professional Equipment

+	−
(a) 560	

Accounts Payable

−	+
	(a) 560

Accounts Receivable

+	−
(b) 870	

Professional Fees

−	+
	(b) 870

Rent Expense

+	−
(c) 1,000	

Cash

+	−
	(c) 1,000

Supplies Expense

+	−
(d) 220	

Accounts Payable

−	+
	(d) 220

Utilities Expense

+	−
(e) 110	

Cash

+	−
	(e) 110

Cash

+	−
(f) 920	

Accounts Receivable

+	−
	(f) 920

Accounts Payable

−	+
(g) 700	

Cash

+	−
	(g) 700

Salary Expense

+	−
(h) 900	

Cash

+	−
	(h) 900

Office Equipment

+	−
(i) 452	

Cash

+	−
	(i) 452

CHAPTER 3

PART 1   True/False

1. F
2. F
3. F
4. F
5. T

6. T
7. F
8. F
9. T
10. F

PART 2   Completion—Language of Business

1. general ledger
2. posting
3. source documents
4. cost principle
5. journalizing
6. Post. Ref. column of the journal
7. account numbers

PART 3   Completing a Journal Entry

GENERAL JOURNAL   PAGE ___33___

	DATE		DESCRIPTION	POST. REF.	DEBIT	CREDIT	
1	20—						1
2	Oct.	29	Cash	111	1,100.00		2
3			Accounts Receivable	113	600.00		3
4			Income from Services	411		1,700.00	4
5			Received partial payment for				5
6			services performed.				6
7							7
8							8

1. $600 ($1,700 − $1,100)
2. $2,800 ($600 + $1,100 + $1,100)
3. $1,300 ($700 + $400 + $200)
4. compound

CHAPTER 4

PART 1 True/False

1.	T	6.	T
2.	F	7.	T
3.	T	8.	F
4.	T	9.	T
5.	T	10.	F

PART 2 Completion—Language of Business

1.	book value	6.	accounting cycle
2.	fiscal period	7.	mixed account
3.	contra	8.	matching principle
4.	adjustments	9.	depreciation
5.	accrued wages		

PART 3 Adjusting Entries

1.

Prepaid Insurance		Insurance Expense	
Bal. 950	Adj. 510	Adj. 510	

2.

Accumulated Depreciation, Equipment		Depreciation Expense, Equipment	
	Bal. 7,500	Adj. 2,500	
	Adj. 2,500		

3.

Wages Expense		Wages Payable	
Bal. 8,100			Adj. 470
Adj. 470			

PART 4   Analyzing the Work Sheet

ACCOUNT NAME	TRIAL BALANCE		ADJUSTMENTS		ADJUSTED TRIAL BALANCE		INCOME STATEMENT		BALANCE SHEET	
	DEBIT	CREDIT	DEBIT	CREDIT.	DEBIT	CREDIT	DEBIT	CREDIT	DEBIT	CREDIT
0. Equipment	X				X				X	
1. Cash	X				X				X	
2. C. Tumi, Capital		X				X				X
3. Advertising Expense	X				X		X			
4. Accounts Receivable	X				X				X	
5. Wages Expense	X		X		X		X			
6. Accumulated Depreciation, Equipment		X		X		X				X
7. Wages Payable				X		X				X
8. C. Tumi, Drawing	X				X				X	
9. Service Revenue		X				X		X		
10. Depreciation Expense, Equipment			X		X		X			

CHAPTER 5

PART 1   True/False

1.	F	6.	F
2.	T	7.	T
3.	T	8.	F
4.	F	9.	T
5.	F	10.	T

PART 2   Completion—Language of Business

1. post-closing trial balance
2. real or permanent
3. interim
4. Income Summary
5. closing
6. nominal or temporary-equity
7. accrual basis
8. modified cash basis

PART 3   Closing Entries

	Debit	Credit
1.	b	d
2.	d	a, f
3.	d	e
4.	e	c

PART 4   Posting Closing Entries

1. $41,000
2. $46,000
3. $5,000 net loss ($46,000 − $41,000)
4. $22,000
5. J. See, Capital; Income Summary
6. J. See, Capital; J. See, Drawing
7. $27,000 decrease ($22,000 + $5,000 net loss)
8. $123,000 ($150,000 − $27,000)

CHAPTER 6

PART 1   True/False

1. F
2. F
3. T
4. T
5. T

6. F
7. T
8. T
9. T
10. F

PART 2   Chart of Accounts

Assets
Cash
Prepaid Insurance
Equipment
Accumulated Depreciation, Equipment
Truck
Accumulated Depreciation, Truck

Liabilities
Accounts Payable

Owner's Equity
L. Barrett, Capital
L. Barrett, Drawing

Revenue
Income from Services

Expenses
Salary Expense
Rent Expense
Advertising Expense
Utilities Expense
Supplies Expense
Insurance Expense
Depreciation Expense, Equipment
Depreciation Expense, Truck
Miscellaneous Expense

PART 3   Combined Journal

Cash Debit and Credit
Other Accounts Debit and Credit
Income from Services Credit
Accounts Payable Debit and Credit
Advertising Expense Debit
Miscellaneous Expense Debit

CHAPTER 7
PART 1 True/False

1. F	6. T
2. T	7. T
3. T	8. F
4. T	9. T
5. T	10. F

PART 2 Completion—Language of Business

1. drawer
2. service charge
3. endorsement
4. denominations
5. canceled checks
6. restrictive endorsement
7. payee
8. ledger balance of cash
9. deposit in transit
10. change fund
11. qualified endorsement
12. bank reconciliation
13. Outstanding checks
14. blank endorsement

PART 3 Reimbursing the Petty Cash Fund

Balance of the Petty Cash Fund, $60

GENERAL JOURNAL   PAGE _____

	DATE		DESCRIPTION	POST. REF.	DEBIT	CREDIT	
1	20—						1
2	June	30	Repair Expense		7.10		2
3			Delivery Expense		4.20		3
4			Miscellaneous Expense		16.48		4
5			H. Ball, Drawing		11.50		5
6			Cash			39.28	6
7			Issued Ck. No. 711 to reimburse				7
8			the petty cash fund.				8
9							9

CHAPTER 8

PART 1   True/False

1.	T	6.	T
2.	F	7.	F
3.	F	8.	F
4.	F	9.	T
5.	T	10.	F

PART 2   Completion—Language of Business

1. gross pay
2. employee
3. exemption
4. net pay
5. independent contractor
6. individual earnings record

PART 3   Calculation of Earnings

Employee's Name	Hours Worked	Regular Hourly Rate	Total Earnings
A. L. Gordon	43	$ 7.60	$338.20
L. A. Larson	47	9.40	474.70
C. W. Neilson	49	11.20	599.20

PART 4   Payroll Entry

GENERAL JOURNAL   PAGE ___79___

	DATE		DESCRIPTION	POST. REF.	DEBIT	CREDIT	
1	20—						1
2	Mar.	14	Sales Salary Expense		72,000.00		2
3			Office Salary Expense		21,640.00		3
4			Employees' Federal Income Tax Payable			9,300.00	4
5			FICA Tax Payable			7,163.46	5
6			Employees' U.S. Savings Bond Deductions				6
7			Payable			900.00	7
8			Employees' Union Dues Payable			1,200.00	8
9			Employees' Medical Insurance Payable			2,000.00	9
10			Salaries Payable			73,076.54	10
11			To record payroll for the week				11
12			ended March 14.				12
13							13

CHAPTER 9
PART 1   True/False

1.	F	6.	T
2.	F	7.	F
3.	T	8.	T
4.	F	9.	T
5.	T	10.	F

PART 2   Completion—Language of Business

1. quarter
2. Form W-2
3. employer identification number
4. Payroll Tax Expense
5. Workers' compensation insurance
6. W-3
7. Form 941

PART 3   Completing Form W-2

a Control number	22222	OMB No. 1545-0000		
b Employer identification number (EIN) 72-1162127		**1** Wages, tips, other compensation 34,218.42		**2** Federal income tax withheld 3,716.22
c Employer's name, address, and ZIP code		**3** Social security wages 34,218.42		**4** Social security tax withheld 2,121.54
Benson Company 1620 Hampton Place Boston, MA 02116		**5** Medicare wages and tips 34,218.42		**6** Medicare tax withheld 496.17
		7 Social security tips		**8** Allocated tips
d Employee's social security number 562-25-6329		**9** Advance EIC payment		**10** Dependent care benefits
e Employee's first name and initial Last name Suff.		**11** Nonqualified plans		**12a**
Jane C. Parker		**13** Statutory employee Retirement plan Third-party sick pay		**12b**
2219 Henderson Street Boston, MA 02121		**14** Other		**12c**
				12d
f Employee's address and ZIP code				

15 State Employer's state ID number MA 42-6916	**16** State wages, tips, etc. 34,218.42	**17** State income tax 1,780.04	**18** Local wages, tips, etc.	**19** Local income tax	**20** Locality name

Form **W-2** Wage and Tax Statement   20___

Copy 1—For State, City, or Local Tax Department

Department of the Treasury—Internal Revenue Service

CHAPTER 10

SALES JOURNAL

PART 1   True/False

1. T
2. F
3. T
4. F
5. F

6. F
7. F
8. F
9. T
10. F

PART 2   Completion—Language of Business

1. sales journal
2. merchandise inventory
3. special journals

4. controlling account
5. subsidiary ledger
6. credit memorandum

PURCHASES JOURNAL

PART 1   True/False

1. F
2. T
3. F
4. T
5. F

6. F
7. F
8. F
9. T
10. T

PART 2   Completion—Language of Business

1. purchase order
2. FOB shipping point
3. internal controls

4. invoice
5. credit memorandum
6. FOB destination

CHAPTER 11

PART 1 True/False

1.	T	6.	F
2.	F	7.	F
3.	F	8.	T
4.	T	9.	T
5.	F	10.	T

PART 2 Completion—Language of Business

1. trade discounts
2. credit period
3. cash discount

PART 3 Matching

1.	P	6.	J
2.	CR	7.	J
3.	CP	8.	CP
4.	CR	9.	S
5.	J	10.	CP

PART 4 Cash Receipts Journal

Other Accounts Credit
Accounts Receivable Credit
Sales Credit
Sales Discounts Debit
Cash Debit

CHAPTER 12

PART 1   True/False

1.	T	6.	T
2.	F	7.	T
3.	F	8.	F
4.	F	9.	T
5.	T	10.	F

PART 2   Identifying Work Sheet Columns

ACCOUNT NAME	INCOME STATEMENT DEBIT	INCOME STATEMENT CREDIT	BALANCE SHEET DEBIT	BALANCE SHEET CREDIT
0. *Rent Income*		✓		
1. Sales Discounts	✓			
2. C. Carr, Drawing			✓	
3. Supplies Expense	✓			
4. Sales		✓		
5. Merchandise Inventory	✓	✓	✓	
6. Purchases Returns and Allowances		✓		
7. Income Summary	✓	✓		
8. C. Carr, Capital				✓
9. Accumulated Depreciation, Equipment				✓
10. Purchases	✓			
11. Sales Returns and Allowances	✓			
12. Purchases Discounts		✓		
13. Unearned Rent				✓
14. Salaries Payable				✓

CHAPTER 13

PART 1   True/False

1.	F	6.	F
2.	T	7.	T
3.	F	8.	F
4.	F	9.	F
5.	F	10.	F

PART 2   Completion—Language of Business

1. Working Capital
2. Gross Profit
3. Cost of Goods Sold
4. Income from Operations
5. Freight In

PART 3   Financial Statement Classifications

	Account Name	Financial Statement	Classification
0.	*Example:* Wages Expense	Income Statement	Operating Expenses
0.	*Example:* Accounts Payable	Balance Sheet	Current Liabilities
1.	Purchases	Income Statement	Cost of Goods Sold
2.	Accounts Receivable	Balance Sheet	Current Assets
3.	Building	Balance Sheet	Property and Equipment
4.	Freight In	Income Statement	Cost of Goods Sold
5.	Interest Expense	Income Statement	Other Expenses
6.	Supplies Expense	Income Statement	Operating Expenses
7.	Sales Discounts	Income Statement	Revenue from Sales
8.	Unearned Subscriptions	Balance Sheet	Current Liabilities
9.	Accumulated Depreciation, Equipment	Balance Sheet	Property and Equipment
10.	Purchases Returns and Allowances	Income Statement	Cost of Goods Sold

NAME _____ DATE _____ CLASS _____

GENERAL JOURNAL

PAGE _____

	DATE		DESCRIPTION	POST. REF.	DEBIT	CREDIT	
1							1
2							2
3							3
4							4
5							5
6							6
7							7
8							8
9							9
10							10
11							11
12							12
13							13
14							14
15							15
16							16
17							17
18							18
19							19
20							20
21							21
22							22
23							23
24							24
25							25
26							26
27							27
28							28
29							29
30							30
31							31
32							32
33							33
34							34
35							35
36							36
37							37
38							38
39							39
40							40
41							41
42							42
43							43
44							44
45							45

GENERAL JOURNAL   PAGE _____

	DATE		DESCRIPTION	POST. REF.	DEBIT	CREDIT	
1							1
2							2
3							3
4							4
5							5
6							6
7							7
8							8
9							9
10							10
11							11
12							12
13							13
14							14
15							15
16							16
17							17
18							18
19							19
20							20
21							21
22							22
23							23
24							24
25							25
26							26
27							27
28							28
29							29
30							30
31							31
32							32
33							33
34							34
35							35
36							36
37							37
38							38
39							39
40							40
41							41
42							42
43							43
44							44
45							45

NAME _____ DATE _____ CLASS _____

GENERAL LEDGER

ACCOUNT _____ ACCOUNT NO. _____

DATE		ITEM	POST. REF.	DEBIT	CREDIT	BALANCE	
						DEBIT	CREDIT

ACCOUNT _____ ACCOUNT NO. _____

DATE		ITEM	POST. REF.	DEBIT	CREDIT	BALANCE	
						DEBIT	CREDIT

ACCOUNT _____ ACCOUNT NO. _____

DATE		ITEM	POST. REF.	DEBIT	CREDIT	BALANCE	
						DEBIT	CREDIT

NAME _____   DATE _____   CLASS _____

ACCOUNT _____   ACCOUNT NO. _____

DATE		ITEM	POST. REF.	DEBIT	CREDIT	BALANCE	
						DEBIT	CREDIT

ACCOUNT _____   ACCOUNT NO. _____

DATE		ITEM	POST. REF.	DEBIT	CREDIT	BALANCE	
						DEBIT	CREDIT

ACCOUNT _____   ACCOUNT NO. _____

DATE		ITEM	POST. REF.	DEBIT	CREDIT	BALANCE	
						DEBIT	CREDIT

ACCOUNT _____   ACCOUNT NO. _____

DATE		ITEM	POST. REF.	DEBIT	CREDIT	BALANCE	
						DEBIT	CREDIT

ACCOUNT _____   ACCOUNT NO. _____

DATE		ITEM	POST. REF.	DEBIT	CREDIT	BALANCE	
						DEBIT	CREDIT

NAME _____ DATE _____ CLASS _____

	ACCOUNT NAME	TRIAL BALANCE	
		DEBIT	CREDIT
1			
2			
3			
4			
5			
6			
7			
8			
9			
10			
11			
12			
13			
14			
15			
16			
17			
18			
19			
20			
21			
22			
23			
24			
25			
26			
27			
28			
29			
30			
31			
32			
33			
34			
35			

ADJUSTMENTS		INCOME STATEMENT		BALANCE SHEET		
DEBIT	CREDIT	DEBIT	CREDIT	DEBIT	CREDIT	
						1
						2
						3
						4
						5
						6
						7
						8
						9
						10
						11
						12
						13
						14
						15
						16
						17
						18
						19
						20
						21
						22
						23
						24
						25
						26
						27
						28
						29
						30
						31
						32
						33
						34
						35